PRAYERS FOR LIFE AND WORSHIP

ROBERT GRIFFITH

GRACE AND TRUTH PUBLISHING
www.graceandtruthpublishing.com.au

ISBN: 978-1-7646132-5-5

CONTENTS

TOPICAL GUIDE

When you are anxious: 33, 34, 38, 40, 63

When you are weary or need rest: 31, 32, 35, 65

When you need guidance or direction: 11, 12, 13, 14

When you are struggling with sin: 21, 22, 23, 24

When you feel distant from God: 25, 26, 27

When you need encouragement: 28, 29, 30

When you are facing difficulty or trial: 36, 37, 39

When you need peace: 33, 34, 65

When you are seeking contentment: 64

When you need strength to persevere: 41, 42, 70

When you are dealing with relationships: 56, 57, 58

When you want to grow spiritually: 15, 16, 17, 18

When you desire a deeper prayer life: 1, 2, 3, 4

When you want to serve others: 66

When you want to share your faith: 67

When you are thinking about work: 61, 62

When you have financial concerns: 63

When you are praying for the Church: 68

When you are seeking revival: 69

When you are thinking about the future: 43, 44, 70

When you are reflecting on life: 45, 46, 47, 48, 49, 50

PREFACE

Prayer is one of the simplest and yet deepest expressions of the Christian life. It is not a performance needing to be mastered, nor a formula to be perfected, but a relationship to be lived. Through prayer, we can come before God as we are - with our gratitude, our burdens, our clarity, our confusion, our strength and also our weakness - and we learn to depend on Him in every part of life.

Yet many believers struggle with prayer. At times, words do not come easily. At other times, prayer can feel repetitive, uncertain, or even distant. This book has been written to help in those moments. It is not intended to replace personal prayer, but to support it - to provide language when words are hard to find, and to guide the heart back to God with clarity and focus.

Within these pages you will find over 400 prayers that reflect the wide range of life: joy and sorrow, strength and struggle, work and rest, faith and doubt. Each prayer is shaped by Scripture and grounded in the grace of God revealed in Jesus Christ. They are written to be used every day, not just simply read. They may be followed as they are, adapted as needed, or used as a starting point for further prayer.

There is no single way to use this book. Some may turn to it daily, others in specific seasons or situations. Some may pray slowly through a single prayer; others may use several at a time. The aim here is not method, but movement - drawing near to God, growing in faith, and learning to trust Him more deeply. Above all, prayer is about our Lord Jesus Christ. Through Him we have access to the Father, and through Him we are sustained in every imaginable circumstance.

In each of the 70 categories there are two longer prayers and four shorter ones. It is my hope that these prayers help you to draw near, remain steady, and live each day in dependence upon God.

Robert Griffith

1. PRAYERS FOR COMING BEFORE GOD

Holy Father, I come before You in the name of Jesus Christ, not because I have earned the right to stand in Your presence, but because Your mercy has opened the way. You are high and holy, yet You welcome those who seek You with humble hearts.

I come to You with my weakness, my need, my gratitude, and my longing to know You more. Quiet the noise within me. Still the distractions that pull at my thoughts. Gather my scattered heart and fix my attention upon You.

Thank You that I do not approach a distant God, but the living God who sees, hears, knows, and loves His people. Thank You that through Christ I may "approach God's throne of grace with confidence, so that we may receive mercy and find grace to help us in our time of need." (Hebrews 4:16).

I need that mercy today. I need that grace today. I need Your wisdom, Your strength, Your cleansing, and Your peace.

As I come before You, search me and know me. Expose what is false within me and deepen what is true. Let pride fall silent. Let fear lose its grip. Let unbelief be answered by Your promises. Teach me not merely to say prayers, but to meet with You.

Draw me near, and let me know the joy of Your presence. Lift my eyes above my circumstances and set my heart again upon Your greatness, Your goodness, and Your glory.

I come to listen, to worship, to trust, and to belong myself afresh to You. Guard this time from haste and from wandering thoughts.

Let the secret place become a place of healing, honesty, surrender, and renewed affection for Christ. Teach me to love Your presence more than the gifts of Your hand. Through Jesus Christ my Lord. **Amen.**

Gracious God, I come before You at the threshold of prayer, aware that You are God and I am not. You are eternal, wise, righteous, and full of steadfast love. I am a creature of dust, dependent on Your breath, upheld by Your kindness, and sustained by Your faithfulness. Yet You invite me to seek Your face. You do not turn away the one who comes in repentance, faith, and need. So, I come, not pretending to be strong, but confessing that apart from You I can do nothing.

I bring You the burdens I have carried, the thoughts that have troubled me, the sins that have weighed upon me, and the desires that I barely know how to express. Receive me with the tenderness of a Father and the mercy You have shown to me in Christ.

Wash away the self-reliance that clings so stubbornly to my heart. Teach me to pray with honesty. Teach me to wait without restlessness. Teach me to speak, and teach me also to be still before You.

Your word says, "Come near to God and He will come near to you." (James 4:8). I cling to that promise now. Let my coming to You be more than habit. Let it be surrender. Let it be worship. Let it be the turning of my soul toward its true home.

Meet me in this quiet moment. Reorder my loves. Renew my mind. Calm my spirit. Remind me that I am not abandoned to my own resources, but held in the strong and gentle hands of my Saviour.

May this time before You shape the rest of my day and the whole direction of my life. Let me rise from prayer with clearer vision, deeper peace, and a greater readiness to obey You. Give me grace to leave behind pretence and to stand before You in truth. Make me grateful for access, eager for holiness, and glad to belong to You.

Let prayer become not a duty I merely perform, but a refuge I cherish and a pathway of communion with You. I ask this through Jesus Christ, who lives and reigns forever. **Amen.**

Lord God, I come before You with a thankful heart. You have kept me, provided for me, and drawn me again to this place of prayer.

I do not come because I am worthy, but because Christ has made a way for me to draw near.

Cleanse my thoughts, quiet my heart, and help me to seek You sincerely. Let this not be a moment of empty words, but a true meeting with the living God.

Lift my mind above the noise of life and fix my heart upon Your goodness.

Speak, Lord, for Your servant is listening. Keep me near to You and teach me to treasure this quiet meeting with You. **Amen.**

Father in heaven, I come to You with all that I am and all that I carry.

You know my needs before I speak, and still, You welcome me into Your presence.

Thank You for Your amazing grace. Help me come always with reverence, honesty, and faith. Remove from me all distraction, pride, and unbelief.

Teach me to rest in Your love and trust in Your wisdom.

As I draw near to You, let my soul find peace, my conscience find cleansing, and my heart find fresh delight in You. Let Your smile be enough for me in this hour of prayer.

Through Jesus Christ my Lord. **Amen.**

Merciful God, here I am before You. I bring no claim except Your mercy and no confidence except Your promise.

Thank You that You are ready to receive those who call upon You in truth.

As I come, humble me, steady me, and open my heart to Your voice.

Let my prayers be shaped by Your word and governed by Your will. Keep me from rushing, keep me from wandering, and keep me near to You.

May this quiet approach to Your throne leave me more grateful, more trusting, and more obedient.

Receive my praise, my fears, and my deepest needs. **Amen.**

Holy and loving Father, I pause before You now.

The day may be busy, my mind may be restless, and my heart may be unsettled, but You remain unchanged.

You are faithful, near, and full of grace.

Draw me out of myself and into the light of Your presence. Let me come with childlike trust and holy reverence.

Forgive what is sinful in me, strengthen what is weak, and awaken what is dull.

As I begin this time of prayer, make me conscious of Your nearness and glad in Your love.

Let this first turning of my heart toward You shape all that follows. **Amen.**

2. PRAYERS FOR BEGINNING THE DAY

Heavenly Father, as this new day begins, I turn my heart toward You with gratitude and dependence. Thank You for the gift of life, for the mercy that has carried me through the night, and for the fresh kindness of this morning. Your word reminds me that, "Because of the Lord's great love we are not consumed, for His compassions never fail. They are new every morning; great is Your faithfulness." (Lamentations 3:22-23).

I begin this day under that truth. Before I face responsibilities, decisions, conversations, burdens, or opportunities, I come first to You.

Set my mind upon Christ and anchor my heart in Your peace. Guard me from beginning the day in haste, anxiety, distraction, or self-reliance. Teach me to walk slowly enough in spirit to notice Your hand, to hear Your word, and to follow Your leading. Go before me into every hour that lies ahead. Be Lord over my thoughts, my speech, my attitude, my work, and my reactions. Let nothing today pull me away from trust in You.

Where I will be tested, strengthen me. Where I will be tempted, protect me. Where I will be called to serve, make me willing. Where I will meet people in need, make me kind. Where I will face pressure, make me calm. Where I will need wisdom, make me teachable. Do not let me waste this day on things that do not matter. Help me to live it with purpose, humility, and glad obedience.

I commit to You my plans and also the things I cannot foresee. If joy comes, let me receive it thankfully. If difficulty comes, let me endure it faithfully. If interruptions come, let me meet them graciously. Keep me mindful that this day is not mine to control but Yours to govern. May I walk through it in fellowship with You, conscious of Your presence and eager to honour You. Let the first movements of my soul this morning shape the rest of the day, so that from beginning to end I may live as one who belongs to Jesus Christ. **Amen.**

Lord my God, I place this day before You while it is still fresh and unspent. Before its demands have crowded in and before my thoughts have scattered in many directions, I bring myself to You. I offer You my body, my mind, my time, my words, my work, my relationships, and my hidden thoughts.

Let nothing in me be withheld from Your gracious rule. This day belongs to You, and I ask for grace to live it in a way that reflects that truth.

Thank You for waking me again to see the light of another morning. Thank You that I do not step into this day alone. You are with me before I rise, beside me in every task, and ahead of me in all that is still unknown. I confess my need of You at the very start.

Without Your help, I will lean on my own understanding, speak careless words, and be ruled by passing moods. But with Your Spirit strengthening me, I may walk in wisdom, patience, and love.

Order my steps today. Let Your word guide my thinking and Your peace govern my heart. Deliver me from needless worry about things that may never happen. Keep me from resentment, irritation, and self-pity. Make me quick to listen, slow to speak, and ready to forgive. Help me to do the next thing faithfully, whether it seems great or small. Let my ordinary duties become acts of quiet worship as they are done for Your glory.

I pray also for a heart that remains sensitive to You all day long. When I am busy, keep me prayerful. When I am tired, keep me gentle. When I am pressed, keep me honest. When I am uncertain, keep me trusting. When I am blessed, keep me thankful. Let me not merely begin with You and then forget You, but walk with You hour by hour.

And when this day closes, may I look back not with regret over wasted hours, but with gratitude for Your sustaining grace. I ask this in the strong and worthy name of Jesus. **Amen.**

Father, thank You for this new day. Before I do anything else, I bring myself before You.

Fill my mind with truth, my heart with peace, and my hands with willingness to serve.

Keep me from anxiety, pride, and impatience. Help me to walk through this day in a manner worthy of Christ.

Let my words be gracious, my thoughts be pure, and my actions be shaped by love.

Go before me in all I must do, and keep me close to You from morning until night. May this day begin with trust and continue in obedience.

I place all that lies ahead into Your faithful hands. Amen.

Lord God, as I rise to meet the day, I ask for Your presence to go with me.

Thank You for rest, for life, and for mercy that is new again this morning.

Guide my steps, guard my heart, and give me wisdom for every decision. Keep me from rushing ahead of You or shrinking back in fear.

Help me to meet each task with faithfulness and each person with kindness. Let me remember throughout the day that I belong to You.

May the work of my hands and the meditation of my heart be pleasing in Your sight.

Lead me in peace and truth today. In the precious name of Jesus, I pray. **Amen.**

Gracious Father, I begin this day by acknowledging that I need You. I do not know all that today will bring, but You do.

You are already present in every moment that is still hidden from me.

So, I ask You for calmness in pressure, courage in duty, and patience in every interruption.

Teach me to trust You with what I cannot control and to obey You in what is plainly before me.

Let my first thoughts be directed toward Your goodness and my first desires be shaped by Your will.

Keep me grateful, watchful, and ready to honour Christ in all things. **Amen.**

Lord God, this day is Yours, and I am Yours.

Receive my thanks for the gift of a new beginning.

Cleanse me from yesterday's failures and help me not to carry old burdens as I step into this morning.

Fill me with fresh hope, fresh strength, and fresh resolve to walk with You. Be present in my speaking, my working, my waiting, and my serving.

Help me to do what is right, to love what is good, and to remain faithful in small things.

Whatever this day holds, let me meet it with a steady heart and an eye fixed upon You.

In Jesus' name and for Jesus' glory, I pray. **Amen.**

3. PRAYERS FOR ENDING THE DAY

Heavenly Father, as this day draws to its close, I come before You with gratitude, humility, and need. You have carried me through its hours, upheld me in ways I have seen and, in many ways, I have not seen, and shown me mercies that I could never fully count. Thank You for every kindness, every strength supplied, every danger prevented, every burden lightened, and every reminder that my life is held in Your faithful hands. The day now lies behind me, and I bring it back to You.

I thank You for what was good in it - for duties completed, help received, encouragement given, joy experienced, and truth remembered. I thank You also that even where the day has been hard, confusing, or heavy, You have not abandoned me. You have been present in all of it. Your word says, "The Lord is my shepherd, I lack nothing." (Psalm 23:1). Tonight I rest again in that assurance. You have shepherded me through another day, and You will not fail me in the night.

I confess that this day has not been perfect. I have sinned in thought, word, attitude, and action. There were moments when I was impatient, distracted, fearful, proud, or slow to trust You. Forgive me for all that was displeasing in Your sight. Cleanse my conscience through the blood of Christ. Do not let me go to rest burdened by guilt or hardened by excuses. Give me a tender heart, a clear spirit, and the quiet confidence that comes from Your pardoning grace.

As darkness falls, I place into Your hands all that remains unfinished, unresolved, or uncertain. Guard my mind from anxious thoughts and my heart from needless striving.

Teach me to leave with You, what I cannot change tonight. Grant me peaceful rest, renewing sleep, and a deeper awareness that You neither slumber nor sleep. Prepare me for another day, if it is Your will, and let me lie down under the shelter of Your love. Into Your keeping I commit my body, soul, and spirit, through Jesus Christ my Lord. **Amen.**

Gracious God, the day is ending, and I return to You, who have been my help from morning until now. Before I sleep, I want to pause and remember that every breath, every step, and every moment of strength has come from You.

Whether this day has seemed fruitful or frustrating, peaceful or demanding, bright or shadowed, You have remained constant. You have not changed with my moods, nor withdrawn because of my weakness. You have been faithful, and I praise You for Your steadfast care.

I bring to You now the record of this day. Where there has been joy, I thank You. Where there has been sorrow, I ask for comfort. Where there has been failure, I ask for mercy. Where there has been obedience, I ask that all glory would go to You.

Save me from the pride that clings to successes and from the despair that clings to shortcomings. Teach me to view this day not through self-importance or self-condemnation, but through the grace of Christ and the wisdom of Your word.

Your word says, "In peace I will lie down and sleep, for You alone, Lord, make me dwell in safety." (Psalm 4:8). I rest on that promise tonight. Watch over this home. Protect those I love. Give calmness to my thoughts and stillness to my body. Let sleep be a gift, not a struggle. If my mind is troubled, quiet it. If my heart is burdened, lighten it. If my spirit is weary, refresh it. Teach me to trust You enough to rest.

I also place tomorrow before You, though it has not yet arrived. Whatever it will contain is already known to You. I do not need to carry tomorrow tonight. I do not need to solve tonight what belongs to another day. Give me grace to let go, to be still, and to remember that I am upheld not by my own vigilance but by Your unceasing care.

Receive my thanks, my repentance, and my trust. Let the end of this day be marked by peace with You, peace in my conscience, and peace in my heart, through Jesus Christ my Saviour. **Amen.**

Father, thank You for bringing me safely to the end of this day. Thank You for the mercies I noticed and the many I did not.

I praise You for every kindness, every provision, and every help You gave along the way.

Forgive me for the sins of this day - for anxious thoughts, careless words, selfish attitudes, and failures to trust You fully.

Wash me again in Your grace and quiet my heart in Your peace.

As I prepare to rest, I place into Your hands all that remains unfinished or unresolved.

Watch over me through the night and grant me sleep in safety, peace, and confidence in Your faithful love. **Amen.**

Lord God, the day is over, and I come to You for rest. Thank You for sustaining me through every hour.

You were with me in things I handled well and in things I struggled to carry.

I confess my need of Your mercy for all that was wrong in me today. Cleanse me, renew me, and let no unconfessed sin remain between us.

Calm my thoughts and free me from worry about tomorrow. Help me to lie down with trust instead of striving.

Keep me through the night, refresh my body and mind, and let me wake, if it is Your will, ready to serve You again with a thankful heart.

I commit this prayer to you in Jesus' name. **Amen.**

Merciful Father, I end this day by returning thanks to You. Whatever has filled these hours, You have remained faithful.

For every joy, I thank You. For every sorrow, I ask Your comfort. For every failure, I seek Your forgiveness.

For every burden still pressing on me, I ask Your peace.

Teach me now to leave in Your hands what I cannot change. Guard me from restless thoughts and needless fears.

Cover me with Your care and give me deep and quiet sleep.

Let the close of this day remind me that my life is safely held by the One who watches over His children without ceasing. **Amen.**

Holy Father, I come to the end of another day under Your gracious care.

Thank You that You have not left me to myself.

Thank You for Your patience, Your provision, and Your presence.

I ask You now to search my heart, forgive my sins, and settle my spirit.

Remove the agitation that clings to me and replace it with the calm that comes from trusting You.

Bless those I love and keep them safe tonight.

As darkness falls and silence comes, help me to rest beneath Your sovereign care, knowing that the God who guided me through the day will also keep me through the night.

In Jesus' name. **Amen.**

4. PRAYERS FOR WORSHIP IN PRIVATE

Holy Father, I come aside from the noise and demands of life to worship You in private. In this quiet place, away from the gaze of others and the pressure of appearances, I desire to meet with You sincerely and wholeheartedly. You are worthy of worship, whether my feelings are strong or weak, whether my heart is light or burdened. You remain glorious, unchanging, and altogether good. Teach me to worship You not merely with words upon my lips, but with truth in my inward being.

Thank You that private worship is not empty solitude, but holy communion with the living God. Here, in secret, I may come honestly before You. I do not need to pretend strength, holiness, or calmness. I may bring You my praise and my weakness, my delight and my weariness, my gratitude and my need. Thank You that through Christ I am welcomed into Your presence. Thank You that I draw near with confidence, because my acceptance rests on His finished work, not my worth.

Your word says, "But when you pray, go into your room, close the door and pray to your Father, who is unseen. Then Your Father, who sees what is done in secret, will reward you." (Matthew 6:6). Keep me mindful of that gracious truth. Let this hidden place become a place of joy, reverence, repentance, and renewal. Free me from the desire to impress and from the shallowness that so easily creeps into spiritual habits. Teach me to prize the secret place because I prize You.

As I worship You now, lift my thoughts above earthbound concerns and set my heart again on Your beauty and majesty. Fill my mind with Your truth, my mouth with sincere praise, and my spirit with holy stillness. Let Scripture become living bread to me. Let prayer become more than petition - let it be adoration, surrender, confession, thanksgiving, and glad delight in who You are. Shape me in secret so that I may live faithfully in public. May private worship deepen my love for Christ, strengthen my obedience, and make my soul more at home in the presence of God. **Amen.**

Gracious and loving God, I seek You now in the quietness of private worship. I thank You for this sacred opportunity to step away from clamour and return my soul to its true centre in You. The world pulls at my attention in many directions. Duties press in, distractions multiply, and my own heart can become scattered and dull. But here, in this quiet turning toward You, I ask that my spirit may be gathered, calmed, and awakened to Your presence.

You are not honoured merely by outward activity or public expressions of devotion. You desire truth in the inner life. You call me to love You with heart, soul, mind, and strength. So I ask You to make this time before You real and unhurried. Let me not race through familiar words while my mind wanders elsewhere. Let me not confuse routine with communion. Instead, teach me to worship You with reverence, affection, humility, and joy. Open the eyes of my heart to behold again the wonder of who You are - holy, sovereign, merciful, wise, and full of steadfast love.

I thank You that in Christ I do not worship from a distance. I am brought near, by His blood, welcomed by Your grace, and indwelt by Your Spirit. Because of that, even this hidden moment matters deeply. You see what no one else sees. You know the longings I can barely express and the sins I would rather hide. Yet You invite me closer. You do not despise the quiet cry of the seeking heart.

Let this private worship renew my whole inner life. Search me where I am compromised. Correct me where I am drifting. Strengthen me where I am weak. Comfort me where I am troubled. Teach me again to delight in Your word, to rest in Your promises, and to treasure Christ above all things. May worship in secret guard me from spiritual emptiness and keep me rooted in reality before You. Then, when I return to the duties of daily life, let me carry with me the fragrance of time spent in Your presence - more peaceful, more grateful, more watchful, and more ready to obey. I ask this in the name of Jesus, my Saviour and my King. **Amen.**

Father, I come to worship You in private, away from noise, distraction, and the eyes of others.

Teach me to value this hidden place where I may meet with You sincerely.

Let my worship be true, not mechanical, and warm, not cold. Lift my heart above the clutter of the day and fix my thoughts on Your greatness, mercy, and holiness.

Thank You that through Christ I may draw near with confidence and peace. Search me, cleanse me, and renew me as I wait before You.

May this quiet time with You deepen my love, strengthen my faith, and shape my life in ways that honour Christ.

I offer You my praise and my heart. **Amen.**

Lord God, in the stillness of this moment I turn aside to worship You.

You are worthy of my attention, my affection, and my highest praise.

Forgive me for the many times my mind is restless and my devotion shallow.

Gather my thoughts and settle my spirit in Your presence. Let Your word speak freshly to me and Your Spirit awaken in me reverence, gratitude, and joy.

Keep me from treating private worship as a duty alone. Make it a delight and a refuge. Teach me to seek You when no one sees, and to find in Your presence the strength and peace my soul truly needs. **Amen.**

Gracious Father, thank You for the gift of secret worship. In this quiet place, remind me that You see, You know, and You welcome me through Jesus Christ.

Help me to be honest before You, humble under Your word, and glad in Your love.

Strip away pretence and renew what is tired and dull within me.

Let my praise be sincere, my confession be real, and my thanksgiving be full. As I worship You in private, prepare me to live for You in public.

May hidden faithfulness before You become visible fruit in my words, choices, and conduct throughout the day.

Keep me near to You and teach me to treasure Your presence. In Jesus' name I pray. **Amen.**

Holy Father, I set apart this time to seek and worship You.

Draw me away from hurried thoughts and divided loyalties.

Make me attentive to Your voice and responsive to Your will.

Thank You that private worship is never lonely, for You are here. Fill this quiet moment with the reality of Your nearness.

Let my soul find rest, my conscience find cleansing, and my heart find fresh delight in Christ.

Teach me to love the secret place where my faith is strengthened and my motives are purified.

May what is formed in private before You shape all that I do and say when I step again into the world. **Amen.**

5. PRAYERS FOR STILLNESS BEFORE GOD

Holy and gracious Father, I come before You and ask for the grace to be still. My mind is often crowded, my heart often hurried, and my soul too easily pulled in many directions at once. Even when I come to pray, I can bring with me the noise of unfinished tasks, anxious thoughts, recalled conversations, and restless concerns about what lies ahead. Yet You call me not only to speak, but also to be still before You. Teach me that holy stillness is not emptiness, but trust. It is not withdrawal from reality, but quiet confidence in the God who reigns.

Psalm, 46:10 says, "Be still, and know that I am God." Let that word settle upon me now. Help me to lay down for a while the need to manage, fix, explain, and control. Save me from the illusion that everything depends on me. Remind me that You are on the throne, wise in all Your ways, perfect in all Your works, and faithful in all Your promises. When my thoughts race, slow them by Your peace. When my heart is agitated, steady it by Your presence. When my spirit is tired, renew it by Your nearness.

In this stillness, make me attentive to You. Teach me to wait without impatience, to listen without resistance, and to worship without performance. Search the hidden places of my heart. Reveal the fears I have disguised as busyness and the unbelief I have hidden beneath activity. Quiet what is sinful in me, and strengthen what is weak. Let this stillness become a place of honesty, cleansing, and renewal.

I ask not merely for an outward pause, but for an inward resting in You. Let my soul become settled under Your care. Let me be content to sit before You without striving, trusting that You know me fully and love me faithfully in Christ. If You speak through Your word, help me to receive it. If You simply hold me in peace, help me to be thankful. Teach me that stillness before God is itself a form of worship, a declaration that You are enough and that I am safe in Your hands. Through Jesus Christ my Lord I pray. **Amen.**

Heavenly Father, I come to You longing for the stillness that this world cannot give. So much around me is loud, urgent, and demanding. So much within me is unsettled and quick to react. I confess that I often carry noise in my soul even when outward surroundings are quiet. I bring to You a heart that is easily distracted, a mind that is quick to wander, and a spirit that struggles to rest. Yet You are patient, and You invite me to wait before You.

Thank You that I do not need to manufacture peace for myself. I do not need to force my soul into calmness by my own strength. True stillness comes from knowing that You are God, that You are near, and that You are trustworthy. I thank You that in Christ I am not an outsider trying to find my way in, but a beloved child welcomed into Your presence. Because of Him, I may come with all my restlessness and ask You to quiet me with Your love.

Your word says, "Truly my soul finds rest in God; my salvation comes from Him." (Psalm 62:1). Let that become my experience now. Quiet the inner arguments. Keep me from imagining that stillness is wasted time. Help me to understand that often my soul needs to be silent before it can hear clearly, repent deeply, or worship sincerely.

As I sit before You, let Your Spirit do His gentle work in me. Untangle what is knotted. Soften what is hard. Expose what is false. Heal what is bruised. If my mind runs ahead, bring it back. If my heart sinks into anxiety, lift it again with the promises of Your word. If my soul grows dull, awaken it to the beauty of Christ. Teach me to wait before You with expectancy and humility.

May this stillness before You become part of the deep rhythm of my life - not occasional escape, but regular surrender. Let it shape the way I listen, the way I speak, the way I carry burdens, and the way I trust You in daily life. Give me the grace to rise from this quiet place less driven, less fearful, and more anchored in the peace of God. I ask this in the name of Jesus, my refuge and my rest. **Amen.**

Father, quiet my restless heart before You.

So much within me feels hurried, crowded, and unsettled, yet You remain calm, sovereign, and near.

Teach me to be still in Your presence and to trust that You are God.

Help me to lay down anxious thoughts, impatient striving, and the need to control what belongs to You alone.

Let this quiet moment become a place of peace, honesty, and renewed faith.

Speak through Your word, calm me by Your Spirit, and steady me with Your love.

May stillness before You teach me that I am safe in Your hands and upheld by Your faithful care. **Amen.**

Lord God, I pause before You and ask for inward stillness. My mind wanders, my heart races, and my thoughts are often noisy, but You call me to rest in You.

Draw me away from distraction and settle my soul under Your gracious rule. Help me not to fear silence, but to welcome it as a place where I may know You more deeply.

Search me, cleanse me, and strengthen me as I wait before You.

Let Your peace quiet what is troubled in me and Your truth silence what is false.

Teach me to listen, to trust, and to remain before You with a calm and willing heart. **Amen.**

Gracious Father, in this moment of stillness I bring to You all that is unsettled within me.

I lay before You my worries, my distractions, my weariness, and the burdens I have carried too tightly.

Quiet me with the assurance of Your presence. Remind me that You are not absent, rushed, or uncertain. You are the God who reigns in wisdom and love.

Help me to stop striving for a little while and simply rest in You. May stillness before

You become a place where my faith is strengthened, my soul is restored, and my eyes are lifted again to Christ. Keep me near and teach me peace. **Amen.**

Holy Father, teach me the grace of being still before You.

Not every need requires many words, and not every burden must be carried in haste.

Sometimes I simply need to sit in the light of Your presence and remember that You are God.

So, calm my thoughts, steady my breathing, and settle my heart.

Let the noise within me grow quiet as I fix my mind on Your greatness and Your goodness.

In this silence, remind me that I am loved, forgiven, and held secure in Christ.

Let this stillness prepare me to walk more peacefully and faithfully through all that lies ahead. **Amen.**

Faithful Father, I come before You confessing that trust does not always come easily to me. I believe Your word, yet I often feel the pull of fear, uncertainty, and self-reliance. I know that You are good, yet in difficult moments I am tempted to question Your wisdom, Your timing, or Your care. So I bring You my wavering heart and ask You to strengthen it. Teach me to trust You more fully - not only when life is calm and clear, but also when the way is dark and I cannot see what lies ahead.

Your word says, "Trust in the Lord with all your heart and lean not on your own understanding." (Proverbs 3:5). I confess how often I do lean on my own understanding. I look for certainty where You call me to faith. I search for control where You call me to surrender. I want answers when You are calling me to rest in Your character. Forgive me for the pride that thinks I must know everything before I can obey. Forgive me for the fear that imagines I am safer in my own hands than in Yours.

Thank You that Your faithfulness will never depend on the strength of my feelings. You remain trustworthy because of who You are - wise in all Your ways, good in all You permit, and perfect in all You do. You have never failed Your people, never forgotten Your promises, and never abandoned those who belong to You in Christ.

When I remember the cross, I am reminded that Your love is not uncertain. When I remember the resurrection, I am reminded that Your power is not limited. When I remember Your promises, I am reminded that my future is secure in You.

Teach me to trust You in practical, daily ways. When I do not understand, help me still to obey. When I am afraid, help me still to rest. When I feel weak, help me still to hope. Keep me from making worry my refuge or circumstances my measure of truth. Let Your word speak more loudly to me than my fears. I place my present, my future, and all that concerns me into Your wise and loving hands, through Jesus Christ my Lord. **Amen.**

Gracious God, I ask You today for the grace to trust You. There are times when my heart feels steady and faith comes readily, but there are other times when trust feels like hard work. In such moments, I am conscious of my weakness. I see how quickly I become anxious when plans change, unsettled when answers do not come, and fearful when life does not unfold as I expected. Yet even then, You remain the same. You are not shaken by what shakes me. You are not confused by what confuses me. You are not threatened by what overwhelms me.

Thank You that I am not called to trust in fate, in chance, or in my own strength, but in the living God who knows all things and rules all things well. Thank You that my life is not drifting without purpose, but held within the care of a heavenly Father who works for the good of His children. Even when I cannot trace Your hand, I can trust Your heart. Even when the path is hidden, the Shepherd is near. Even when I am uncertain, You are never unsure.

Your word says, "When I am afraid, I put my trust in You." (Psalm 56:3). That is what I choose to do now. Not because all fear has vanished, but because You are worthy of trust in the midst of fear. Help me not to wait until I feel brave before I believe. Help me instead to bring my fears into the light of Your promises and let faith rise there. Deliver me from the exhausting effort to secure myself apart from You. Teach me the freedom of leaning my full weight upon Your faithfulness.

As I walk through this day, let trust become active and visible. Let it shape my decisions, soften my anxieties, calm my spirit, and steady my words. Keep me from panicked thinking and from the unbelief that assumes the worst. Give me a quiet confidence that You will supply what I need, guide where I cannot see, and sustain me in all that comes.

And if the path remains difficult, let me still say with sincerity that You are good, Your wisdom is perfect, and Your love endures forever. I ask this through Jesus Christ, who is Himself my assurance and my peace. **Amen.**

Father, teach me to trust You with all my heart.

I am often tempted to lean on what I can see, explain, or control, but You call me to rest in Your wisdom and goodness.

Forgive me for anxious striving and unbelieving thoughts. Remind me that You are faithful in all Your ways and kind in all Your dealings with Your children.

When I do not understand, help me to obey. When I feel afraid, help me to rest.

Let Your promises speak more strongly to me than my fears. Keep my heart steady in Christ and teach me to place my whole life, present and future, into Your loving and sovereign hands. **Amen.**

Lord God, You know how quickly my heart can become troubled when life feels uncertain.

Yet You remain unchanging, wise, and good. Help me to trust You today, not only in words but in truth.

Keep me from leaning on my own understanding or trying to carry what belongs to You.

Give me grace to leave with You the things I cannot fix, answer, or foresee.

Fill me with quiet confidence that my life is not outside Your care.

May trust in You calm my thoughts, govern my choices, and steady my spirit through every circumstance I face.

Let my heart rest in the God who never fails. **Amen.**

Gracious Father, I bring You my fears, my questions, and my uncertainty.

I confess that trust can feel difficult when the path ahead is unclear.

Yet I know that You are faithful and that Your love for me in Christ is sure.

Help me not to measure Your goodness by my circumstances, but to remember Your character and Your promises.

Teach me to walk by faith and not by sight.

Strengthen me to believe that You are working even when I cannot yet see the outcome.

Let trust in You become the anchor of my heart and the calm beneath all the shifting things of life. **Amen.**

Holy Father, I place before You all that concerns me today.

The burdens I carry, the uncertainties I feel, and the questions I cannot answer are all known to You.

Thank You that I do not have to pretend strength when I am weak.

I can trust You as a child trusts a wise and loving father.

Help me to leave behind restless striving and to rest instead in Your perfect care.

Whatever You appoint is wise, whatever You permit is known to You, and whatever lies ahead is already under Your rule.

Keep me near to Christ and teach me to trust You with a peaceful and obedient heart. **Amen.**

7. PRAYERS FOR RESTING IN GOD

Gracious Father, I come before You longing not merely for relief from pressure, but for true rest in You. My life can become so full of demands, responsibilities, thoughts, and concerns that even when my body pauses, my soul continues to strain. I know what it is to be busy, to be burdened, and to be inwardly weary. Yet You invite me not only to work for You and trust You, but also to rest in You. Teach me what that means. Teach me that rest is not laziness, indifference, or an escape, but quiet confidence in the God who rules wisely and loves faithfully.

Your word says, "Come to me, all you who are weary and burdened, and I will give you rest." (Matthew 11:28). I come to that invitation now. I bring You the burdens I have carried too long, the pressures I have allowed to master me, and the anxieties that have crowded out peace. I confess that I often live as though everything depends upon me. I hurry, I worry, I overthink, and I carry what I was never meant to carry alone. Forgive me for that proud restlessness.

Thank You that in Christ there is rest for the conscience, rest for the heart, and rest for the weary soul. Because He has finished the work of salvation, I do not need to strive to make myself accepted before You. Because He intercedes for me, I do not need to fear that I am left unsupported. Because He reigns, I do not need to live as though the future is hanging on my strength. Let the gospel itself become the bedrock of my rest.

Help me to rest in Your character - in Your wisdom when I lack understanding, in Your power when I feel weak, in Your love when I feel uncertain, and in Your faithfulness when the path ahead is unclear. Quiet the part of me that always wants to rush ahead. Free me from inward agitation and the endless need to prove, fix, or secure everything by my own effort. Let my soul grow still under Your care. Teach me to live from rest rather than merely collapse into it. May I find in You a refuge deeper than sleep, stronger than circumstance, and sweeter than all the false comforts of this world. **Amen.**

Holy and loving Father, I come to You with a tired spirit and ask You to teach me the grace of resting in You. There are days when I am weary not only in body, but in mind and heart. Thoughts spin, responsibilities weigh heavily, and concerns about tomorrow steal strength from today. Even in moments when there should be peace, my soul can remain tense, alert, and burdened. Yet You have not made me to live in constant inward strain. You call me to cast my cares upon You because You care for me. Help me to do that truly and not just in words.

I thank You that Your rest is not fragile. It does not depend on ideal circumstances, perfect health, or the absence of difficulty. It is rooted in who You are. You are the everlasting God, never hurried, never weary, never threatened, never uncertain. All things remain under Your command. Nothing catches You by surprise. rest in You is not denial of reality, but submission to the deepest reality of all - that You are God, and I am safely in Your hands.

Your word says, "Yes, my soul, find rest in God; my hope comes from Him." (Psalm 62:5). Let that be the posture of my heart. Teach my soul to settle itself in You. When fears arise, let me rest in Your promises. When unanswered questions press upon me, let me rest in Your wisdom. When weakness makes me feel vulnerable, let me rest in Your strength. Keep me from seeking refuge in distractions, comforts, or habits that cannot truly satisfy. Bring me back again and again to the calm strength of Your presence.

Let rest in You shape how I live. Make me less driven by anxiety and more governed by peace. Let me work diligently when duty calls, but without inward panic. Let me carry responsibility faithfully, but not as though I were the saviour of my own life. Teach me when to stop, when to pray, when to release, and when simply to be still. May my soul become more deeply rooted in Christ, who is my peace. And in resting in You, may I become more patient, more gentle, more joyful, and more free. I ask this in the name of Jesus, my Sabbath and my rest. **Amen.**

Father, I come to You weary and in need of rest.

My thoughts are too often crowded and my heart too easily burdened, but You invite me to rest in Your care.

Teach me to lay down what I have been carrying too tightly. Help me not to live as though everything depends upon me. Remind me that You are wise, faithful, and near.

Let the peace of Christ quiet my restless spirit and the promises of Your word steady my heart.

Keep me from false refuges and draw me back to the deep and lasting rest found only in You.

Settle my soul under Your loving rule and teach me to trust Your care. **Amen.**

Lord God, thank You that You do not call me to endless striving, but to rest in You.

I confess how often I hurry, worry, and carry those burdens that should be left in Your hands.

Forgive my restless self-reliance.

Teach me to live and work from a heart at peace in Your presence. When my spirit is agitated, quiet me.

When my mind is racing, calm me. When my strength is low, uphold me.

Let Your nearness become my refuge and Your faithfulness my resting place.

May my soul find in You the peace that this world cannot give and the strength that I cannot produce for myself. **Amen.**

Gracious Father, I ask You to teach me the holy art of resting in You. Not idleness, but trust. Not passivity, but peace.

Help me to remember that my life is upheld by Your power and surrounded by Your love.

Keep me from seeking comfort in things that cannot truly satisfy.

Let me find in Christ a refuge for my conscience, my fears, and my weariness.

As I bring my burdens to You, grant me grace to release them and not snatch them back again.

Give me a heart that is still before You, confident in Your goodness, and glad to be held by Your faithful care. **Amen.**

Holy Father, my soul needs the rest that only You can give.

The world is noisy, life is demanding, and my own heart is often unsettled.

Yet You remain untroubled, sovereign, and kind. Draw me into the calm of Your presence.

Help me to stop striving for a little while and remember that You are God.

Teach me to rest in Your wisdom when I do not understand, in Your strength when I feel weak, and in Your love when I feel uncertain.

Let Your peace govern my inner life and make me more patient, gentle, and steady in all I do.

Through Jesus Christ my peace, **Amen.**

8. PRAYERS FOR THANKFULNESS

Gracious Father, I come before You with a heart that desires to be more thankful. So often I move quickly past Your mercies, noticing my needs more readily than Your gifts and my burdens more quickly than Your blessings. Forgive me for the dullness that forgets Your kindness and for the selfishness that receives so much while pausing so little to give You praise. Open my eyes again to the countless signs of Your goodness. Teach me to live not with a spirit of complaint, but gratitude.

Thank You first for who You are. You are holy, wise, faithful, and good. Your love does not waver with my circumstances, and Your mercy does not run dry when I am weak. You have given me far more than daily provision. In Christ You have given me forgiveness, reconciliation, peace with You, adoption into Your family, and the certain hope of eternal life. Your word says, "Give thanks to the Lord, for He is good; His love endures forever." (Psalm 107:1). Let that truth guide me all my days.

Thank You also for the daily mercies I too easily overlook - for breath and strength, for food and shelter, for friendships and fellowship, for moments of beauty, for answered prayers, and for help quietly given. Thank You for preserving me through many dangers seen and unseen, for guiding me when I could not see the way clearly, and for sustaining me in times when I felt weaker than I wished anyone knew. Thank You for all the ways You have been patient with me, corrected me, forgiven me, and drawn me back when my heart has wandered.

Teach me to give thanks not because pain is pleasant, but because Your faithfulness remains constant. Let gratitude guard me from bitterness, envy, and self-pity. Let it soften my spirit, enlarge my joy, and deepen my worship. May thankfulness become one of the steady habits of my soul, shaping my prayers, my speech, my relationships, and my whole outlook on life. And when I struggle to see reasons for gratitude, remind me again that Christ is enough, Your promises are sure, and Your mercies are new every morning. **Amen.**

Heavenly Father, I thank You for the grace of gratitude. In a world that trains the heart to notice what is missing, You call me to remember what has already been given. You have not dealt with me according to my sins, nor repaid me according to my failures, but have lavished mercy upon me in Christ. Even now, when I can be hurried, distracted, and slow to praise, You remain generous and patient. I acknowledge that every good thing I have comes from Your hand.

Thank You for the gift of salvation. Thank You that I was not left in darkness, guilt, and spiritual death, but was sought, awakened, and brought near through the saving work of Jesus Christ. Thank You for the cross, where my sin was answered by Your mercy, and for the empty tomb, where my fear was answered by Your triumph. Thank You that I belong to You, that Your Spirit dwells within me, and that nothing can separate me from the love of God that is in Christ Jesus my Lord. These are mercies too great for me to measure and too precious for me ever to treat as ordinary.

I thank You also for all the common mercies of daily life. Thank You for the rhythm of days and nights, for work and rest, for conversation and companionship, for the beauty of creation, for provision in times of need, and for the quiet faithfulness that surrounds so much of ordinary life. Thank You for people who have loved me, encouraged me, strengthened my hands when I was weary and prayed for me. Thank You for lessons learned through hardship and for growth that has come through trials.

Your word says, "And whatever you do, whether in word or deed, do it all in the name of the Lord Jesus, giving thanks to God the Father through Him." (Colossians 3:17). Let thankfulness be at the core of my life. Keep me from living as though blessings are owed to me. Deliver me from resentment and the envy that poisons joy. Make me quick to notice grace, quick to give thanks, and quick to speak of Your goodness. May gratitude not remain a passing feeling, but become a settled disposition of heart. I ask this through Jesus Christ, with deep thanks for all that You are and all that You have given. **Amen.**

Father, thank You for Your goodness to me.

So much of Your kindness fills my days, yet I confess that I often notice my troubles more quickly than Your mercies.

Forgive my forgetfulness and teach me to live with grateful eyes.

Thank You for life, for daily provision, for the people You have placed around me, and above all for salvation through Jesus Christ.

Let thankfulness shape my words, my thoughts, and my prayers. Keep me from grumbling, envy, and self-pity. Instead, make me quick to remember that every good and perfect gift comes from You.

May a thankful heart deepen my joy, strengthen my faith, and lead me into warmer worship of Your holy name. **Amen.**

Lord God, I pause to thank You for all that You are and all that You have done.

You have been faithful in every season, patient in all my weakness, and generous beyond my deserving.

Thank You for mercies seen and unseen, for prayers answered and for grace given in ways I did not even recognise at the time.

Most of all, thank You for Christ, for forgiveness, and for the sure hope of eternal life.

Teach me to be truly thankful, not only when life is easy, but in every circumstance.

Let gratitude guard my heart from bitterness and help me to walk through this day with joy, humility, and peace. **Amen.**

Gracious Father, I thank You that Your mercies are new every morning and Your faithfulness never fails.

Thank You for the ordinary blessings that sustain me and the eternal blessings that secure me in Christ.

Keep me from taking Your gifts for granted.

Make me mindful of Your hand in daily life and eager to give You praise.

Whether I have much or little, whether the day is bright or difficult, let my heart still find reason to thank You.

Shape in me a spirit of gratitude that honours You, blesses others, and strengthens my soul.

May thanksgiving become one of the steady rhythms of my life before You. **Amen.**

Holy Father, You have been better to me than I deserve and kinder than I often remember.

Thank You for preserving me, providing for me, correcting me, and loving me with steadfast mercy. Thank You for the gift of prayer, the gift of Your word, the gift of Your Church, and the gift of Christ my Saviour.

Let thankfulness rise in me more naturally than complaint. Help me to speak often of Your goodness and to receive each blessing with humility and praise.

When troubles come, keep me from forgetting that Your love still endures and Your grace still holds me fast.

I give You thanks with all my heart. **Amen.**

9. PRAYERS FOR PRAISE

Lord God, I come before You to praise You for who You are. Before I ask for anything, before I speak of my needs or burdens, I lift my heart to adore You. You alone are worthy of all honour, glory, blessing, and praise. You are the Creator of heaven and earth, the Lord of history, the King over all nations, and the God of my salvation. There is none like You in majesty, none like You in holiness, none like You in wisdom, and none like You in steadfast love.

I praise You for Your holiness. You are utterly pure, unstained by evil, perfect in righteousness, and glorious in all Your ways. I praise You for Your power. You spoke, and the world came into being. You uphold all things by Your will.

Nothing is too hard for You, nothing escapes Your rule, and nothing can overturn Your purposes. I praise You for Your wisdom. Your judgments are perfect, Your ways are higher than mine, and Your understanding is beyond measure. I praise You for Your mercy.

Your word says, "Great is the Lord and most worthy of praise; His greatness no one can fathom." (Psalm 145:3). Let my praise rise with that truth. Teach me not to offer You thin and hurried words, but heartfelt worship rooted in wonder. Keep me from the dullness that speaks of You lightly. Awaken my soul to the splendour of Your name. Open my eyes to behold more of Christ, for in Him Your glory shines with saving beauty. In His life, death, resurrection, and reign, I see Your justice, love, wisdom, and power joined perfectly together.

Let praise become more natural to me than complaint, more instinctive than fear, and more constant than self-concern. Even in hardship, give me a heart that remembers You are still worthy. Even in weakness, let me boast in the Lord. Even when answers tarry, let me praise You for Your unchanging character. May my life, not only my lips, become a testimony to Your worth. Receive the worship of my heart, through Jesus Christ, to whom be glory forever and ever. **Amen.**

Gracious and glorious God, I praise You today because You are worthy, whether my feelings rise easily or not. You do not become more glorious when I praise You, nor less glorious when I forget. You are eternally majestic, eternally good, and eternally blessed. Yet You have made me to know You and to delight in You, and so praise is both my duty and my joy. Lift my thoughts above myself and fix them upon Your greatness, for you are the God who is from everlasting to everlasting.

Before mountains were born and before the world was formed, You are God. You are not limited by time, weakened by change, or surprised by anything that unfolds in this world. You are faithful in every generation. What You promise, You perform. What You begin, You complete. What You speak, stands forever. I praise You that my life rests not upon shifting sand, but upon the eternal God who does all things well.

I praise You also as the God of redemption. You saw me in my need and did not leave me to perish. In Your love You sent Your Son. In Your mercy You laid my sin upon Him. In Your power You raised Him from the dead.

In Your grace You called me to Yourself. What can I do but praise You? Your word says, "Praise the Lord, my soul; all my inmost being, praise His holy name." (Psalm 103:1). Let all that is within me respond. Let mind, heart, memory, and desire be summoned into worship.

Where praise has grown weak in me, renew it. Where I have become preoccupied with myself, enlarge my vision of You. Where sorrow or weariness has dimmed my song, remind me that Christ is still risen, Your throne is still secure, and Your promises are still true. Let praise strengthen my faith, steady my heart, and sanctify my perspective.

Teach me to bless You not only in public worship, but in private devotion, in ordinary work, in times of joy, and in days of testing. May praise become a habit of holy remembrance and loving response. I offer You my adoration through Jesus Christ, my Lord and my song. **Amen.**

Father, I praise You for Your greatness, holiness, wisdom, and love.

You are worthy of far more honour than I can ever give. Thank You that You are not only the Maker of all things, but also the Saviour of all who trust in Christ.

Lift my heart above my own concerns and fix my thoughts upon Your glory.

Keep me from cold and careless worship. Awaken in me sincere wonder, gratitude, and delight in who You are. Whether life feels light or heavy today, let my soul still bless Your name.

May praise be more than words on my lips - may it become the true response of my whole life to Your goodness and grace. In Jesus' mighty name I pray. **Amen.**

Lord God, I praise You because You are worthy.

Your greatness cannot be measured, Your mercy cannot be exhausted, and Your faithfulness never fails.

Thank You for every evidence of Your goodness in creation, providence, and redemption.

Above all, thank You for Jesus Christ, in whom Your glory and grace shine so clearly. Teach me to praise You with reverence, joy, and sincerity.

Let my heart not be slow to worship or quick to forget.

Make praise a steady rhythm in my life, so that in all circumstances I may remember who You are and rest in the beauty of Your unchanging character. **Amen.**

Gracious Father, praise belongs to You. You are holy in all Your ways, wise in all Your works, and loving in all Your dealings with Your people.

I thank You that I may come before You through Christ and lift my voice in adoration.

Help me to praise You not only when blessings are obvious, but also when faith must rise in the dark.

Let praise lift my eyes above fear, disappointment, and self-preoccupation.

Fill my mind with the truth of who You are and my heart with gladness in Your presence.

May my soul learn to say again and again, "The Lord is good; His love endures forever." (Psalm 100:5). **Amen.**

Holy Father, I bless Your name and thank You that You are altogether worthy of praise.

There is no flaw in Your character, no failure in Your promises, and no shadow in Your goodness.

You are the God who reigns, the God who saves, and the God who keeps His people.

Let my worship be sincere and glad. Deliver me from empty familiarity and restore to me a fresh sense of wonder before You.

Teach me to praise You in the ordinary moments of life and in the difficult ones too.

May praise strengthen my faith, soften my heart, and keep Christ at the centre of all I am and do. **Amen.**

Gracious Father, I come before You longing for spiritual renewal. There are times when my heart feels warm and responsive to You, but there are other times when I feel dull, distracted, weary, and inwardly dry. I know what it is to keep going outwardly while inwardly losing freshness, tenderness, and delight in You. Forgive me for the ways I have allowed routine to replace wonder, busyness to crowd out devotion, and lesser things to weaken my appetite for what is eternal.

Thank You that You are not only the God who first saves, but also the God who restores, revives, and renews His people. You do not cast off Your children when they are weary, nor abandon them when they are spiritually flat. In mercy You call us back. In love You draw near again through Christ. Your word says, "He refreshes my soul." (Psalm 23:3). I ask You to do that for me now. Refresh my soul. Restore what has faded. Rekindle what has cooled.

Renew my love for Christ. Let me see Him again with clearer eyes and greater affection. Renew my hunger for Scripture, so that Your word may not feel distant or familiar in a lifeless way, but living, searching, nourishing, and precious. Renew my desire for prayer, so that communion with You is not neglected or hurried. Renew my joy in salvation, so that I may remember with gladness the mercy You have shown me in Jesus.

Guard me from chasing shallow emotion while neglecting the deeper work of true renewal. I do not merely ask to feel different for a moment, but to be renewed in the inner person. Strengthen faith, deepen humility, enlarge gratitude, and restore obedience. Let renewal reach my thoughts, motives, habits, and desires. If there is sin that has deadened me, expose it. If there is sorrow that has drained me, comfort me. If there is unbelief that has weakened me, correct me by Your truth. Make me spiritually alive, watchful, and glad in You again. I ask this through Jesus Christ my Lord, who is able to revive the fainting soul and keep me near to Himself. **Amen.**

Holy Father, I bring before You the need of my inner life. Others may see the outward shape of my days, but You alone know the true condition of my soul. You know when I am spiritually fresh and when I am merely going through motions. You know when worship is sincere and when my mind is wandering. You know when love for Christ is active and when it has grown dim beneath layers of weariness, distraction, and neglect. So, I come honestly and ask for renewal.

Thank You that renewal is possible because Your mercy is constant. You do not say to the tired believer, the wandering believer, or the discouraged believer that there is no way back to freshness. Instead, You call us to return to You. You delight to renew the humble and revive the contrite.

Thank You that the Holy Spirit is still at work, that Your word is still living and active, and that the grace of Christ is still sufficient for all my need. I do not need to remain in spiritual dryness as though it were normal or unchangeable.

Your word says, "I will refresh the weary and satisfy the faint." (Jeremiah 31:25). Fulfil that promise in me. Refresh what is weary in faith, faint in hope, and cold in love. Restore spiritual alertness where I have become careless. Restore joy where I have become joyless. Restore first love where affection for Christ has grown thin. Restore discipline where I have drifted. Restore courage where fear has taken hold. Do in me the quiet, deep work that only You can do.

Renewal does not mean making me impressive. It means making me alive to You again. So, turn my eyes away from self and back to Christ. Give me the grace to seek You earnestly, to open Your word expectantly, and to pray with new honesty. Let my heart be softened, my conscience tender, and my spirit responsive to Your leading. And may this renewal bear fruit in daily life - greater patience, greater faithfulness, greater gentleness, greater purity, and greater readiness to obey. Let the freshness You give me not remain hidden in feeling alone, but appear in steadfast godliness. **Amen.**

Father, I ask You to renew my soul. Where I have grown weary, refresh me.

Where I have grown dull, awaken me. Where I have drifted, draw me back please Lord.

Forgive me for allowing routine, distraction, and lesser desires to crowd out love for You.

Restore to me the joy of Your salvation and renew in me a willing spirit.

Let Your word become precious again, prayer become living again, and Christ become the glad centre of my heart again. Keep me from settling into spiritual dryness as though it were normal.

Revive me by Your Spirit and make me eager to seek, love, and obey You with fresh sincerity and strength. **Amen.**

Lord God, You know the true state of my inner life, and I ask You for spiritual renewal.

I do not want merely to appear faithful outwardly while my heart grows cold within.

Breathe fresh life into my soul. Renew my hunger for Scripture, my delight in prayer, my tenderness toward sin, and my joy in Christ.

Rescue me from spiritual laziness and restore holy desire.

Let Your Spirit stir what has become sluggish and strengthen what has become weak. Teach me again the blessedness of walking closely with You.

May renewal in secret lead to greater faithfulness, humility, peace, and obedience in all of life. **Amen.**

Gracious Father, I bring You my spiritual weariness and ask You to refresh me.

Thank You that You do not despise the weak, the tired, or the fainting believer. You invite me to return to You and find grace for my need.

So, restore what has faded in me. Rekindle love for Christ, sharpen my spiritual sight, and make me more responsive to Your word.

Free me from dullness of heart and from habits that drain spiritual life.

Let this be a season not of decline, but of renewal.

Revive me inwardly, so that my worship, service, and obedience may once again be marked by gladness and sincerity. **Amen.**

Holy Father, I need the renewing work of Your Spirit.

Without You I become dry, distracted, and slow to seek You. But You are the God who restores souls and revives weary hearts. Turn me again toward Christ.

Renew my mind with truth, my heart with love, and my will with holy strength. Search out whatever is grieving, quenching, or resisting Your work in me, and lead me into repentance and fresh obedience.

Let renewal be more than a passing feeling.

Make it deep, real, and fruitful. May I rise from this prayer more awake to Your presence, more thankful for Your grace, and more ready to walk with You. **Amen.**

Heavenly Father, I come before You seeking guidance. There are decisions before me, uncertainties around me, and limitations within me that make me feel my need of You afresh. I do not know all that lies ahead. I do not always see clearly what is wise, what is timely, or what is best. My own understanding is partial, my motives can be mixed, and my heart is sometimes pulled by fear, impatience, or self-interest. Do not leave me to my own wisdom.

Your word says, "I will instruct you and teach you in the way you should go; I will counsel you with my loving eye on you." (Psalm 32:8). I hold on to that promise now. Thank You that You are not a distant God who leaves His children to stumble through life alone. You are the Shepherd who leads, the Father who counsels, and the Lord who directs the steps of those who trust in You. Teach me to seek Your guidance with humility, patience, and sincerity. Keep me from demanding instant answers when You are teaching me to wait. Keep me also from ignoring the light You have already given in Your word.

Guide my mind by truth. Let Your word shape my thinking more than my feelings, circumstances, or preferences. Guard me from choices that may appear attractive but are not pleasing to You. If I am being driven by fear, quiet me. If I am being led by pride, humble me. If I am resisting Your will because it is costly, soften me and make me obedient. Give me a heart that truly wants Your way more than my own.

I ask not only for guidance in major decisions, but in the ordinary paths of daily life. Direct my speech, my attitudes, my reactions, and my responsibilities. Show me how to honour Christ in the small choices as well as the large ones. Open the right doors in Your time and close the wrong ones in mercy. Give me peace when I must wait, courage when I must act, and wisdom to recognise the difference. Above all, let guidance lead me closer to You, not merely closer to answers. Through Jesus Christ my Lord. **Amen.**

Gracious God, I ask You for guidance because I know how easily I can lose my way. Left to myself, I can act too quickly, hesitate too long, or mistake my own desires for Your leading. I can be influenced by pressure, by emotion, or by the opinions of others more than by Your truth. Yet You are wise without limit, faithful in all Your ways, and kind in the way You lead us. So, I come not trusting my instincts, but trusting You.

Thank You that You have not hidden from us all that we need in order to walk faithfully. You have given us Your word as a lamp to our feet and a light for our path. You have given us Your Spirit to illumine truth, convict the conscience, and incline the heart toward obedience. You have given us Christ, in whom all the treasures of wisdom and knowledge are found. So, I need not live in confusion as though guidance is unreachable. Help me to seek it in the right place and in the right spirit.

Your word says in James, "If any of you lacks wisdom, you should ask God, who gives generously to all without finding fault." I ask You now for that wisdom. Give me clarity where I am uncertain, restraint where I am impulsive, and patience where I am restless. Keep me from the folly of forcing outcomes that You have not appointed. Save me from reading signs into everything while neglecting the plain teaching of Scripture. Teach me to value holiness more than mere success and faithfulness more than visible results.

Guide me step by step. If the whole path is not shown at once, help me to trust You with the next step. If the answer is delayed, help me not to grow bitter or frantic. If the way becomes difficult, keep me from assuming that difficulty means You are absent. Lead me in paths of righteousness for Your name's sake. And when the way becomes plain, give me a willing heart to follow without delay.

Let Your guidance produce peace without passivity, action without presumption, and trust without fear. May I walk in such a way that, looking back, I will be able to say that the Lord directed my path in wisdom and love. I ask this through Jesus Christ, my Shepherd and my guide. **Amen.**

Father, I need Your guidance. My understanding is limited, my heart can be uncertain, and the way ahead is not always clear to me.

Please lead me in the path that is right. Keep me from being ruled by fear, impatience, pride, or self-interest.

Let Your word shape my thinking and Your Spirit guide my heart into obedience.

Give me wisdom for the decisions before me and peace for the things that are not yet clear. Help me to trust You when I must wait and to act faithfully when the way becomes plain.

Above all, let Your guidance keep me close to Christ and walking in a way that honours You. **Amen.**

Lord God, I ask You to guide me today.

Direct my steps, guard my choices, and keep me from wandering into paths that are unwise or displeasing to You.

I do not want merely what seems easiest or most attractive. I want what is true, right, and good in Your sight.

Give me wisdom to discern what matters most and courage to obey what You make clear.

If I am confused, calm me.

If I am hesitant, steady me. If I am rushing ahead, restrain me.

Teach me to walk humbly, prayerfully, and obediently before You.

Let Your loving eye be upon me, and lead me in the way everlasting. **Amen.**

Gracious Father, thank You that You do not leave Your children to guide themselves alone.

You are wise, faithful, and attentive to all my ways. As I seek direction, help me to listen to Your word, submit to Your will, and trust Your timing.

Keep me from forcing doors that You have not opened and from resisting the path You have marked out for me. Give me patience in uncertainty and faith for each next step.

Let my desire be not simply to know the future, but to walk closely with You in the present.

Guide me in such a way that my life becomes more obedient, more peaceful, and more centred on Christ. **Amen.**

Holy Father, I place before You the choices, questions, and uncertainties that weigh on my mind.

You know the way ahead perfectly, and I ask You to lead me in wisdom.

Shine the light of Your truth upon my path.

Make me attentive to Scripture, honest in prayer, and willing in heart.

Deliver me from confusion caused by my own desires and from anxiety caused by what I cannot yet see.

Teach me to trust that Your guidance is good, even when it unfolds slowly.

Lead me step by step, and grant that each decision I make may be shaped by love for You, faith in Christ, and a sincere desire to do Your will. **Amen.**

Heavenly Father, I come before You asking for wisdom. I need more than information, more than intelligence, and more than quick opinions. I need the kind of wisdom that comes from above - wisdom that is shaped by Your truth, governed by Your fear, and expressed in humble obedience. In a world full of noise, competing voices, and confident advice, I confess how easily I can become uncertain, impulsive, or led by what seems right in the moment. So, I ask You Lord to make me wise.

Your word says, "The fear of the Lord is the beginning of wisdom, and knowledge of the Holy One is understanding." (Proverbs 9:10). Teach me first that wisdom begins not with cleverness, but with reverence. Deliver me from the pride that assumes I already see clearly. Deliver me from the impatience that wants shortcuts rather than steady, godly discernment.

Grant me wisdom for decisions, conversations, responsibilities, and relationships. Help me to know not only what is lawful, but what is fitting; not only what is possible, but what is best; not only what is urgent, but what is truly important. In moments of tension, make me gentle. In times of uncertainty, make me prayerful. In situations that require courage, make me steadfast. Give me wisdom to speak when speech is needed and wisdom to remain silent when silence is better. Help me to avoid rash judgment, shallow thinking, and reactions driven by emotion rather than truth.

Your word also says, "If any of you lacks wisdom, you should ask God, who gives generously to all without finding fault." (James 1:5). I thank You for that promise. I come not as one who deserves wisdom, but as one who needs it and trusts Your generosity. Give me a mind shaped by Scripture, a conscience tender before Your Spirit, and a heart ready to obey what You make clear. Let wisdom appear not merely in my thoughts, but in my conduct - in patience, humility, integrity, and peace. Make me wise in Christ, and let that wisdom steady my life and bless those around me. Through Jesus Christ my Lord. **Amen.**

Gracious God, I ask You for the wisdom that comes from above. I live in a world where many voices claim authority and where foolishness often presents itself as confidence. I know how easy it is to mistake quick reactions for discernment, strong feelings for truth, or experience alone for wisdom. Yet true wisdom belongs to You. You are perfectly wise in all Your works and perfectly righteous in all Your ways. Nothing is hidden from Your sight, nothing confuses Your understanding, and nothing can overturn the goodness of Your purposes. So, I ask You to share with me, in measure, the wisdom that reflects Your own.

Teach me to think rightly. Let Your word renew my mind so that I do not simply absorb the spirit of the age or follow the instincts of my own heart. Guard me from worldly wisdom that is self-centred, proud, and driven by ambition.

Instead, let me know the wisdom Your word describes as "pure; then peace-loving, considerate, submissive, full of mercy and good fruit, impartial and sincere." (James 3:17). Form that kind of wisdom in me. Make me not merely sharp in thought, but godly in judgment and gentle in spirit.

I ask for wisdom in the ordinary places of life. Give me wisdom in work, in family relationships, in ministry, in speech, in stewardship, and in the use of time. Keep me from saying too much, promising too quickly, or deciding too rashly. Help me to pause before You, weigh things carefully, and move in step with Your truth. Where I am tempted to act out of fear, give me wisdom. Where I am tempted to act out of pride, humble me. Where I am confused, guide me patiently.

Above all, teach me the wisdom of knowing Christ more deeply. Let me value godliness above cleverness and faithfulness above appearance. Help me to remember that wisdom is not proved merely by what I know, but by how I live. Make my life thoughtful, prayerful, measured, and fruitful. And in all things, let Your wisdom guard me from folly and keep me walking in the way of peace. I ask this through Jesus Christ, in whom are hidden all the treasures of wisdom and knowledge. **Amen.**

Father, I ask You for wisdom.

I do not want merely quick thoughts or human cleverness. I want the wisdom that comes from fearing You, listening to Your word, and walking in humble obedience.

Teach me to think clearly, judge carefully, and respond in ways that honour Christ.

Guard me from rash decisions, proud assumptions, and foolish speech. Help me to know what is right, what is fitting, and what is most pleasing in Your sight.

Let Your Holy Spirit make me teachable and Your truth make me steady.

In all the ordinary choices of life, grant me wisdom that is pure, peace-loving, merciful, and sincere. **Amen.**

Lord God, You are perfectly wise, and I confess how much I need wisdom from You.

My understanding is limited, my perspective is small, and my heart can be too easily influenced by fear or pride.

So, I ask You to guide my mind and govern my choices.

Help me to look at life through the light of Scripture and not through impulse or pressure.

Give me wisdom to speak well, act patiently, and choose faithfully.

Keep me from the folly of leaning on myself. Let Your wisdom shape my thoughts, soften my spirit, and make my life more peaceful, more fruitful, and more like Christ. **Amen.**

Gracious Father, in the many demands and decisions of life, I ask for wisdom.

Help me to see beyond appearances and to value what truly matters.

Keep me from being impressed by what is loud, urgent, or merely successful.

Teach me instead to seek what is good, true, and lasting. Let wisdom guide my words, my priorities, and my relationships.

May I not be hasty in judgment or careless in counsel.

Make me humble enough to learn, patient enough to wait, and brave enough to obey when the right path becomes clear.

Let the wisdom You give bring peace to my heart and steadiness to my life. **Amen.**

Holy Father, I need wisdom for today.

There are things I do not understand, questions I cannot answer, and decisions I do not want to make foolishly.

Thank You that You invite those who lack wisdom to ask, and that You give generously. So, I come asking with trust.

Shape my mind by Your truth and my heart by Your grace.

Keep me from confusion, presumption, and shallow thinking. Help me to think clearly, pray sincerely, and act faithfully.

In all things, let wisdom keep me near to Christ and lead me in ways that are humble, godly, and full of peace. **Amen.**

13. PRAYERS FOR DISCERNMENT

Heavenly Father, I come before You asking for discernment. I need more than general wisdom. I need the grace to distinguish between truth and error, between what is merely attractive and what is truly good, between what seems right for a moment and what is right in Your sight. I live in a world full of voices, claims, opinions, pressures, and appearances. My own heart can also be unreliable, for it can be drawn by emotion, impatience, pride, or fear. So, I ask You to make me discerning.

Your word says in Philippians 1:9-10, "And this is my prayer: that your love may abound more and more in knowledge and depth of insight, so that you may be able to discern what is best." Let that prayer be fulfilled in me. Help me not merely to spot what is obviously wrong, but to discern what is best. Teach me to recognise the difference between what is lawful and what is wise, between what is good and what is better, between what flatters the flesh and what truly honours Christ. Guard me from shallow judgments and hasty conclusions.

Give me discernment in doctrine, so that I may not be carried along by teaching that sounds persuasive but departs from Your word. Give me discernment in relationships, so that I may recognise what helps or harms my walk with You. Give me discernment in decisions, so that I may not mistake urgency for calling or outward success for Your deep blessing. Give me discernment in my own heart, that I may see where hidden motives, self-deception, or quiet compromises may be at work. Search me and expose what I would rather not see.

I ask that discernment would be shaped by love, holiness, and humility. Do not let me become suspicious, harsh, or proud in the name of discernment. Let it be governed by truth and kindness together.

Make me thoughtful, prayerful, and steady. Help me to test all things by Scripture, to listen carefully, and to act with integrity. Where there is confusion, clarify. Where there is subtle danger, warn me. Through Jesus Christ my Lord. **Amen.**

Gracious God, I ask You for spiritual discernment in a world where not everything is as it first appears. There are things that look wise but are empty, things that sound good but are false, and things that promise life while quietly leading the heart away from You. I confess that I do not always see clearly. Sometimes I am too quick to trust, too slow to question, or too influenced by what is visible and immediate. Yet You see all things perfectly. Nothing deceives You, and no darkness is hidden from Your sight. So, I ask You to share with me the discernment that comes from Your Spirit and Your word.

Thank You that You have not left Your people without light. You have given us the Scriptures to train our minds and steady our judgments. You have given us the Holy Spirit to illumine truth, convict the conscience, and help us recognise what accords with godliness. You have given us Christ Himself, who is truth incarnate and the pattern of perfect spiritual clarity. Help me to look to Him and hold thoughts shaped not by the confusion of the world, but by the truth of Your kingdom.

In Romans 12:2, Your word says, "Do not conform to the pattern of this world, but be transformed by the renewing of your mind." I ask for that renewing work in me. Renew my thinking so that I may test and approve what Your will is - Your good, pleasing, and perfect will. Keep me from being conformed to the values, assumptions, and instincts of a world that does not know You. Teach me to recognise compromise before it hardens into disobedience. Teach me to sense when something is spiritually unhealthy, though culturally admired.

Give me discernment also in daily living. Help me to know when to speak and when to be silent, when to act and when to wait, when to engage and when to withdraw. Make me alert to what strengthens faith and alert also to what weakens it. Guard me from deception, from foolish influences, and from the self-deception that can live within my own heart. Let discernment make me neither fearful nor proud, but sober, humble, and anchored in truth. I ask this through Jesus Christ, who is my wisdom and my light. **Amen.**

Father, I ask You for discernment.

Help me to distinguish between what is true and what is false, between what is merely appealing and what is truly good.

Guard me from shallow judgments, hasty choices, and the subtle pull of deception.

Let Your word train my mind and Your Spirit sharpen my conscience.

Keep me from being led by appearances, emotions, or the pressure of others. Teach me to test all things carefully and to hold fast to what is good.

Make me humble, watchful, and clear-sighted, so that I may walk in truth, honour Christ, and avoid the paths that would quietly lead me away from You. **Amen.**

Lord God, in a world full of so many competing voices, I need discernment from You.

I do not want to be gullible, careless, or spiritually dull. Help me to recognise what pleases You and what does not.

Show me where danger lies beneath smooth words or attractive appearances.

Expose in me any mixed motives, hidden pride, or willingness to compromise.

Let Scripture be the measure of my thinking and Christ the centre of my judgment. Teach me not only to avoid what is wrong, but to choose what is best.

Keep me steady in truth, tender in conscience, and wise in the way I live each day before You. **Amen.**

Gracious Father God, grant me discernment in my decisions, relationships, and spiritual life.

Keep me from confusing activity with fruitfulness, success with faithfulness, or confidence with truth. Help me to see clearly where I am vulnerable and where I need to be watchful.

Guard me from influences that would weaken my love for Christ or dull my appetite for holiness.

Give me insight to recognise what leads toward life and what leads away from it.

Let me not be naïve, but neither let me become cynical.

Make me discerning, with a heart ruled by love, humility, and obedience to Your word. **Amen.**

Lord God, search me and give me discernment.

Show me what I do not naturally see and correct what I have wrongly judged.

Renew my mind so that I may recognise Your will and resist what is false.

Help me to listen carefully, pray thoughtfully, and move cautiously where caution is needed.

Deliver me from self-deception and from the quiet compromises that can harden the heart over time.

Let discernment be a safeguard to my soul and a servant to my obedience.

Keep me near to Christ, grounded in Scripture, and sensitive to the leading of Your Spirit in all things. **Amen.**

14. PRAYERS FOR WAITING FOR GOD'S TIMING

Heavenly Father, I come before You in a season of waiting and ask for grace to trust Your timing. Waiting is not easy for me. I often want clarity quickly, answers immediately, and change without delay. I want doors to open when I think they should open and burdens to lift when I think they should lift. Yet again and again You teach me that Your timing is not hurried, uncertain, or late. It is wise, good, and perfectly governed by Your love. So I ask You to teach my heart how to wait well.

Your word says, "I wait for the Lord, my whole being waits, and in His word I put my hope." (Psalm 130:5). Let that become true of me. Help me not to wait with resentment, unbelief, or inward agitation, but with hope rooted in Your promises. Keep me from the impatience that tries to force outcomes. Save me from the fear that assumes delay means neglect. Guard me from interpreting silence as absence.

Teach me to believe that waiting is not wasted time in Your hands. Use it to deepen my faith, purify my motives, expose my idols, and make me more willing to receive Your will rather than merely demand my own. If I must wait longer than I want, let me not grow bitter. If I do not understand why the delay continues, let me not accuse You in my heart. Instead, make me quiet in trust and steady in obedience. Help me to continue praying, listening, serving, and hoping.

I place before You the specific things for which I am waiting - the answers I long for, the changes I hope to see, the guidance I seek, and the burdens I wish were lifted. I ask You to act in mercy and power. But until Your time comes, give me the grace to wait with a surrendered spirit. Keep me from grasping at what You have not yet given.

Keep me from despair when the way seems slow. Let waiting become for me a school of trust, where I learn that You are enough even before the answer arrives. And when Your time comes, may I see that Your way was better than my haste. Through Jesus Christ my Lord. **Amen.**

Gracious God, I confess that waiting can be one of the hardest disciplines of faith. It is difficult to live in the space between promise and fulfilment, between prayer and answer, between longing and arrival. In those spaces, my heart can become restless, doubtful, and weary. I can be tempted to run ahead of You or to sink into discouragement. Yet You remain sovereign over every season. You are never delayed by weakness, never hindered by confusion, and never late in accomplishing what You have purposed. So, I come asking not only for answers, but for grace to wait under Your hand.

Your word says, "There is a time for everything, and a season for every activity under the heavens." (Ecclesiastes 3:1). Help me to believe that truth in a personal way. I do not need to panic because I do not control the timetable. I do not need to force what should be received. I do not need to despair when what I long for remains out of reach. You know the right time. You know what must happen in me before what I seek is entrusted to me. You know what dangers You are sparing me from and what good You are quietly accomplishing in delay.

Teach me to wait with prayerfulness, bringing my desires honestly before You without demanding that You obey my timetable. Teach me to wait with watchfulness, so that I remain ready to respond when Your time does come. And teach me to wait with thankfulness, remembering that even now I am not deprived of Your goodness. Christ is mine. Your Spirit is with me. Your promises stand firm.

If the waiting continues, strengthen me. If disappointment presses on me, comfort me. If envy tempts me as I watch others receive what I desire, guard my heart. Keep me from measuring Your love by speed. Make me patient without becoming passive, hopeful without becoming demanding, and faithful while the answer still tarries.

In Your perfect time, do what is best. Until then, keep me trusting, worshipping, and at peace beneath Your wise and fatherly care. I ask this through Jesus Christ, who waited in perfect obedience to Your will. **Amen.**

Father, teach me to wait for Your timing with trust and peace.

I confess that I want quick answers and immediate change, but You are wise in all Your ways and good in all You do.

Keep me from impatience, fear, and the urge to force what You have not yet given.

Help me to believe that delay is not abandonment and silence is not absence. While I wait, strengthen my faith, steady my heart, and keep me obedient in the present moment.

Let waiting become a place where I learn deeper trust in You.

Hold me back from rushing ahead and keep me near to Christ while I wait for Your wise and perfect time. **Amen.**

Lord God, I place before You the things I am waiting for and the burdens that feel unresolved.

You know how hard it can be to live with unanswered prayers and uncertain timing.

Yet I thank You that Your clock is never wrong and Your purposes are never delayed.

Help me to wait without bitterness, anxiety, or unbelief. Teach me to rest in Your wisdom when I cannot understand Your timing.

Make me patient in hope and faithful in prayer.

Let my soul be anchored not in quick outcomes, but in Your unchanging character.

Keep me watchful, surrendered, and at peace until Your time becomes clear. **Amen.**

Gracious Father, in this season of waiting I ask You for grace.

Guard me from discouragement and from the temptation to take matters into my own hands.

Help me to trust that what You delay, You delay wisely, and what You give, You give well. Use this time to deepen my faith and to loosen my grip on my own plans.

Let waiting teach me dependence, humility, and hope.

May I not waste this season in frustration, but receive it as part of Your loving work in me.

Keep me prayerful, steady, and ready to follow when Your time arrives. Until then, let Your promises sustain my heart. **Amen.**

Father God, I wait before You with unfulfilled desires and questions that remain unanswered.

You know them all, and I place them again into Your hands.

Teach me not to measure Your care by how my circumstances change.

Remind me that Your faithfulness is constant even when the path feels slow. Give me a willing spirit to wait and a quiet heart to trust.

Keep me from envy, from restlessness, and from despair. Let me continue to walk obediently in today's light while tomorrow remains with You.

May waiting not weaken my faith, but strengthen it as I learn that Your timing is always wise and always good. **Amen.**

15. PRAYERS FOR NEW BEGINNINGS

Gracious Father, I come before You at the threshold of a new beginning. Whether this new season has arrived by joyful choice, unexpected change, or difficult necessity, I place it into Your hands. New beginnings can stir hope, but they can also awaken uncertainty, fear, and a deep awareness of my weakness. I do not know all that lies ahead. I cannot foresee every challenge, every blessing, or every demand. But I thank You that I do not step into it alone. You go before me, remain with me, and hold the future in Your sovereign care.

Your word says, "See, I am doing a new thing! Now it springs up; do you not perceive it?" (Isaiah 43:19). Help me to receive that truth with faith. Open my eyes to the work You may be doing, even if it does not look exactly as I expected. Guard me from clinging too tightly to the past, whether from regret, nostalgia, disappointment, or fear. Do not let old failures define me or old comforts imprison me. Teach me to believe that Your mercies are new every morning and that Your faithfulness extends into every unfamiliar place.

As I begin this new season, purify my motives and steady my steps. Keep me from rushing ahead in self-confidence and from shrinking back in unbelief. Let this beginning be shaped by prayer, guided by Scripture, and strengthened by trust in Christ. If there are decisions to make, grant me wisdom. If there are relationships to build, grant me grace. If there are responsibilities to carry, grant me strength. If there are disappointments ahead, prepare me with patience. If there are blessings ahead, keep me humble and thankful.

Above all, let this new beginning draw me closer to You. Use it to deepen my dependence, enlarge my faith, and renew my love for Christ. Teach me to take the next step faithfully and leave the unseen parts of the path in Your hands. May this new beginning become not a monument to my plans, but a testimony to Your guidance, provision, and grace. Through Jesus Christ my Lord, my Saviour, and my Redeemer. **Amen.**

Heavenly Father, thank You that with You there is always grace for new beginnings. I praise You that You are the God who restores, calls, leads, and renews. You are not limited by my past, discouraged by my weakness, or surprised by the changes that now stand before me. What feels new and uncertain to me is fully known to You. Before I arrived at this moment, You were already here. Before I take the first step, You have already prepared the way. Thank You that the future is not a place where I must find my own strength, but a place where I will continue to discover Your faithfulness.

I confess that beginnings can unsettle me. Even when they are good, they often expose how much I like familiarity, control, and visible certainty. Yet You call me to walk by faith and not by sight. Your word says, "Forget the former things; do not dwell on the past." (Isaiah 43:18). Teach me rightly to remember the past without being trapped by it. Let me learn from it, thank You for Your mercies in it, and repent of what needs repentance, but help me not to live looking backward when You are calling me forward. Free me from the fear of change and the burden of trying to secure everything before I move.

I pray for courage for this new beginning. Courage to obey, courage to trust, courage to adapt, and courage to persevere if the path proves harder than I hoped. Keep me from idealising what lies ahead, but also from dreading it. Let me meet it soberly, prayerfully, and hopefully, knowing that the same God who has kept me until now will keep me still. If this season brings opportunities, help me use them faithfully. If it brings stretching and discipline, help me receive them humbly. If it brings hidden blessings, let me recognise them with gratitude.

Let Christ be at the centre of this beginning. May I not seek simply a better situation, but a deeper walk with You. Make me attentive to Your voice, teachable in spirit, and steady in daily obedience. Let this new chapter begin well and if I am tempted to fear what is unknown, remind me that the One who holds tomorrow is the same One who loved me at the cross. I entrust this new beginning to You, through Jesus Christ, my hope and my future. **Amen.**

Father, I place this new beginning into Your hands.

What lies ahead is not fully known to me, but it is fully known to You.

Thank You that I do not need to fear the future when You are already there.

Give me grace to step forward with trust, humility, and courage. Keep me from clinging to the past or from rushing ahead in self-confidence.

Let this new season begin with prayer, be guided by Your word, and be shaped by obedience to Christ. Where I feel uncertain, steady me. Where I feel weak, strengthen me.

May this beginning become a place of growth, faith, and fresh dependence on Your faithful care. **Amen.**

Lord God, thank You that Your mercies are new and that in You there is always grace for a new beginning.

As I enter this season, help me to do so with a willing and peaceful heart.

Free me from fear, from regret, and from the burden of trying to control what only You can govern.

Give me wisdom for each step and patience for all that will unfold gradually.

Let Christ remain at the centre of all my plans and hopes.

Teach me to walk by faith and not by sight.

May this new beginning not simply change my circumstances, but deepen my trust, purify my motives, and draw me nearer to You. **Amen.**

Gracious Father, I come to You with both hope and uncertainty as I face this new beginning.

Thank You that You are the same yesterday, today, and forever. When everything around me feels unfamiliar, You remain unchanging and faithful. Guide me as I step into what is next.

Help me not to dwell on what is behind in a way that weakens my courage or clouds my vision.

Renew my mind, steady my spirit, and direct my path.

Let me begin not in anxiety, but in prayer, not in pride, but in dependence.

Lead me forward in peace, and let this season bear good fruit for Your glory. **Amen.**

Holy Father, this new beginning feels significant, and I ask for Your help.

Go before me into every detail I cannot yet see.

Prepare me for the responsibilities, relationships, opportunities, and challenges that lie ahead.

Keep me from fear of failure and from the pride of self-reliance.

Give me a heart that is ready to learn, willing to obey, and quick to trust.

Let the future not be a source of torment to me, but a place where I discover again Your guidance and grace.

May this beginning be marked by hope, sustained by faith, and made fruitful by Your presence with me. **Amen.**

Heavenly Father, I come before You asking for a teachable spirit. Left to myself, I can be slow to listen, quick to defend myself, and reluctant to be corrected. Pride rises easily in my heart. I can prefer my own opinions, cling to familiar ways, and resist the very truth that would help me grow. Yet You are a wise and gracious Father, and Your corrections are never unnecessary or cruel. You teach because You love. You discipline because You are committed to my holiness. So, I ask You to soften my heart and make me ready to learn.

Your word says, "Whoever heeds life-giving correction will be at home among the wise." (Proverbs 15:31). Help me to believe that correction is a gift and not merely an irritation. Deliver me from the foolishness that resents instruction and assumes it already knows enough. Keep me from being defensive when Your word and Spirit exposes me, when wise counsel challenges me, or when circumstances reveal weaknesses I would rather ignore.

Teach me first through Your word. Give me ears that are eager to hear, a mind that is willing to think carefully, and a conscience that responds honestly to truth. Do not let me read Scripture merely to confirm what I already think. Instead, let me come with humility, ready to be corrected, strengthened, and guided. Where I have been stubborn in attitude, humble me. Where I have been blind to my own faults, open my eyes.

Teach me also through wise believers, through the Church, and through the providences of daily life. Help me to recognise when You are speaking through encouragement, disappointment, warning, delay, or rebuke. Save me from the pride that dismisses others too quickly. Give me discernment to receive what is true and the grace to act upon it. Above all, make me teachable before Christ. Let me sit at His feet with a willing heart. May a teachable spirit guard me from folly, deepen my maturity, and make my life more fruitful in every good work. Through Jesus Christ my Lord. **Amen.**

Gracious God, I ask You for the humility and openness that belong to a teachable spirit. There is much I do not know, much I do not yet understand, and much in me that still needs to be changed. Yet I confess that I do not always welcome the process by which growth comes. I can want maturity without correction, wisdom without listening, and progress without the humbling work of being shown where I am wrong. Forgive me for this resistance. Teach me to receive Your instruction with gratitude.

Thank You that You are patient with me. You do not abandon Your children to ignorance, folly, or spiritual immaturity. You teach us by Your word, by Your Spirit, by faithful believers, and by the experiences You appoint in Your wise providence. You are committed to finishing the good work You have begun in me. Because of that, I do not need to fear being corrected. I may welcome Your teaching because it comes from a Father who loves me and from a Saviour who gave Himself for me.

Your word says, "Instruct the wise and they will be wiser still; teach the righteous and they will add to their learning." (Proverbs 9:9). Make that true of me. Let me not reach a point where I think I have outgrown the need to learn. Keep me from spiritual self-satisfaction, from the blindness of pride, and from the stubbornness that resists change. If there are attitudes in me that are proud, expose them. If there are habits that are unwise, correct them. If there are truths I have neglected, bring them freshly before me.

Give me a spirit that listens well. Help me to receive counsel without resentment, correction without bitterness, and instruction without defensiveness. Teach me to weigh what I hear carefully by Scripture, but never to use discernment as a cover for pride. Let me grow not only in knowledge, but in humility, gentleness, and obedience. May a teachable spirit make me more useful in Your service, more peaceful in my relationships, and more like Christ in daily life. I ask this through Jesus Christ, who learned obedience in suffering and now teaches His people by grace and truth. **Amen.**

Father, give me a teachable spirit.

Save me from pride, defensiveness, and the foolishness that resists correction. Help me to listen carefully to Your word and to receive truth with humility and obedience.

When You expose sin in me, keep me from excuses. When You show me a better way, keep me from stubbornness.

Teach me to welcome instruction as a gift of Your love and not as a threat to my pride.

Make me eager to grow, willing to repent, and glad to be shaped by Your hand.

Let humility open the way for wisdom, and let a teachable spirit make me more fruitful, peaceful, and more like Christ. **Amen.**

Lord God, I confess that I do not always find it easy to be taught. My heart can be slow to listen and quick to defend itself.

Forgive me for resisting what would help me grow.

Give me grace to hear Your voice in Scripture, in wise counsel, and in the circumstances You appoint.

Help me to receive correction without bitterness and instruction without resentment.

Keep me from thinking I know enough already. Instead, make me humble, curious, and willing to learn.

May Your truth not simply pass through my mind, but shape my heart, govern my choices, and lead me into greater obedience to Christ. **Amen.**

Gracious Father, make me teachable before You.

Open my ears to hear, my mind to understand, and my heart to respond.

Deliver me from the pride that rejects instruction and from the fear that avoids correction.

Let me not confuse stubbornness with strength or defensiveness with wisdom.

Teach me to receive Your truth with gratitude and to act upon it with sincerity.

Give me discernment to recognise where You are showing me something I need to learn.

May I never outgrow the posture of a disciple.

Keep me at the feet of Christ, ready to be corrected, strengthened, and led in the ways of righteousness. **Amen.**

Holy Father, I ask You to form in me a spirit that is willing to be taught. There is still much in me that needs Your shaping grace.

So, soften what is hard, humble what is proud, and awaken what is dull. Help me to welcome the truth even when it searches me deeply.

Keep me from resisting Your work because it is uncomfortable. Let Your word have full authority over my thoughts, attitudes, and decisions.

And when others speak wisely into my life, grant me grace to listen with honesty and patience. Make me teachable, so that I may grow in wisdom, holiness, and likeness to Christ. **Amen.**

17. PRAYERS FOR DEEPER FAITH

Heavenly Father, I come before You asking for deeper faith. I believe in You, I trust in Christ, and I know that salvation is by grace through faith, yet I also know how often my faith feels small, fragile, and easily shaken. There are times when I rest in Your promises with glad confidence, but there are other times when fear rises, doubts press in, and my heart becomes more aware of circumstances than of Your faithfulness. So I ask You to deepen my faith - not merely to increase my religious feeling, but to root me more firmly in the truth of who You are.

Your word says, "Immediately the boy's father exclaimed, 'I do believe; help me overcome my unbelief!'" (Mark 9:24). That is often the cry of my own heart. I do believe, yet I also see unbelief still lingering within me. I confess how easily I lean on what I can see, predict, and control. Forgive me for the ways I live as though Your promises were uncertain and Your care needed to be doubted. Strengthen what is weak in me and correct what is false in me.

Deepen my faith by leading me again to Christ. Let me look away from myself and fix my eyes upon Him - upon His perfect obedience, His atoning death, His victorious resurrection, and His present reign. Remind me that my security does not rest on the strength of my grip on Him, but on the strength of His grip on me. When my faith feels small, teach me that its power lies not in its size, but in its object. And the object of my faith is the living Saviour who cannot fail.

Deepen my faith also through Your word. Let Your promises become more precious to me than my fears and more persuasive than my doubts. When answers are delayed, let faith wait. When suffering presses hard, let faith cling to Your character. Keep me from the shallow desire for a faith that is merely comfortable. Give me instead a faith that is steady, resilient, humble, and fruitful. May deeper faith make me calmer in uncertainty, stronger in obedience, and more joyful in Christ. I ask this through Jesus Christ my Lord. **Amen.**

Gracious God, I ask You to deepen my faith because I know how much I need it. Faith is not only for the beginning of the Christian life, but for every step of it. I need faith to pray, faith to obey, faith to wait, faith to endure, and faith to die well. Yet I confess that faith does not always come easily. Sometimes I am strong in confidence, and at other times I am weak, hesitant, and unsettled. I can be distracted by what is visible, discouraged by what is painful, and worn down by the long struggle of trusting You in a fallen world. So, I ask You to strengthen and deepen my faith.

Thank You that You are not offended by the honest cry of a weak believer. You do not despise those who come to You asking for help. You know our frame. You remember that we are dust. Yet You also delight to strengthen what is weak and to mature what is young and fragile. Thank You that faith itself is Your gift and that the One who began the good work in me will carry it on to completion.

Your word says, "So then faith comes from hearing, and hearing through the word of Christ." (Romans 10:17). Make me one who listens well. Let me sit under Your word not as a mere observer, but as one who needs life, light, and strength. Let Your truth expose unbelief where it has lodged in my heart. Let Your promises feed confidence in Your goodness. Let the gospel steady me again and again. When faith weakens, bring me back to what is unchanging - Christ crucified, Christ risen, Christ reigning, Christ returning.

Let deeper faith show itself in daily life. May it make me less anxious, less self-reliant, less controlled by appearances, and less shaken by delays. Let it make me more ready to obey even when I do not see the whole path, more patient in waiting, and more peaceful in hardship. Keep me from a faith that speaks boldly in public but collapses under private pressure. Make my faith real, durable, and quietly strong. And in all of this, let deeper faith produce not self-confidence, but greater dependence upon You and greater love for Christ. Through Jesus Christ, the author and perfecter of faith. **Amen.**

Father, deepen my faith. I believe in You, yet I know how often my heart is shaken by fear, delay, and uncertainty.

Forgive the unbelief that lingers within me and strengthen what is weak.

Help me to trust Your character when I cannot trace Your hand and to rest in Your promises when circumstances feel unsettled.

Let faith rise above what I can see and hold firmly to what You have said.

Keep me near to Christ, and remind me that He is faithful even when I feel fragile.

Make my faith steady, sincere, and fruitful, so that I may walk with greater peace, obedience, and confidence in Your loving care. **Amen.**

Lord God, I ask You for deeper faith - not a passing feeling, but a stronger trust in who You are.

Teach me to believe Your word more than my fears and Your promises more than my questions.

When my faith is weak, do not let me drift from You, but draw me closer.

Strengthen me through Scripture, through prayer, and through remembering the grace that is mine in Christ.

Help me to walk by faith and not by sight, to obey without demanding full explanation, and to wait without losing heart.

Let deeper faith shape the way I think, pray, endure, and serve. In Jesus' name I pray. **Amen.**

Gracious Father, I know that faith must grow, and I ask You to deepen it in me.

Rescue me from shallow trust that depends too much on visible comfort and easy answers.

Teach me to trust You in the dark as well as in the light, in weakness as well as in strength, and in waiting as well as in receiving.

Let trials drive me nearer to You and not away from You.

May every season of life become a place where faith is tested, purified, and strengthened.

Keep my eyes on Christ, and let deeper faith make me calmer in trouble, hopeful in prayer, and willing in obedience. **Amen.**

Holy Father, increase and deepen my faith.

I confess that I often lean too heavily on what I can measure, manage, and understand.

But You call me to trust You with my whole heart. Help me to do that more truly.

Give me a faith that listens carefully to Your word, prays honestly, and obeys readily. When doubts press in, remind me of Your faithfulness.

When fears rise, remind me of Your power. When I feel spiritually weak, remind me that Christ is enough.

Let deeper faith root me more firmly in Your love and make my life more peaceful, strong, and Christ-centred. **Amen.**

18. PRAYERS FOR ASSURANCE OF SALVATION

Heavenly Father, I come before You asking for deeper assurance of salvation. I thank You that my hope does not rest in my feelings, or my ability to hold myself close to You, but in Your grace given to me in Jesus Christ. Yet there are times when doubts rise, when I see my sin more clearly than Your mercy, and when I am tempted to question whether I truly belong to You. That's when, I need You to steady me.

Your word says, "Therefore, there is now no condemnation for those who are in Christ Jesus." (Romans 8:1). Let that truth sink deeply into my soul. Thank You that if I am in Christ, my guilt has been answered, my condemnation removed, and my standing before You secured by His finished work. I do not stand before You on the basis of my record, but on the basis of His righteousness. I do not live under the shadow of judgment, but in the light of mercy. Teach me to rest there.

I confess that sometimes I look too much at the weakness of my faith instead of the strength of my Saviour. I look at my failures, my inconsistencies, my coldness, and my struggles, and I begin to fear. But remind me that assurance is not found in pretending sin is small. It is found in knowing that Christ is sufficient. His blood truly cleanses. His righteousness truly covers. His intercession truly continues. His promises truly stand. Keep me from listening to the accusing voice that would drive me away from the cross.

Grant me the witness of Your Spirit through Your word. Let the truths of the gospel shine more brightly than my doubts. Give me a heart that trusts what You have said, a conscience that finds peace in Christ, and a life that increasingly bears the fruit of Your saving work. When I sin, lead me quickly to repentance, not to despair. When I feel weak, draw me again to the throne of grace. Let assurance make me humble, thankful, and eager to obey - not careless, but secure in Your love. May I live as one who is truly forgiven, truly adopted, and truly kept by the power of God through faith. **Amen.**

Gracious God, I thank You for the salvation You have provided in Jesus Christ, full, free, and sufficient for all who believe. I praise You that You do not save partially, temporarily, or uncertainly, but with a salvation grounded in Your eternal purpose and secured by the work of Your Son. Yet I confess that I do not always live in the comfort of that truth. I ask You now to strengthen my assurance and anchor me more firmly in what You have promised.

Your word says, "I write these things to you who believe in the name of the Son of God so that you may know that you have eternal life." (1 John 5:13). Thank You that assurance is not presumption when it rests upon Christ. You desire Your children to know the security of Your saving grace. You do not call us to live in constant uncertainty, but in confident dependence upon the One who saves to the uttermost. Help me, then, to receive with faith what You have said. Where unbelief clouds my peace, correct me by Your truth. Where sin has robbed me of joy, restore me through repentance.

Keep me from building assurance on unstable foundations. Let me not rest in spiritual impressions, past emotions, or comparison with others. Let my confidence be rooted in Christ crucified and risen, in the promises of Your word, and in the quiet witness of a life being changed by grace. Teach me that assurance grows as I look outward to Christ, upward to Your promises, and inward only in the sober and humble recognition of Your sanctifying work. Make me thankful for every evidence of grace, yet never tempted to trust those evidences more than the Saviour Himself.

Let assurance bring peace to my soul and strength to my obedience. May it free me from slavish fear and deepen trust. When accusations rise, remind me that Christ has answered them. When doubts press hard, remind me that Your word stands firm. When I grow weary, remind me that the Shepherd who sought me will also keep me. Let me live and die in the comfort of belonging to Jesus, secure in His love and upheld by His grace. **Amen.**

Gracious Father, I thank You that my salvation rests not on my feelings, but on Your finished work in Christ.

Yet I confess that there are times when my assurance feels weak and uncertain.

Doubts can arise, and my heart can become unsettled.

So, I ask You to strengthen my assurance.

Remind me that I am saved by grace through faith, not by my performance or consistency.

Help me to rest in the promises of Your word and not in the shifting experience of my emotions. Let the truth of the gospel anchor me firmly.

May I grow in confidence, knowing that I belong to You and that You will never let me go. **Amen.**

Faithful God, I ask You to deepen my assurance of salvation. When doubts arise, help me to return to what is true.

You have called me, saved me, and secured me in Christ. Let me not look inward for certainty, but outward to the cross.

Remind me that Jesus has done all that is necessary for my salvation.

Keep me from fear that I may be lost or forgotten.

Instead, fill my heart with the quiet confidence that I am known and loved by You.

Strengthen my faith so that I may live with peace and joy, resting in the certainty of Your saving grace. **Amen.**

Lord, when my heart feels uncertain, draw me back to Your promises.

You have said that whoever believes in the Son has eternal life, and I hold onto that truth.

Help me not to be shaken by passing doubts or changing emotions.

Give me a steady confidence rooted in Your word.

Let Your Spirit bear witness within me that I am Your child. Teach me to rest in what Christ has accomplished and to trust that my salvation is secure in Him.

May assurance grow in me, bringing peace to my heart and stability to my faith. **Amen.**

Gracious God and Father, I bring before You my desire for greater assurance.

I do not want to live in uncertainty, but in the confidence of Your grace.

Help me to remember that my salvation depends on Christ alone.

When I feel unworthy, remind me that He is sufficient.

When I feel unsure, remind me that Your promises do not change.

Strengthen my faith and quiet my doubts.

Let me walk in the joy of knowing that I am forgiven, accepted, and secure in You. May this assurance shape my life and deepen my love for You. **Amen.**

Lord of truth, I come before You asking for a deeper hunger for Your word. I know that Scripture is not merely a book, but Your living voice to Your people. It is light for the path, food for the soul, and truth that sets the heart free. Yet I confess that my appetite for it is not always what it should be. There are times when I approach Your word with eagerness and joy, but there are other times when I feel distracted, dull, or easily drawn to lesser things. Forgive me for treating lightly what is of greatest value. Awaken in me a renewed desire to know You through Your word.

You have said that Your word is "living and active, sharper than any double-edged sword." (Hebrews 4:12). Help me to believe that. Keep me from approaching Scripture as something familiar, predictable, or optional. Instead, let me come with expectancy, knowing that You speak through what You have written. Open my mind to understand, my heart to receive, and my will to obey.

I ask You to cultivate in me a true spiritual appetite. Just as the body longs for food, let my soul long for Your word. Your word says, "Like newborn babies, crave pure spiritual milk, so that by it you may grow up in your salvation." (1 Peter 2:2). Create that craving in me. Where my desire is weak, strengthen it. Where my attention wanders, focus it. Where my heart resists, soften it. Let me not be content with a surface reading, but draw me into deeper meditation, reflection, and delight.

Guard me from reading without listening, from studying without applying, and from knowing without loving. Let Your word shape my thinking, correct my errors, expose my sin, and comfort my heart. Make it precious to me in times of joy and essential to me in times of trial. Let it become a steady companion, a source of wisdom, and a means by which I grow in Christ. May hunger for Scripture deepen my faith, guide my steps, and keep me anchored in truth. Through Jesus Christ, the living Word, **Amen.**

God of all wisdom, I thank You for the gift of Scripture. You have not left us to guess what is true or to wander in confusion. You have spoken clearly, faithfully, and sufficiently in Your word. Yet I confess that I do not always treasure this gift as I should. I can neglect it, rush through it, or treat it as a task rather than a delight. I ask You now to renew in me a deep and lasting hunger for Your truth.

Your word says, "Your words were found, and I ate them; they were my joy and my heart's delight." (Jeremiah 15:16). Let that be my experience. Teach me not only to read Scripture, but to feed upon it. Let it nourish my faith, strengthen my soul, and shape my inner life.

Deliver me from the habit of turning first to other voices for guidance while neglecting the voice of God. Reorder my priorities so that Your word holds the central place it deserves.

I ask for more than discipline - I ask for desire. Give me a heart that wants Your word, not merely one that knows it should read it. When I am tempted to neglect it, draw me back. When I am distracted, refocus me. When I feel no appetite, awaken it again. Help me to see that time in Scripture is never wasted, but always fruitful when approached with faith and humility.

Let Your word dwell in me richly. Let it guide my decisions, steady my emotions, and correct my thinking. In moments of temptation, let it guard me. In moments of confusion, let it direct me. In moments of sorrow, let it comfort me. In moments of joy, let it deepen my gratitude. May it become the lens through which I see life and the foundation upon which I stand.

Above all, let Scripture lead me to Christ. Keep me from treating it as an end in itself. Let me see in its pages the glory of my Saviour, the beauty of His work, and the certainty of His promises.

And as I behold Him, may my hunger for Your word grow stronger, my love for You grow deeper, and my life become more aligned with Your truth. Through Jesus Christ, **Amen.**

Lord, give me a deep and growing hunger for Your word.

I confess that my appetite for Scripture is not always what it should be.

I can easily turn to other things for comfort, distraction, or guidance, while neglecting the very truth that nourishes my soul.

Forgive me for this and awaken in me a genuine desire for Your word. Help me to come to it not out of duty alone, but with expectation and longing.

Open my eyes to see its beauty and my heart to receive its truth. Let Scripture become a daily source of strength, shaping my thinking, guiding my decisions, and drawing me closer to You.

May I delight in Your word and find in it the life You promise. In Jesus' name I pray. **Amen.**

Gracious God, stir within me a renewed love for Scripture.

Your word is living, powerful, and full of wisdom, yet I confess that I do not always treat it with the attention it deserves.

Too often I approach it hurriedly or set it aside altogether. Change that in me, I pray.

Give me a steady desire to read, reflect, and meditate on what You have spoken.

Help me to make time for it and to guard that time carefully. As I read, give me understanding. As I think on Your word, give me clarity. As I apply it, give me obedience.

Let Your word take root deeply in my life, so that it shapes not only what I know, but who I become. **Amen.**

Faithful Father, thank You that You have spoken clearly through Your word.

You have not left me without guidance, but have given me truth that is reliable and life-giving.

Help me to treasure this gift more deeply. Keep me from reading Scripture casually or without attention. Instead, give me a focused mind and a receptive heart.

Let me hear Your voice as I read and respond with faith and obedience. Guard me from knowledge that does not lead to change.

May Your word dwell richly within me, shaping my attitudes, correcting my thinking, and strengthening my faith. Let it become a constant source of nourishment, guiding me in every part of life. **Amen.**

Holy Lord, I bring before You my desire to grow in love for Your word.

Draw me to it regularly and keep me from neglecting it when life becomes busy or distracting.

When I feel dry, refresh my heart through its truth.

When I feel uncertain, guide me through its wisdom. Help me to read slowly, to think carefully, and to respond faithfully.

Let Scripture become central in my life, shaping how I think, speak, and live each day. Give me joy in discovering its riches and patience in understanding its depth.

May Your word dwell in me richly and lead me into a deeper walk with You. **Amen.**

20. PRAYERS FOR A LIFE OF PRAYER

Our Father in heaven, I ask You to shape my whole life into one of prayer. I do not want prayer to be an occasional refuge only in times of crisis, nor a habit performed with little thought, but a living and steady communion with You. You have opened the way for me through Jesus Christ. You invite me to come boldly to the throne of grace. Yet I confess that prayer can so easily become neglected, hurried, distracted, or confined to the edges of life. Forgive me for living as though I can manage without the privilege and power of drawing near to You.

Teach me that prayer is not a burden laid upon me, but a gift given to me. It is the place where weakness meets grace, where fear meets peace, where confusion meets wisdom, and where the burdened heart finds rest in the God who knows all things. Your word says, "Pray continually." (1 Thessalonians 5:17). Help me to understand that call rightly. Let prayer become not merely a few moments set apart, though I need those too, but the quiet posture of my heart throughout the day. Train me to turn to You often, naturally, and sincerely.

Where prayer has become dry, renew it. Where prayer has become formal, warm it. Where prayer has become sporadic, steady it. Guard me from speaking many words while my heart remains distant. Keep me also from the discouragement that gives up too quickly when answers seem delayed. Teach me to persevere. Teach me to listen as well as speak.

I ask that prayer would touch every part of my life. Let it enter my work, my relationships, my decisions, my fears, my gratitude, my repentance, and my hopes. Make me quick to pray before I rush, quick to pray when I am troubled, quick to pray when I am thankful, and quick to pray when I am tempted. Let prayer become the atmosphere in which I live, because it is in prayer that I remember who You are, who I am, and where true help is found. Build in me a life of prayer that is honest, reverent, childlike, and full of dependence on Your grace. Through Jesus Christ my Lord. **Amen.**

God of mercy, I come before You confessing how much I need to grow in prayer. I know that prayer should not be a small corner of the Christian life, but one of its great rhythms. Yet I also know how easily I let other things crowd it out. Busyness, tiredness, distraction, and self-reliance all conspire to make prayer seem less urgent than it truly is. I can speak about prayer more readily than I practise it and value its idea more than its discipline. So, I ask You to form in me a true life of prayer.

You have given me every reason to pray. I am Your child by grace. I am welcomed through Christ. I am helped by the Holy Spirit, who intercedes for the saints according to the will of God. I am invited to bring before You every burden, every need, and every concern. Thank You that prayer is not shouting into emptiness, but speaking to the living God who listens with wisdom, love, and perfect attention. Thank You that no sincere prayer offered in faith is wasted.

Your word says, "Devote yourselves to prayer, being watchful and thankful." (Colossians 4:2). I ask You for that devotion. Make me watchful in prayer, aware of my need, alert to temptation, and attentive to Your hand at work. Make me thankful in prayer, not merely asking for what I lack, but remembering and praising You for what You have given. Deliver me from a life that only turns to prayer when all other options have failed. Teach me to begin with prayer because You are my first resort, not my last.

Let prayer become both anchor and pathway in my life - an anchor that steadies me and a pathway by which I walk with You. Teach me to pray in secret and in the ordinary moments, in joy and in sorrow, in confidence and in weakness. Let prayer deepen my holiness, soften my spirit, and align my will more closely with Yours. If I falter, draw me back. If I grow weary, refresh me. If I become distracted, gather me again. And let my life increasingly bear the marks of a praying believer - peace, humility, dependence, perseverance, and a growing likeness to Christ. In His worthy name I pray. **Amen.**

Lord, teach me to live a life of prayer. I do not want prayer to sit at the edge of my days, used only in moments of trouble or urgency.

I want it to become a steady rhythm of my life and a constant turning of my heart toward You. Forgive me for prayerlessness, for self-reliance, and for the many times I have carried burdens alone instead of bringing them to You.

Draw me into deeper communion with You. Help me to pray in the morning, in the demands of the day, and in the quiet of the evening. Let prayer become as natural to me as breathing and as necessary to me as daily bread.

May I live close to You, speak honestly with You, and depend upon You in all things. **Amen.**

Gracious God, form in me the habit and joy of prayer.

I confess that I can be distracted, hurried, and inconsistent. My mind wanders, my heart grows dull, and prayer can become irregular when life feels crowded. Yet I know that I am never stronger than when I live in dependence on You.

So, teach me to return to prayer again and again.

Give me discipline when I feel sluggish, desire when I feel dry, and perseverance when answers seem delayed.

Help me to pray not only with words, but with faith, reverence, and expectation.

Let prayer shape my thoughts, calm my anxieties, and align my will with Yours. Make me a believer who is not merely familiar with prayer, but formed by it and sustained through it each day. **Amen.**

Faithful Father, thank You for the privilege of prayer and for the access I have to You through Jesus Christ. I ask You to make prayer a living reality in my daily walk.

Keep me from treating it as a duty to be checked off or a practice reserved for special moments. Instead, teach me to seek You continually and sincerely. Help me to bring before You my work, my decisions, my temptations, my fears, my gratitude, and my needs.

Let prayer become the place where my heart is softened, my mind is renewed, and my burdens are lifted. Strengthen me to keep praying when I feel weak, and remind me that no sincere prayer offered in faith is ever wasted before You.

Teach me to value fellowship with You above hurried living and self-sufficient thinking. **Amen.**

Holy Lord, I ask You to make my life a life of prayer. Let communion with You become a deep and steady habit, not a neglected corner of my faith.

Help me to turn to You quickly in every season - in joy, in sorrow, in uncertainty, in temptation, and in thankfulness. Teach me to pray without pretending, to wait without frustration, and to trust without wavering.

Guard me from empty words and from a heart that speaks to You while thinking of a hundred other things. Instead, draw me into honest, thoughtful, and wholehearted prayer.

Let prayer strengthen my faith, deepen my love for Christ, and make me more peaceful, watchful, and dependent on Your grace in every part of life.

Make me quick to seek You and slow to drift from You. **Amen.**

21. PRAYERS FOR REPENTANCE

Merciful God, I come before You in repentance, aware of my sin and my need for Your grace. I do not come to excuse myself, to minimise what I have done, or to shift blame elsewhere. I come to acknowledge that I have sinned against You in thought, word, and action. I have failed to love You with all my heart and to love others as I should. I have known what is right and not always done it. I have turned aside in ways both obvious and hidden. Yet I thank You that You invite sinners to return, not to be rejected, but to be forgiven.

Your word says in 1 John 1:9, "If we confess our sins, He is faithful and just and will forgive us our sins and purify us from all unrighteousness." I hold on to that promise now. Thank You that forgiveness rests not on my ability to make things right, but on the finished work of Christ. At the cross, my sin was answered with mercy.

Search me, O God, and know my heart. Show me where I have been careless, proud, impatient, unkind, or unbelieving. Expose sins I have ignored, habits I have excused, and attitudes I have allowed to grow unchecked. Do not let me remain comfortable with what grieves You. Yet as You expose, also heal. As You convict, also restore. Let repentance not lead me into despair, but into the freedom of being made clean again.

Grant me true repentance - not merely regret over consequences, but sorrow over sin itself. Give me a broken and contrite heart that You will not despise. Turn me away from what is wrong and toward what is right. Strengthen my resolve to walk in obedience, not by my own strength, but by the power of Your Spirit. Let repentance become a regular grace in my life, keeping me humble, honest, and near to Christ.
May I rise from this prayer forgiven, cleansed, and renewed. Not hardened by sin, but softened by grace. Not burdened by guilt, but freed by mercy. And may that forgiveness lead me to deeper gratitude, greater watchfulness, and a more faithful walk with You. Through Jesus Christ my Saviour. **Amen.**

Holy and gracious Father, I come to You confessing my sin and seeking Your mercy. I know that nothing is hidden from Your sight. You see the outward actions and the inward motives, the words I have spoken and the thoughts I have entertained. You know the places where I have fallen short and the ways I have resisted Your will. Yet I thank You that I may come openly before You, not to hide, but to be restored.

I confess that sin is not a small matter. It offends Your holiness, disrupts my fellowship with You, and distorts my life. Forgive me for treating it lightly, for justifying it, or for delaying repentance. Forgive me for the times I have been more concerned about how I appear to others than about the true state of my heart before You. Cleanse me from all unrighteousness and renew a right spirit within me.

Your word says, "Create in me a pure heart, O God, and renew a steadfast spirit within me." (Psalm 51:10). I ask You to do that work in me. Create what I cannot produce by myself. Renew what has grown weak or compromised. Restore the joy of Your salvation and grant me a willing spirit to sustain me. Let repentance not be a moment only, but a turning that continues into a changed life.

Keep me from returning to the same patterns without struggle. Strengthen me to resist temptation and to walk in the light. Surround me with truth, guide me by Your word, and make me sensitive to the voice of Your Spirit. When I stumble again, keep me from hiding in shame. Instead, draw me quickly back to the cross, where grace is greater than all my sin.

Let repentance lead me into deeper love for Christ. The more I see my sin, the more I see the wonder of His mercy. The more I confess, the more I experience Your cleansing. The more I turn, the more I find life. Make me a repentant believer, not crushed by guilt, but shaped by grace and growing in holiness day by day. I ask this through Jesus Christ, who died and rose again for my forgiveness. **Amen.**

Holy God, I come before You with a heart that needs to confess. You know me completely, and nothing is hidden from Your sight.

Yet I can still avoid, excuse, or minimise my sin. Forgive me for this. Give me honesty before You.

Help me to see my sin clearly, not defensively, but truthfully and humbly.

Let me not compare myself with others or soften what You call wrong.

Instead, teach me to bring my sin into the light, trusting in Your mercy. Thank You that in Christ I am already forgiven, and that confession is not about earning grace, but about walking in it.

Cleanse my conscience, restore my fellowship, and renew my desire to walk closely with You in sincerity and truth. **Amen.**

Gracious Father, I thank You that I can come to You freely because of Christ. I do not need to hide or pretend, for You already know my heart.

I confess that I have sinned in thought, word, and action. There have been things I have done that I should not have done, and things I have left undone that I should have done.

Yet I thank You that Your grace is greater than my sin. Help me to confess with humility and without fear.

Let me not rush through confession, but take time to acknowledge my need and Your mercy.

Restore to me the joy of walking openly before You, and strengthen me to turn from sin and pursue what is right. **Amen.**

Faithful God, I ask You to give me a heart that is quick to confess and slow to hide.

Keep me from becoming hardened to sin or comfortable with what grieves You. When I fall, draw me back to You quickly. Let me not delay in confession or make excuses for what I know is wrong.

Thank You that I am already forgiven in Christ, and that confession restores the joy of that forgiveness in my life. Cleanse my heart and renew my spirit.

Help me to walk in the light, not carrying hidden burdens, but living in the freedom of Your grace. May confession become a regular and honest part of my walk with You. **Amen.**

Merciful Lord, I bring my sin before You and ask for a deeper work of honesty within me.

You are holy, and I do not want to treat sin lightly. At the same time, I thank You that I do not come in fear of rejection, but in the assurance of Your grace.

Help me to confess not only outward actions, but inward attitudes, motives, and desires.

Search me and reveal what needs to be brought into the light.

Let confession lead not to despair, but to renewed joy in the gospel.

Strengthen me to turn away from sin and to walk in obedience.

May my life be marked by humility, honesty, and a deep reliance on Your mercy each day. **Amen.**

God of all grace, I come before You with deep gratitude that forgiveness is already mine in Jesus Christ. I do not stand before You as one trying to earn mercy or persuade You to be kind. I come as one who has been received in the Beloved, cleansed by the blood of Christ, and welcomed through the finished work of the cross. Thank You that in Him my sin has been judged, my guilt has been borne, and my condemnation has been removed forever. What I could never secure for myself, You have freely given by grace.

Yet I confess that although forgiveness is mine in Christ, I do not always live in the freedom and joy of it. Sometimes sin troubles my conscience, accusation clouds my heart, and shame lingers in ways that dim my peace and weaken my fellowship with You. So, I ask You not for a new cross or a fresh atonement, but for the living reality of Your forgiveness to be deeply known and freshly enjoyed in my life. Let the grace already given in Christ become vivid again to my heart.

Thank You that forgiveness is not fragile, partial, or uncertain. It rests entirely on Christ and on the riches of Your grace. Deliver me from living as though I am still trying to pay for what Jesus has already fully answered. Deliver me also from taking forgiveness lightly, as though grace were small. Let forgiveness humble me, steady me, and fill me with worship.

Where my heart has grown cold, let the wonder of grace warm it again. And where I have wronged others, give me humility to seek reconciliation. Let the forgiveness that is mine in Christ bear fruit in repentance, gratitude, and renewed obedience.

Teach me to live as one who is truly forgiven. Let me not drag chains that Christ has broken, nor return to darkness as though grace had not dawned. May the assurance of forgiveness make me more watchful over sin, more tender toward others, and more ready to forgive as I have been forgiven. Through Jesus Christ my Saviour and my righteousness. **Amen.**

Faithful Father, I thank You that forgiveness is not a distant hope but a present possession for all who are in Christ. You have not left me under guilt, nor placed me on probation, nor required me to earn back Your favour each time I fail. In Your Son, You have dealt with my sin fully and finally. Thank You for such mercy. Thank You that the gospel is not the announcement of possible forgiveness, but of forgiveness accomplished through the death and resurrection of Christ.

I confess, however, that my heart does not always rest there. I can carry guilt after it should have been surrendered. I can rehearse failure more readily than I remember grace. I can speak of forgiveness doctrinally while struggling to live in its comfort personally. So I ask You to make the forgiveness already secured in Christ more powerful in my daily life.

Your word says, "As far as the east is from the west, so far has He removed our transgressions from us." (Psalm 103:12). Thank You that this is not poetic exaggeration, but covenant mercy fulfilled in Christ. Thank You that my sins are not merely overlooked, but removed. Thank You that Your grace does not leave me half-cleansed and uncertain, but fully accepted in Your Son. Let that truth restore peace where sin has unsettled me and restore confidence where failure has weakened me.

At the same time, keep me from abusing grace. Let forgiveness never become an excuse for spiritual carelessness. Instead, let it deepen my hatred of sin and enlarge my love for Christ. The more I know the cost of my forgiveness, the more I want to walk in holiness. The more I understand the greatness of mercy, the more I want to live in grateful obedience. So renew me by Your Spirit. Cleanse what has been soiled, restore what has been weakened, and make me eager to walk in the light.

And as I rest in the forgiveness that is mine in Christ, teach me also to extend forgiveness to others. Let the mercy I have received shape the mercy I show. Make me a forgiving believer because I belong to a forgiving Saviour. I ask this in the name of Jesus Christ, through whom grace reigns. **Amen.**

Gracious Father, I thank You that forgiveness is not something I must earn, but something You have freely given in Christ.

Yet I confess that I do not always live in the good of that forgiveness. At times I carry guilt unnecessarily, or I return to what You have already dealt with at the cross.

So, I ask You to help me receive and rest in Your forgiveness more fully. Remind me that through Jesus, my sin has been paid for completely.

Let me not doubt what You have declared. Cleanse my conscience, quiet my heart, and restore my joy.

Help me to walk in the freedom of being forgiven, not bound by what You have already removed. **Amen.**

Faithful God, I thank You that in Christ I am forgiven, fully and finally.

You have not left my sin unresolved, nor do You hold it over me.

Yet I confess that I can struggle to believe this deeply. I can feel unworthy, uncertain, and hesitant to draw near.

So, I ask You to strengthen my faith in the reality of Your forgiveness. Let Your word speak more clearly to me than my feelings.

Help me to trust what You have promised and to rest in what Christ has accomplished.

Remove lingering guilt and give me confidence to come before You with peace, knowing that I am accepted and loved. **Amen.**

Merciful Lord, thank You that Your forgiveness is complete and unchanging.

You have removed my sin and remembered it no more. Help me to live in that truth. Keep me from returning to past failures as though they still define me.

Instead, teach me to see myself as You see me in Christ. When my heart condemns me, remind me that You are greater than my heart.

Let forgiveness not only be something I know, but something I experience deeply.

Restore to me the joy of salvation and give me a renewed desire to walk in holiness, not out of fear, but out of gratitude for Your grace. **Amen.**

Holy Lord, I ask You to help me extend forgiveness to others as I have received it from You.

At times I find it difficult to let go of wrongs done against me. Hurt can linger, and I can hold on to it more than I should.

Yet You have forgiven me completely in Christ. So I ask You to soften my heart.

Help me to release bitterness and to choose forgiveness, even when it is costly.

Let Your grace shape my response.

Teach me to forgive sincerely, just as I have been forgiven.

May forgiveness bring freedom to my heart and reflect the mercy You have shown me. **Amen.**

O God of mercy, I thank You that in Jesus Christ I am not left under the weight of guilt, but brought into the freedom of Your grace. You have not merely offered relief, but accomplished redemption. In Christ, my sin has been judged, my debt has been paid, and my conscience has a true and lasting answer. I come, therefore, not as one trying to escape guilt by my own effort, but as one asking that the freedom already secured in Christ would be more fully realised in my life.

Yet I confess that guilt can still cling to me in ways that trouble my heart. There are times when I carry what You have already removed, when I replay failures, rehearse regrets, and allow accusation to cloud the peace You have given. I can live as though forgiveness were uncertain, as though grace were fragile, and as though the cross were not enough. Teach me to live in the light of what is true, not in the shadow of what has already been dealt with by Christ.

Your word says, "How much more, then, will the blood of Christ… cleanse our consciences from acts that lead to death, so that we may serve the living God!" (Hebrews 9:14). Let that cleansing reach deeply into my conscience. Where guilt remains, bring clarity. Where shame lingers, bring the light of the gospel. Where accusation rises, silence it with the truth.

At the same time, keep me from confusing true conviction with false guilt. Where sin remains, make me honest and responsive. Let me not excuse what needs to be confessed, nor ignore what needs to be put right. But once brought into the light, let me not remain burdened by what You have already forgiven. May the freedom I have in Christ, lead to peace of heart, steadiness of mind, and joy in Your presence. Let it free me to serve You without fear, to pray without hesitation, and to live without the heavy burden of self-condemnation. And may that same grace make me gentle toward others, patient with weakness, and ready to extend mercy as I have received it. Through Jesus Christ, who has set me free. **Amen.**

Faithful and gracious Lord, I praise You that the gospel does not leave me trapped in guilt, but leads me into freedom. In Christ, there is no condemnation. In Him, I am not defined by my past, my failures, or my worst moments, but by Your grace and by His righteousness. Thank You that You have not called me to carry guilt as a permanent burden, but to lay it down at the cross and walk in newness of life.

Still, I acknowledge how easily guilt can return. Memories can accuse, conscience can be unsettled, and the enemy can use past failures to weaken present faith. I can begin to measure my standing before You by how I feel rather than by what You have said. I can become hesitant in prayer, slow in worship, and uncertain in my walk. So, I ask You to make the freedom of the gospel more powerful in my daily experience.

Your word says, "Therefore, there is now no condemnation for those who are in Christ Jesus." (Romans 8:1). Let that truth stand firm in my heart. When guilt rises without cause, help me to reject it. When conscience rightly convicts, lead me quickly to repentance and then quickly to rest in Your grace. Keep me from living in a cycle of sin, guilt, and distance from You. Instead, draw me into a pattern of confession, cleansing, and renewed fellowship.

Teach me to distinguish between the voice of Your Spirit and the voice of accusation. Your Spirit convicts to restore; accusation condemns to destroy. Help me to listen to the one and resist the other. Let the cross be the answer to every charge. Let the empty tomb be the assurance that the work is complete.

As I grow in freedom from guilt, let my life reflect that freedom. Make me more joyful in worship, more confident in prayer, and more willing in obedience. Let me not carry burdens You have removed, nor live as though grace were uncertain.

And where others are weighed down by guilt, make me a bearer of the good news that there is forgiveness, cleansing, and true freedom in Christ. Through Jesus my Saviour. **Amen.**

Gracious God, I thank You that in Christ my guilt has been fully dealt with.

Yet I confess that I do not always live in that freedom. At times I carry a weight that You have already lifted, and I revisit what You have already forgiven.

My heart can hold onto guilt long after Your word has declared me clean. So, I ask You to set me free.

Help me to believe that the cross is sufficient, that nothing remains unpaid, and that I am no longer under condemnation.

Quieten the accusing voice within me and replace it with the truth of Your promises.

Let me walk in the freedom You have given, with a clear conscience and a renewed sense of peace before You. **Amen.**

Faithful Father, I ask You to release me from the burden of guilt that lingers in my heart.

You know the things I regret and the ways I have fallen short. Yet You also know that Christ has paid for every sin.

Help me to stop carrying what no longer belongs to me.

Teach me to rest in Your grace and to accept Your forgiveness without hesitation.

When my thoughts return to past failures, remind me that they have been dealt with fully at the cross.

Let Your truth speak louder than my memory.

Give me a settled confidence that I am forgiven, cleansed, and accepted in Your sight. **Amen.**

Merciful Lord, thank You that You do not hold my guilt against me.

Through Jesus, my record has been cleared, and I stand before You as one who is forgiven.

Yet I confess that my heart can still feel condemned. I ask You to renew my mind with Your truth.

Help me to see myself as You see me in Christ, not defined by past sin, but by present grace.

Remove the heaviness that guilt brings and replace it with the peace that comes from knowing I am right with You.

Let me live in that freedom, not returning again and again to what You have already removed. **Amen.**

Holy God, I bring before You the weight of guilt that sometimes settles on me.

I do not want to live under a burden that You have already lifted.

Help me to distinguish between conviction that leads me to You and guilt that keeps me trapped in the past.

Lead me into the freedom of Your grace.

When I confess, help me to believe that I am truly forgiven.

When I remember past sin, help me to rest in Your promise that it is no longer held against me.

Let my heart be lightened, my mind be settled, and my life be marked by the joy of being fully forgiven in Christ. **Amen.**

God of all grace, I thank You that in Jesus Christ I am not only forgiven, but also freed from shame. You have not simply dealt with my guilt before Your law, but have also covered my shame before Your presence. In Christ, I am not exposed, rejected, or cast aside, but clothed in righteousness, received as Your child, and welcomed into Your presence. Thank You that the gospel speaks not only to what I have done, but to who I now am in Him.

Yet I confess that shame can still linger in my heart. There are memories I would rather hide, failures that still echo, and weaknesses that make me feel small, exposed, or unworthy. I can shrink back, not because Your grace is insufficient, but because I struggle to believe how complete it truly is. So, I ask You to make the freedom You have given more real to me.

Lift my eyes from myself to Christ. Let me look to Him again and again, not with hesitation, but with confidence. As I behold Him, let shame lose its grip. Let the light of His grace drive out the shadows that linger in my heart. Teach me that I am not what I once was. I am now Yours, cleansed, accepted, and new.

Guard me from confusing humility with shame. True humility acknowledges sin and weakness, but rests in grace. Shame, by contrast, keeps me looking inward, weighed down, and hesitant to draw near. Deliver me from that false burden. Let me come to You freely, worship You openly, and serve You without the sense that I must hide.

Let freedom from shame reshape how I live. May it give me courage to be honest, freedom to be open, and joy to walk in the light. Let it deepen my gratitude, strengthen my identity in Christ, and make me more compassionate toward others who struggle under similar burdens.

May I live as one who is no longer hiding, but known and loved. Through Jesus Christ, who has removed my shame and clothed me in grace. **Amen.**

Lord of mercy and truth, I praise You that the gospel brings freedom from shame. In a world where failure, weakness, and sin can leave deep marks on the heart, You speak a better word. You do not expose Your people to humiliate them, but to heal them. You do not uncover to destroy, but to restore. In Christ, You have taken what was shameful and dealt with it. Thank You that I do not stand before You in disgrace, but in grace.

Still, I acknowledge that shame can linger in ways that affect how I think, feel, and live. It can make me hesitant in prayer, reserved in worship, and guarded in relationships. It can whisper that I am less than what Your word declares me to be. It can keep me looking back rather than walking forward. So, I ask You to bring the truth of the gospel to bear on these hidden places in my heart.

Your word says, "So if the Son sets you free, you will be free indeed." (John 8:36). Let that freedom reach even into the places where shame has taken root. Teach me to believe that Christ's work is sufficient not only to forgive, but to restore dignity and identity. Remind me that I am no longer defined by past sins, past failures, or past labels. I am defined by Christ - by His righteousness, His love, and His grace.

Where shame has distorted my thinking, renew my mind with truth. Where it has affected my confidence, strengthen me with assurance. Where it has led me to hide, draw me out into the light of Your presence. Let me not fear being known, because in Christ I am already fully known and fully loved. Keep me from returning to the hiding places You have called me out of.

As I grow in freedom from shame, let it produce visible fruit. Give me boldness to pray, openness in fellowship, and joy in worship. Make me more willing to speak of Your grace and more ready to walk in the light. Let this freedom shape how I treat others - with patience, understanding and gentleness. May I reflect the grace I have received, pointing others to the One who restores what has been broken. Through Jesus Christ my Lord. **Amen.**

Gracious Father, I thank You that in Christ I am not only forgiven, but also restored and accepted.

Yet I confess that shame can still linger within me. It can make me feel unworthy, distant, and hesitant to draw near to You.

At times I define myself by past failures rather than by Your grace. So, I ask You to free me from shame.

Help me to believe that in Christ I am made new, not merely improved, but redeemed.

Remove the weight of feeling rejected or unclean. Let me see myself as You see me - clothed in righteousness and welcomed into Your presence.

May I walk with confidence and peace, knowing I am fully accepted in Your love. **Amen.**

Faithful God, I ask You to break the hold of shame over my heart.

You know the things that cause me to feel exposed, unworthy, or diminished. Yet You have not turned away from me. Instead, You have drawn me near through Christ.

Help me to stop hiding in shame and to come into the light of Your grace. Teach me that I do not need to cover myself, for You have covered me completely.

Let Your truth silence the lies that tell me I am less than what You have declared.

Give me courage to live openly before You, resting in Your acceptance and no longer bound by shame. **Amen.**

Merciful Lord, thank You that You remove not only my sin, but also the shame that comes with it.

I confess that I can still carry a sense of unworthiness, as though I must hold onto what You have already taken away.

Help me to let it go.

Teach me to believe that I am clean, restored, and made new in Christ.

When shame tries to return, remind me of the cross, where my guilt was dealt with and my shame was covered.

Let me not shrink back from You, but draw near with confidence.

May I live in the dignity and freedom of being
Your child. **Amen.**

Holy Lord, I bring before You the hidden shame that sometimes weighs on me.

You see it clearly, yet You do not reject me. Instead, You call me to come near and receive grace.

Help me to step out of hiding and into the light of Your presence.

Replace shame with assurance, fear with confidence, and silence with truth.

Let me no longer define myself by past failures or by the opinions of others, but by Your word and Your grace.

Restore my sense of worth in Christ and help me to live freely, joyfully, and openly as one who has been fully accepted and loved by You. **Amen.**

Holy God, I come before You with a deep awareness that You have called me to a life of holiness. You have not saved me merely to forgive my past, but to shape my present and future into the likeness of Christ. Thank You that holiness is not the price of my acceptance, but the fruit of Your grace at work within me. I stand before You accepted in Christ, clothed in His righteousness, and loved with an everlasting love. Yet because I belong to You, I ask that my life would reflect Your character.

Your word says, "But just as He who called you is holy, so be holy in all you do." (1 Peter 1:15). I feel both the beauty and the seriousness of that call. Holiness reaches into every part of life - my thoughts, my speech, my desires, my choices, my habits, and my hidden life before You. It is not enough for me to appear respectable outwardly while cherishing compromise within. So, Lord, search me deeply and work in me thoroughly.

Thank You that holiness is not something I must create by my own strength. It is the gracious work of Your Spirit in the life of one who belongs to Christ. Still, I confess that I can resist that work. I can tolerate what should be forsaken, excuse what should be confessed, and delay what should be obeyed. Forgive me for every casual attitude toward sin and every divided loyalty of heart. Renew in me a clear sight of the beauty of holiness and the ugliness of sin.

Train my heart to desire what is pleasing to You. Make me holy in what I think. Guard my mind from impurity, bitterness, pride, and unbelief. Make me holy in what I say. Let my words be truthful, gracious, pure, and wise. Make me holy in what I do. Let integrity, kindness, obedience, and self-control mark my conduct.

Let holiness not make me proud, severe, or self-righteous, but humble, gentle, and Christlike. May growing holiness deepen my gratitude for grace and enlarge my love for the Saviour who has made me His own. Through Jesus Christ my Lord. **Amen.**

God of all grace, I thank You that You are committed to making Your people holy. You do not leave us as we are, nor abandon us to spiritual weakness and compromise. In Christ, You have claimed us for Yourself, and by Your Spirit You are shaping us into His likeness. I praise You that holiness is not an impossible ideal held over me in condemnation, but a real work of grace being formed within me day by day. So, I ask You to continue that work in me with power, patience, and mercy.

Your word says, "For it is God's will that you should be sanctified." (1 Thessalonians 4:3). Help me to welcome that will and not resist it. There are times when holiness seems costly, when obedience requires sacrifice, and when letting go of sinful patterns feels hard. Yet teach me to believe that Your will is always wiser, better, and more life-giving than anything sin can offer. Keep me from imagining that compromise will bring peace. True peace is found only in walking closely with You.

I confess that holiness often feels slow in its progress. I long for quicker change, clearer victory, and greater purity. Yet remind me that You are patient in Your work and faithful in all You begin. Keep me from discouragement when I see how much still needs changing. Let me not grow careless because the battle continues, nor despair because growth feels gradual. Instead, teach me to pursue holiness steadily, prayerfully, and dependently.

Use Your word to cleanse me. Use prayer to keep me near You. Use the fellowship of Your people to encourage and sharpen me. Use even trials and disappointments to loosen my grip on this world and deepen my love for what is eternal. Let every part of life become an instrument in Your hand for shaping me. And as holiness grows, let it be clear that all glory belongs to You. Keep me from comparing myself to others or taking pride in progress that is only the fruit of grace. Make me tender toward those who struggle, patient with the weak, and eager to point others to Christ. Let holiness shine not as cold severity, but as the beauty of a life increasingly governed by the love, truth, and purity of Jesus. In His name I pray. **Amen.**

Holy God, I thank You that in Christ I have been set apart for You and called to a life of holiness.

Yet I confess that I do not always pursue holiness as I should.

I can tolerate what should be resisted and become comfortable with what grieves Your Spirit. Forgive me for this.

Renew in me a desire to live a life that reflects Your character.

Help me to take sin seriously, not out of fear of rejection, but out of love for You.

Shape my thoughts, my words, and my actions so that they honour You.

Let holiness become not a burden, but a joy - the natural response of a heart that belongs to You. **Amen.**

Gracious Father, I ask You to grow holiness within me.

I know that this is Your work by Your Spirit, yet I also know that I must pursue it with intention.

Help me to be watchful in the small things and faithful in the daily choices that shape my life.

Guard me from compromise, from hidden sin, and from a divided heart.

Give me a growing desire for what is good, pure, and pleasing to You. When I am tempted, strengthen me.

When I fail, restore me. Let my life reflect a steady pattern of obedience, not to earn Your love, but because I have already received it fully in Christ. **Amen.**

Faithful God, thank You that You are committed to making me holy.

You do not leave me unchanged, but continue to work in me day by day. Help me to cooperate with that work.

When You reveal sin, give me humility to confess it.

When You call me to obedience, give me courage to follow. Let me not resist Your Spirit or delay in responding to Your leading. Teach me to love what is right and to turn from what is wrong.

May holiness grow in my inner life, shaping my desires and motives as well as my outward conduct. Let me become more like Christ in every part of my life. **Amen.**

Lord, I bring before You my desire to live a holy life.

You are holy, and You have called me to reflect that holiness in all I do.

Help me to live with integrity, sincerity, and a clear conscience before You.

Guard my heart from pride and self-righteousness as I pursue holiness.

Let it be marked by humility and dependence on Your grace.

When growth feels slow, give me patience.

When the path is difficult, give me strength.

May holiness become a visible mark of Your work in me, pointing not to my effort, but to Your transforming power at work within me each day. **Amen.**

Holy God, I come before You asking for purity of heart, mind, and life. You have called me to belong to You, to walk in the light, and to reflect the beauty of Christ in both my inner life and outward conduct. Thank You that in Christ I am already cleansed, accepted, and made new. I do not seek purity in order to earn Your favour, but because I have already received Your grace. Yet I know how much I need Your ongoing work within me, for my heart can be divided, my thoughts can be careless, and my desires can be drawn toward what is unclean. So I ask You to make me pure.

Your word says, "Blessed are the pure in heart, for they will see God." (Matthew 5:8). Let that promise and that calling settle deeply in me. Purity is not merely outward restraint. It is an inward sincerity, a singleness of heart, and a life increasingly free from corruption, compromise, and hidden defilement. I ask You, then, to work beyond appearance and reach the deeper places of my soul. Search my motives. Examine my desires. Reveal what is false, mixed, or unworthy in me.

Guard my mind. Keep me from thoughts that stain, degrade, or pull me away from holiness. Guard my eyes. Help me to turn away from what weakens the soul and feeds sinful desire. Guard my speech. Let my words be clean, truthful, and gracious. Guard my imagination. Let it not become a place where impurity is entertained and quietly strengthened. And guard my habits. Where I have allowed things into my life that make purity harder, give me courage to put them away. I confess that impurity can present itself subtly, not only in obvious sin, but in compromise, indulgence, and the quiet tolerance of what should be resisted. Forgive me where I have been careless. Strengthen me to pursue purity actively, not passively. Help me to fill my life with what is good, true, beautiful, and worthy of Christ. Let Your word renew my thinking and Your Spirit strengthen my resolve. May purity become not a fearful avoidance alone, but a joyful pursuit of what honours You. Through Jesus Christ my Lord. **Amen.**

God of light, I thank You that You are pure in all Your ways and that You call Your people to walk in purity before You. In a world that often treats impurity lightly, mocks holiness, and celebrates what degrades the soul, I ask You to keep me distinct. Do not let me be shaped by the spirit of the age. Let me be shaped by Your truth. You have given me Your Spirit, Your word, and the grace of Christ, so that I may live in a way that pleases You.

Your word says, "Finally, brothers and sisters, whatever is true, whatever is noble, whatever is right, whatever is pure… think about such things." (Philippians 4:8). Teach me to obey that command. Help me not merely to reject impurity, but to set my mind positively on what is pure. Fill my thoughts with truth, my heart with reverence, and my life with what strengthens holiness. Let me not starve impurity one day only to feed it the next by what I watch, read, entertain, or dwell upon.

I ask especially for purity in secret. Keep me from the hypocrisy of appearing respectable outwardly while harbouring uncleanness within. Let me be the same before You in private as I seek to be before others in public. Give me an undivided heart. Make me sincere, watchful, and honest. If there are places where I have compromised, expose them in mercy and lead me into the freedom of the light.

At the same time, keep purity from becoming a harsh or self-righteous thing in me. Let it be humble, grateful, and grace-shaped. I do not ask for purity so that I may think more highly of myself, but so that Christ may be honoured in me. Let purity make me more gentle, more disciplined, more peaceful, and more free. And where others are struggling, make me compassionate, wise, and helpful, not condemning.

Keep me close to Christ, for purity flourishes where love for Him is strong. Let seeing more of His beauty make sin less attractive and holiness more desirable. Shape me by His grace until purity is not merely something I pursue in moments of battle, but a growing quality of the whole life I offer to You. Through Jesus Christ, who is holy, blameless, and pure. **Amen.**

Holy God, I ask You to form in me a heart of purity.

You see beyond outward actions into the thoughts, desires, and motives within me. I confess that impurity can take root quietly, not only in what I do, but in what I allow my mind to dwell on.

Forgive me where I have been careless. Cleanse my thinking, guard my imagination, and shape my desires so that they honour You.

Help me to turn away quickly from what is unclean and to pursue what is true and pure. Let my heart be undivided and sincere before You.

May purity grow within me as a reflection of Your grace at work in my life. **Amen.**

Gracious Father, thank You that in Christ I have been made clean.

I ask You now to help me live in that reality each day. Guard me from influences that weaken my walk and from habits that lead me toward compromise.

Give me wisdom to recognise what draws my heart away from You and courage to turn from it.

Let Your word shape my thinking and Your Spirit guide my choices.

Help me to pursue purity not only outwardly, but inwardly, where true change begins.

May my life reflect integrity, sincerity, and a deep desire to please You in all things. **Amen.**

Faithful God, I bring before You my desire to walk in purity.

You know the areas where I am most vulnerable and the patterns that can easily lead me astray.

Strengthen me in those places.

Help me to be watchful, disciplined, and quick to turn to You when temptation arises.

Let me not entertain what I should reject or excuse what I should resist.

Instead, fill my mind with what is good and my heart with a love for holiness.

May purity grow steadily in my life, shaping both my private thoughts and my public actions. **Amen.**

Merciful Lord, I ask You to keep me pure for Your glory.

In a world filled with distraction and temptation, help me to remain focused on what is right and pleasing to You.

Guard my eyes, my thoughts, and my choices.

Let me not drift into compromise, but remain firm in faith.

At the same time, keep me humble, knowing that any growth in purity is the result of Your grace.

Let my life reflect not self-effort alone, but the transforming work of Your Spirit.

May I walk in purity with joy, freedom, and a deep awareness of Your presence with me. **Amen.**

27. PRAYERS FOR VICTORY OVER TEMPTATION

Lord our Deliverer, I come before You aware that temptation is a real and present battle in my life. You know my weaknesses, my history, and the patterns that can easily draw me aside. Yet I thank You that in Jesus Christ I am not left powerless. I do not stand in this struggle alone. You have given me Your Spirit, Your word, and the assurance that sin no longer reigns over me. So, I ask that the victory already secured in Christ would be increasingly lived out in my daily experience.

Your word says, "No temptation has overtaken you except what is common to mankind. And God is faithful; He will not let you be tempted beyond what you can bear." (1 Corinthians 10:13). Help me to believe that in the moment of testing. When temptation feels strong, remind me that You are stronger.

I confess that temptation often begins subtly. It starts with a thought, a desire, a small compromise that seems harmless. Teach me to be watchful at the beginning, not only at the point of failure. Let me recognise the early signs and turn to You quickly. Guard my mind from wandering into places where sin takes root. Guard my heart from entertaining what should be rejected.

Strengthen me inwardly. Let my love for Christ outweigh the appeal of sin. Let the memory of the cross remind me of the cost of sin, and let the promise of Your presence remind me of the joy of obedience. Give me not only resistance, but a growing desire for holiness. Make me quick to say no to what is wrong and eager to pursue what is right.

And when I stumble, do not let me remain in defeat. Draw me quickly back into the light. Restore my focus, renew my strength, and set me again on the path of obedience. Let each battle, whether won or lost, drive me closer to You. May victory over temptation become more evident, not because I am strong, but because Your grace is at work within me. Through Jesus Christ my Lord. **Amen.**

Faithful God, I thank You that temptation does not have the final word in my life. In Christ, I have been brought into a new relationship with You, and sin no longer holds authority over me. Yet I know that the struggle remains. There are moments when temptation feels persuasive, familiar, and difficult to resist. I ask You to strengthen me to stand firm and to walk in the freedom You have given.

Your word says, "Watch and pray so that you will not fall into temptation. The spirit is willing, but the flesh is weak." (Matthew 26:41). Teach me to live in that posture. Keep me from overconfidence that assumes I can stand without vigilance. At the same time, keep me from discouragement that assumes I cannot stand at all. Let me walk humbly, aware of my weakness, yet confident in Your strength.

Help me to be watchful. Let me not drift carelessly into situations that make obedience harder. Give me wisdom to avoid what feeds temptation and to pursue what strengthens faith. Help me to take practical steps to guard my life - my time, my habits, and my influences.

Teach me also to pray in the moment of testing. Not only in set times, but in the instant when temptation arises. Draw my heart quickly to You. Let me seek Your help honestly and rely on Your presence. Let prayer become my immediate refuge and my steady defence.

Let Christ be central in this battle. He was tempted in every way, yet without sin. He understands my weakness and provides grace in my time of need. Let His example guide me and His strength uphold me. And as I grow, let victory over temptation become more consistent. Not perfect, but real.

And let this victory produce humility and compassion. Keep me from judging others who struggle. Instead, make me patient, wise, and ready to encourage. May my life reflect both the seriousness of sin and the greater power of Your grace. Through Jesus Christ my Saviour. **Amen.**

Lord, I ask You to strengthen me in the face of temptation.

You know the areas where I am weak and the patterns that can easily draw me aside.

I do not want to rely on my own strength, for I know how quickly I can fall.

Instead, help me to depend on You in the moment of testing.

Give me clarity to recognise temptation early and courage to turn away without hesitation.

Remind me that there is always a way of escape in You. Let my love for Christ be stronger than the pull of sin.

Strengthen my resolve, steady my heart, and help me to walk in the freedom that is mine in Him. **Amen.**

Gracious God, I bring before You my struggle with temptation. At times it feels strong, familiar, and difficult to resist.

Yet I thank You that I am not without help.

You have given me Your Spirit and Your word to guide and strengthen me.

Teach me to be watchful and not careless.

Help me to avoid situations that make obedience harder and to pursue what strengthens my faith.

When temptation arises, draw me quickly to prayer. Let me not delay or entertain what I know is wrong.

Give me strength to choose what is right, trusting that Your grace is sufficient in every moment. **Amen.**

Faithful Father, thank You that in Christ I share in victory over sin.

I ask You to help me live in that reality.

When I am tempted, remind me of who I am in Christ and of what He has done for me.

Guard my thoughts and keep my heart from drifting toward what is harmful.

Help me to act decisively, not hesitating between obedience and compromise.

Let each victory strengthen my faith and weaken the hold of sin.

And when I fail, draw me back quickly, restoring me by Your grace and renewing my desire to walk closely with You each day. **Amen.**

Holy Lord, I ask You to make me strong in the battle against temptation.

Not strong in myself, but strong in Your grace.

Teach me to rely on You continually and not to trust my own ability to stand.

Keep me humble, watchful, and dependent. Let me not grow careless in times of ease or discouraged in times of struggle.

Instead, help me to persevere, knowing that You are at work in me.

May my life show increasing freedom from sin and a growing desire for holiness, bringing honour to Your name. **Amen.**

God of all grace, I come before You asking for the gift of self-control. You have called me to a life that is not ruled by impulse, desire, or circumstance, but shaped by Your truth and governed by Your Spirit. Yet I confess how easily I can lose control in small and subtle ways. My words can be careless, my thoughts undisciplined, my reactions quick, and my habits inconsistent. So I ask You to strengthen me inwardly, that I may live with a growing measure of self-control in every part of life.

Your word says that self-control is a fruit of the Spirit (Galatians 5:23). Thank You that this is not something I must manufacture by sheer effort alone, but something You produce within me as I walk with You. Still, I know that I must actively pursue it. So I ask You to help me cooperate with Your work. Make me attentive to the moments where self-control is needed - in speech, in thought, in desire, in reaction, and in action.

Guard my words. When I am tempted to speak quickly, sharply, or unwisely, help me to pause and consider. Let my speech be measured, truthful, and gracious. Guard my thoughts. Keep me from dwelling on what is unhelpful, impure, or distracting.

Help me also in my habits and daily choices. Give me discipline in how I use my time, how I order my priorities, and how I respond to desires. Keep me from indulgence that weakens my soul and from patterns that lead me away from You. Instead, shape in me a life that is ordered, thoughtful, and increasingly aligned with Your will.

Where there is pride, humble me. Where there is fear, steady me. Where there is misplaced desire, reorder my affections. Let self-control not be a cold restraint alone, but the fruit of a heart that is being shaped by Your grace. And when I fail, lead me quickly back to You. May self-control grow in me steadily, so that my life reflects the transforming power of Your Spirit. Through Jesus Christ my Lord. **Amen.**

Lord of wisdom and strength, I thank You that You call me to a life of discipline and self-control, not to burden me, but to free me. A life without self-control is easily driven by impulse, swayed by emotion, and weakened by inconsistency. But a life shaped by Your Spirit is steady, thoughtful, and purposeful. I ask You to form that kind of life in me.

Your word says in 2 Timothy 1:7, "For the Spirit God gave us does not make us timid, but gives us power, love and self-discipline." Let that truth take hold of me. You have given me not a spirit of weakness, but of strength. Help me to live in that strength. When I am tempted to give in to impulse, remind me that I have been given power to stand. When I feel overwhelmed, remind me that Your grace is sufficient.

Teach me to practise self-control in the ordinary moments of life. Not only in major decisions, but in daily choices. In how I speak, how I think, how I respond, and how I use my time. Help me to build habits that support faithfulness and to break habits that weaken it. Let me not drift through life, but live intentionally before You.

Guard me especially in areas where I am prone to weakness. You know them well. I ask You to strengthen me there. Give me wisdom to avoid unnecessary temptation and courage to act decisively when I must. Help me to put boundaries in place where needed and to follow through with consistency.

Let self-control be shaped by love for Christ. Not a mere external discipline, but a response to His grace. The more I love Him, the more I want to live in a way that honours Him. Let that love guide my choices and strengthen my resolve.
And as I grow, keep me humble. Let me not take pride in discipline, but recognise Your grace at work in me.

Make me patient with others who struggle and ready to encourage them. May self-control become a quiet strength in my life, reflecting Your work within me and bringing honour to Your name. Through Jesus Christ my Saviour. **Amen.**

Lord, I ask You to grow in me the fruit of self-control.

You know how easily I can act without thinking, speak without restraint, or follow impulses that do not honour You.

I confess that I often rely on my own strength and then fall short. So, I ask You to strengthen me by Your Spirit.

Help me to pause before I speak, to consider before I act, and to choose what is right rather than what is easy.

Guard my thoughts, my words, and my reactions.

Let self-control become a steady mark of my life, not through pressure, but through Your grace at work within me. **Amen.**

Gracious God, I bring before You the areas of my life where I lack discipline.

You know the habits that weaken me and the patterns that pull me away from what is good.

I ask You to help me change.

Give me clarity to recognise what needs to be addressed and courage to act on it.

Strengthen my will so that I may follow through with what is right.

Help me to build habits that reflect faithfulness and to turn away from what leads to compromise.

Let self-control grow not as a burden, but as a freeing work of Your Spirit, enabling me to live wisely and well before You each day. **Amen.**

Faithful Father, thank You that You have given me Your Spirit, who produces self-control in my life.

Help me to walk in step with Him. When I feel overwhelmed by emotion or driven by impulse, steady me.

Remind me that I am not without strength. Teach me to bring my reactions under Your guidance and to respond in ways that honour You.

Let self-control shape my daily choices, my relationships, and my responsibilities.

Keep me from drifting into carelessness or inconsistency.

May my life reflect a growing steadiness that points to Your work within me. **Amen.**

Holy Lord, I ask You to help me live with discipline and purpose.

Guard me from wasting time, from careless speech, and from unwise decisions.

Help me to honour You in both small and large matters.

When I feel tempted to give in to what is easy, remind me of what is right.

When I feel weak, strengthen me by Your grace.

Let self-control be evident in how I live, not as a rigid effort, but as a Spirit-shaped life.

May I grow in maturity, consistency, and faithfulness, bringing honour to You in all I do. **Amen.**

29. PRAYERS FOR CHRISTLIKE CHARACTER

Lord Jesus Christ, I come before You with a longing that my character would increasingly reflect Yours. Thank You that You have not only saved me from sin, but are also shaping me by grace into Your likeness. I know that this work is deep, gradual, and often humbling, yet it is beautiful, because it is Your work. I ask that more and more of what marks You would be formed in me - Your humility, Your gentleness, Your truthfulness, Your purity, Your patience, Your courage, and Your love.

Your word says, "Whoever claims to live in Him must live as Jesus did." (1 John 2:6). I feel both the privilege and the weight of that calling. Left to myself, I do not naturally reflect You as I should. I can be impatient, self-protective, proud, easily irritated, and slow to love. I can speak hastily, judge quickly, and shrink back when courage is needed. So, I ask You to work deeply in me. Let Christlike character be more than an idea I admire.

Shape my heart first. Let me not focus only on outward behaviour while neglecting inward transformation. Purify my motives. Reorder my desires. Expose what is selfish and make me willing to surrender it. Teach me to care more about being holy than appearing impressive. Form in me an inward life that is sincere, tender, and governed by truth.

Make me gentle without becoming weak, courageous without becoming harsh, humble without pretending, and loving without compromise. Let me learn from the way Christ dealt with sinners, with sufferers, with opponents, and with His own disciples. He was full of grace and truth. Teach me to be the same. In conflict, make me measured. In service, make me willing. In disappointment, make me patient. In responsibility, make me faithful.

May the people around me increasingly see not merely my personality, but the imprint of my Saviour upon my life. Through Jesus Christ my Lord. **Amen.**

God of all grace, I thank You that Your purpose for me is not only that I would be forgiven, but that I would be conformed to the image of Your Son. This is a high calling and a glorious one. You are not content to leave me unchanged. Through Your word, Your Spirit, and the events of daily life, You are shaping my character so that I may increasingly resemble Christ.

Your word says, "And we all… are being transformed into His image with ever-increasing glory." (2 Corinthians 3:18). Let that transformation continue steadily in my life. Keep me from settling for surface religion while neglecting the deeper work of true character. I want Christlike character to mark me at home, in Church, at work, in trials, and in the hidden places of life.

Teach me especially the character of Christ in relationships. Let me be more patient with difficult people, more gracious in misunderstanding, more thoughtful in speech, and more ready to forgive. Keep me from defensiveness, from self-importance, and from the need always to be right. Instead, give me the meekness and strength of Christ, who did not insist on His own way, yet never compromised the truth.

Shape my reactions. When I am provoked, keep me calm. When I am disappointed, keep me trusting. When I am praised, keep me humble. When I am overlooked, keep me secure in Your love. Let Christlike character appear not only in my planned actions, but in my instinctive responses.

Let trials assist this work. When life is hard, use it not to harden me, but to deepen Christlikeness in me. Let affliction produce patience, dependence, and maturity. Let success produce gratitude, not pride.

And let all of this be governed by grace. Keep me from trying to imitate Christ in my own strength. Instead, let me abide in Him, behold Him, and be changed by Him. May Christlike character become more and more evident in my life, so that others may see something of His beauty and give glory to You. Through Jesus Christ my Saviour. **Amen.**

Lord Jesus, I ask You to shape my character so that it increasingly reflects Yours.

I do not want to settle for outward religion while my inner life remains unchanged. You know the areas where I fall short - where I am impatient, proud, easily irritated, or slow to love.

So, I ask You to work deeply within me. Form in me humility, gentleness, truthfulness, and compassion. Let my thoughts, my words, and my reactions be shaped by Your Spirit.

Help me to respond as You would respond and to live in a way that reflects Your grace.

May others see something of Your character in me, not for my praise, but for Your glory. **Amen.**

Gracious Father, thank You that You are committed to making me more like Christ.

I ask You to continue that work with patience and power.

Shape my heart so that my motives are sincere and my desires are aligned with Your will.

Help me to grow in patience with others, kindness in speech, and faithfulness in responsibility.

When I am pressed or challenged, let Christ be seen in how I respond. Keep me from reacting in the flesh or retreating into selfishness.

Instead, let Your Spirit guide me in every situation.

May my character be steadily transformed, reflecting the beauty and truth of Jesus in daily life. **Amen.**

Faithful God, I bring before You my desire to grow in Christlike character.

I know that this change does not happen quickly or easily, yet I trust that You are at work in me. Help me to cooperate with that work.

When You reveal areas that need to change, give me humility to respond. When growth feels slow, give me patience to continue. Let my character be shaped not only in planned moments, but in everyday interactions and unguarded responses.

May I become more loving, more gracious, more steady, and more faithful.

Let Christ be formed in me so that my life reflects His presence in all I do. **Amen.**

Holy Lord, I ask You to form in me a character that honours You.

Guard me from pride, from harshness, and from self-centred living.

Teach me to walk with humility and to treat others with grace and respect.

Let my life reflect truth without compromise and love without condition. When I am tempted to defend myself, help me to respond with gentleness.

When I am overlooked, help me to remain secure in Your love.

Let Christlike character become a steady and visible work of Your grace in me, shaping my relationships and guiding my daily life. **Amen.**

God of all grace, I come before You with a desire to walk daily in the grace that is already mine in Jesus Christ. Thank You that I do not begin each day trying to earn Your favour, but standing in the finished work of Christ. I am accepted, forgiven, and secure in Him. Yet I confess that I do not always live in the good of that reality. I can slip into striving, into quiet self-reliance, or into discouragement when I fail. So, I ask You to teach me what it truly means to walk in grace.

Let Your grace teach me. Grace is not only the beginning of my Christian life, but the path I am to walk every day. Help me to depend on it in all things. When I am weak, let me rest in grace. When I am tempted, let grace strengthen me. When I fail, let grace restore me. And when I grow, let grace keep me humble.

Guard me from turning the Christian life into a burden of performance. Keep me from measuring my standing before You by how well I think I am doing. Instead, remind me again and again that my acceptance is rooted in Christ alone. Let that truth free me from anxiety, from comparison, and from the need to prove myself.

At the same time, keep me from misusing grace. Let me never treat it as permission to be careless or indifferent toward sin. True grace leads to holiness, not away from it. Let it shape my desires, my choices, and my conduct. May I walk in a way that honours You, not to earn Your love, but because I have already received it.

Let grace shape how I relate to others. Make me patient, forgiving, and generous. Help me to extend to others the same grace I have received. Keep me from harshness, from pride, and from quick judgment. Let grace soften my heart and guide my words. And let grace become the atmosphere of my life. In every circumstance, teach me to lean on it, trust in it, and live by it. May my life reflect not my effort, but Your abundant and sustaining grace. Through Jesus Christ my Lord. **Amen.**

Faithful Father, I thank You that the whole of the Christian life is grounded in grace. From beginning to end, it is Your work, not mine. You called me, You saved me, and You continue to sustain me. Yet I confess that I often drift from this truth in practice. I can begin well in grace, but then try to continue in my own strength. I can forget that every step forward depends on You. So, I ask You to draw me back into a life that is truly lived in grace.

Help me to continue as I began - by grace. Let me not move away from the simplicity of trusting Christ. Keep me from adding unnecessary burdens or expectations that You have not placed on me. Let me walk steadily, not driven by pressure, but guided by grace.

Teach me to receive grace daily. Not as a distant concept, but as a present reality. When I wake, let me begin in grace. When I work, let me depend on grace. When I face difficulty, let me draw strength from grace. When I fail, let me return to grace. Let every part of life be shaped by this continual dependence on You.

Guard me from discouragement. When I see my weaknesses, remind me that Your grace is sufficient. When I see slow progress, remind me that You are patient and faithful. Keep me from measuring growth too narrowly or becoming disheartened by what remains unfinished. Let me trust that You are at work, even when I cannot see it clearly.

Let grace also produce joy. Not a superficial happiness, but a deep and steady confidence in Your goodness. Let it free me from constant striving and fill me with peace. And let it overflow into my relationships, my service, and my witness.

Above all, keep me close to Christ, for He is the fullness of grace. Let me abide in Him, draw from Him, and walk with Him. May my life increasingly reflect the beauty of a believer who is not striving to earn, but resting and walking in grace. Through Jesus Christ my Saviour. **Amen.**

Gracious God, teach me to walk each day in the grace that is already mine in Christ.

I confess that I often slip into striving, measuring my standing before You by how well I think I am doing. Forgive me for this.

Remind me that I am accepted, not because of my performance, but because of Jesus. Help me to begin each day resting in that truth.

When I feel weak, let grace strengthen me. When I fail, let grace restore me quickly. Guard me from both pride when I succeed and despair when I struggle. Let grace shape my thinking, my choices, and my relationships.

May I live not trying to earn Your favour, but from the security of already having it. Let my life reflect a steady dependence on Your grace in every moment. **Amen.**

Faithful Father, I ask You to make grace the atmosphere of my life. Too often I live as though everything depends on me, carrying burdens You have not asked me to carry.

Teach me to rely on You more fully. Help me to receive Your grace in every situation - in my work, in my struggles, and in my relationships.

When I feel pressure, remind me that Your grace is sufficient. When I feel uncertain, remind me that You are in control. Let grace free me from anxiety, from comparison, and from the need to prove myself.

At the same time, keep me from treating grace lightly. Let it lead me into obedience and shape my desire to live for You. May my life show the quiet confidence of one who is sustained daily by Your unfailing grace. **Amen.**

Merciful Lord, thank You that the whole of the Christian life is lived by grace. I began by grace, and I continue by grace.

Yet I confess that I often forget this and try to move forward in my own strength. Draw me back to simple dependence on You. Help me to trust You in the ordinary moments of each day, not just in times of need.

Let grace steady my heart, guide my thinking, and strengthen my obedience. When I am tempted, let grace empower me to stand. When I am weary, let grace renew me.

Keep me from self-reliance and lead me into a life that is shaped by trust in You.

May I walk steadily in grace, growing in faith and reflecting Your goodness in all I do. **Amen.**

Holy Lord, I ask You to help me live a life that is clearly shaped by grace. Guard me from legalism on one hand and carelessness on the other.

Teach me to walk in the freedom You have given, while also pursuing a life that honours You.

Let grace lead me into humility, gratitude, and steady obedience. When I am tempted to rely on myself, remind me to depend on You.

When I feel discouraged, remind me that Your grace has not run out.

Let me extend grace to others as I have received it, showing patience, kindness, and forgiveness. May my life reflect the beauty of a believer who is not striving to earn, but resting and walking in the grace of God each day. **Amen.**

31. PRAYERS FOR STRENGTH

Almighty God, I come before You aware of my need for strength. Life brings demands, pressures, and challenges that often feel beyond my ability to carry. I confess that in my own strength I am limited, easily wearied, and sometimes overwhelmed. Yet I thank You that I am not left to rely on myself. You are my strength, my refuge, and my ever-present help. I come, therefore, not asking to become strong in myself, but to be strengthened by You.

Your word says, "God is our refuge and strength, an ever-present help in trouble." (Psalm 46:1). Let that truth take hold of my heart. When I feel weak, remind me that You are near. When I feel burdened, remind me that You are able to sustain me. When I feel uncertain, remind me that You are steady and unchanging. Teach me to turn to You quickly, not as a last resort, but as my first response.

I ask for strength in every area of life. Strength for the responsibilities I carry. Strength for the decisions I must make. Strength for the relationships that require patience and grace. Strength for the moments when I feel discouraged or weary. Let Your strength meet me where I am, not where I wish I were. Guard me from the illusion of self-sufficiency. Keep me from trying to carry what belongs in Your hands. Teach me to depend on You, not only in times of crisis, but in the ordinary flow of each day. Let prayer become the place where I draw strength and where I learn to rest in Your provision.

Your word also says, "I can do all this through Him who gives me strength." (Philippians 4:13). Help me to understand that rightly. Strengthen me to be faithful, to persevere, and to honour You in whatever lies before me.

And when I feel weak, let that weakness draw me closer to You. Let it remind me that Your power is made perfect in weakness. May my life show not my strength, but Yours at work in me. Through Jesus Christ my Lord. **Amen.**

Faithful Father, I thank You that You are the source of true strength. You do not ask me to face life alone or to rely on limited human resources. You invite me to draw near and to receive strength from You.

Yet I confess that I often try to manage on my own. I press on in my own ability until I become tired, discouraged, and strained. So, I ask You to teach me a better way - a life of dependence on Your strength.

Your word says, "He gives strength to the weary and increases the power of the weak." (Isaiah 40:29). I come as one who is often weary. Renew my strength. Lift the heaviness that settles on my heart and refresh my spirit.

Help me to wait on You, not in passivity, but in trust. As I wait, renew me so that I may rise again with strength for what lies ahead.

I ask for strength not only for outward tasks, but for inward life. Strength to remain steady when emotions fluctuate. Strength to hold on to truth when doubts arise. Strength to resist temptation and to pursue holiness. Strength to forgive when it is difficult and to love when it is costly. Let Your strength reach into every part of my life.

Teach me to receive strength through the means You have given. Through Your word, speak life to my soul. Through prayer, draw me near and strengthen my heart. Through fellowship, encourage and support me. Through rest, renew me physically and mentally. Let me not neglect these gifts, but use them wisely as part of Your provision.

And when strength feels small, remind me that Your strength is not. Let me not measure my ability and become discouraged. Instead, let me look to You and be strengthened.

May my life be marked by quiet dependence, steady endurance, and a growing confidence in Your sustaining grace. Through Jesus Christ my Saviour. **Amen.**

Almighty God, I come to You for strength because I know how limited I am in myself. There are days when responsibilities feel heavy, pressures feel constant, and my own energy seems too small for what lies before me.

Yet You are never weary, never strained, and never unable to help. So, I ask You to strengthen me today.

Give me strength for my mind when I feel tired, strength for my heart when I feel burdened, and strength for my will when I feel tempted to give up.

Help me not to rely on myself, but to lean fully on You. Remind me that Your power is made perfect in weakness and that You are able to sustain me in every calling You place before me.

Let Your strength steady me, carry me, and keep me faithful in all I must do. **Amen.**

Faithful Father, thank You that I do not have to face life in my own strength. Too often I try to push through by determination alone, only to find myself weary, frustrated, and discouraged.

Teach me a better way. Help me to come to You first, to ask for help quickly, and to depend on Your grace throughout the day.

Strengthen me for the tasks that require patience, for the duties that feel unending, and for the conversations that require wisdom and kindness.

Let me not be overcome by the weight of what is before me. Instead, fill me with quiet endurance, inner steadiness, and the assurance that You are with me.

May I discover in real and practical ways that Your strength is sufficient for every demand, every burden, and every hour of this day. **Amen.**

Gracious Lord, I ask You to renew my strength where I feel depleted. You know the weariness I carry, the pressures I do not easily speak about, and the hidden heaviness of heart that can drain courage and resolve.

I bring all of this to You now. Breathe fresh strength into my soul. Lift what feels heavy and steady what feels weak. Help me to keep going in obedience, even when I do not feel strong.

Let me draw strength from Your word, from prayer, and from the assurance that You are near.

Guard me from self-pity, from discouragement, and from the temptation to withdraw when I most need to trust You. May Your strength become evident in my weakness, so that I continue faithfully and give glory to You alone. **Amen.**

Holy Lord, give me strength not only for outward tasks, but for inward faithfulness. Strengthen me to think clearly, to respond graciously, to endure patiently, and to obey steadily.

When I feel emotionally worn, give me calmness. When I feel spiritually weak, give me renewed faith. When I feel physically tired, help me to rest wisely and continue dependently.

Keep me from trying to appear strong while neglecting the deeper strength that comes from walking closely with You. Teach me to live one step at a time, receiving the grace You provide for each moment.

Let Your strength uphold me in ordinary duties and in difficult seasons alike.

May I become more resilient, more peaceful, and more faithful because I have learned to rely not on my own resources, but on the living God who strengthens His people. **Amen.**

Faithful God, I come before You asking for endurance. You have not called me only to begin the Christian life, but to continue in it with perseverance and steady faith. Yet I confess that I can grow weary along the way. Difficulties, delays, and repeated struggles can wear down my resolve. There are times when I feel like slowing, retreating, or even giving up. So, Lord, strengthen me, that I may endure with patience and trust.

Your word says, "Let us run with perseverance the race marked out for us." (Hebrews 12:1). Help me to see my life as a race that requires endurance. It is not a short sprint, but a long journey. When the path is difficult, give me courage. When progress feels slow, give me patience. When I am tempted to compare myself with others, remind me to focus on the race You have set before me.

Fix my eyes on Jesus, the author and perfecter of my faith. Let me not become distracted by circumstances, nor discouraged by my own limitations. Instead, let me look to Him who endured the cross and now reigns in glory.

I ask for endurance in specific areas of life. In responsibilities that feel demanding, sustain me. In relationships that require patience, strengthen me. In trials that stretch my faith, steady me. Let me not grow bitter or hardened under pressure. Instead, let endurance produce maturity, character, and hope.

Guard me from the temptation to give up too soon. When I feel tired, remind me that Your strength is still available. When I feel discouraged, remind me that Your promises still stand. When I feel alone, remind me that You are with me.

Let endurance grow quietly but steadily, shaping my life over time. And as I endure, keep me humble. Let me not rely on my own determination, but on Your sustaining grace. May my life reflect a quiet perseverance that honours You and points to Your faithfulness. Through Jesus Christ my Lord. **Amen.**

Lord of all strength, I thank You that You call me to endure and that You also provide what I need to do so. You do not ask me to persevere in my own strength, but to depend on You. Yet I confess that I can grow impatient. I can want quick answers, immediate change, and relief from difficulty. When these do not come, my heart can become restless or discouraged. So I ask You to teach me the grace of endurance.

Your word says, "Consider it pure joy… whenever you face trials of many kinds, because you know that the testing of your faith produces perseverance." (James 1:2–3). Help me to understand this rightly. Trials are not meaningless. They are part of Your work in shaping my faith. Teach me to see beyond the immediate difficulty and to trust in what You are producing through it.

Give me endurance in waiting. When answers are delayed, help me to trust Your timing. When circumstances remain unchanged, help me to remain faithful. Keep me from drifting into frustration or losing heart. Let patience take root and grow in me.

Strengthen me also in the daily demands of life. Endurance is not only for great trials, but for the steady faithfulness required in ordinary days. Help me to remain consistent, even when the routine feels long. Let me not lose sight of the importance of small, faithful steps.

Guard my heart from discouragement. When I feel like I am not making progress, remind me that You are at work, even when I cannot see it clearly. When I am tempted to give up, give me renewed strength. Let me press on, not because I feel strong, but because You are faithful.

And let endurance lead me into deeper hope. As I persevere, let me see more clearly that my hope is not in circumstances, but in You. Let that hope sustain me and give me confidence for the future. May my life be marked by steady endurance, shaped by grace, and anchored in Your faithfulness. Through Jesus Christ my Saviour. **Amen.**

Faithful God, I ask You to give me endurance for the path You have set before me.

At times the journey feels long, and I grow tired in both heart and mind. There are responsibilities that do not ease, struggles that do not quickly resolve, and seasons that stretch longer than I expected.

Yet You have not called me to give up, but to press on. So strengthen me to endure. Help me to take each step in faith, even when I cannot see the outcome. Guard me from discouragement and from the quiet temptation to withdraw.

Let me remember that You are with me in every moment, sustaining me and guiding me. May I persevere steadily, trusting that You are working through every part of this journey for Your good purposes. **Amen.**

Gracious Father, teach me to endure with patience and trust. I confess that I often want quick answers, easy paths, and immediate results.

When these do not come, I can become restless and disheartened. Change my perspective, I pray. Help me to see that endurance is part of Your work in me, shaping my character and strengthening my faith.

When the days feel repetitive or the burden feels heavy, give me renewed resolve. Let me not measure progress only by what I can see, but by the faithfulness

You are producing within me. Keep me steady in obedience, even when it feels unnoticed.

May I learn to persevere not by my own strength, but by relying on Your sustaining grace each day. **Amen.**

Merciful Lord, I bring before You my weariness and ask You to renew my endurance. There are moments when I feel like stopping, when the effort seems too great and the reward too distant.

Yet You are faithful, and You call me to continue. Lift my heart and strengthen my spirit.

Help me to remember that nothing done in faith is wasted and that You see every act of obedience.

Guard me from negative thinking that leads to defeat. Instead, fill my mind with truth and my heart with hope.

Let me endure not with resentment, but with quiet confidence in You.

May perseverance grow in me as I learn to trust Your timing and Your purposes more deeply. **Amen.**

Holy Lord, I ask You to give me steady endurance in both the ordinary and the difficult parts of life.

Help me to remain faithful in daily responsibilities, even when they feel routine or unnoticed.

costly or tiring. Keep me from drifting into complacency or giving in to discouragement.

Instead, teach me to press on with a patient and willing spirit. Let endurance become a mark of my life, not driven by stubborn effort, but by trust in Your grace.

May I finish what You have called me to with faithfulness, knowing that You are the One who sustains me from beginning to end. **Amen.**

33. PRAYERS FOR PEACE IN ANXIETY

Lord God, you know how easily my thoughts can become troubled, how quickly my mind can race ahead, and how often I can feel burdened by things I cannot control. Anxiety can press heavily on me, making my heart restless and my spirit unsettled. Yet I thank You that You are not disturbed, uncertain or absent. You remain sovereign. So, I ask You to bring Your peace into the places where anxiety has taken hold.

Your word says, "Do not be anxious about anything, but in every situation, by prayer and petition, with thanksgiving, present your requests to God." (Philippians 4:6). Help me to obey that gracious command. Forgive me for this anxious striving. Teach me to pray instead of spiralling, to trust instead of trying to control, and to give thanks even while I wait.

I place before You the concerns that weigh on me - the things I fear, the uncertainties I cannot resolve, the responsibilities that feel heavy, and the future that I cannot see clearly. You know them all better than I do. I ask You to meet me here, not only by changing circumstances, though I ask for Your help in that too, but by quieting my heart in the midst of them.

Remind me that anxiety is not stronger than Your promises. When fear rises, bring truth to mind. When my thoughts become tangled, untangle them with the clarity of Your word. When I feel inwardly overwhelmed, anchor me again in the certainties of the gospel - that I am Yours, that Christ is reigning, that Your love has not failed, and that Your grace will be sufficient for whatever comes.

Teach me to breathe more deeply in the light of Your presence. Slow the pace within me. Help me to live one day at a time, receiving today's mercies instead of borrowing tomorrow's troubles. And let this peace shape my life so that I become calmer, steadier, and more trusting, not because life is easy, but because You are faithful. Through Jesus Christ, who is Himself my peace. **Amen.**

Faithful Father, I thank You that I may come to You honestly with my anxieties. I do not need to hide them, minimise them, or pretend to be stronger than I am. You know my frame. You understand the burdens that trouble me. You see the pressures that others do not see and the fears that I struggle even to name. Yet You do not turn me away in weakness. Instead, You invite me to cast all my anxiety on You because You care for me. I come now on the strength of that promise.

Your word says, "Cast all your anxiety on Him because He cares for you." (1 Peter 5:7). Teach me what it means to cast my anxieties onto You and not pick them up again a moment later. I can be so quick to pray and yet continue carrying inwardly what I have outwardly handed over. Help me to entrust these things to You in truth. Let prayer become a real release, not merely a form of words.

I ask for peace in the middle of anxious thoughts. Do not let my mind run unchecked. Where my imagination magnifies fears, bring it back under the authority of truth. Where my thoughts loop endlessly, interrupt them with the steadying power of Your promises. Where anxiety drains joy and weakens faith, let Your Spirit strengthen and restore me. Remind me that You are already present in every tomorrow that I fear.

Keep me also from the shame that can accompany anxiety. Let me not think that my struggles place me outside Your care. Instead, let them become occasions to come nearer to You. Teach me that weakness is not the end of hope, but often the place where grace is most deeply known. Help me to receive practical rest where it is needed, wise help where it is available, and spiritual strength from the means You have given - Your word, prayer, fellowship, and honest dependence upon You.

And let Your peace do more than soothe me for a moment. Let it become a steady influence in my life. Make me less reactive, less fearful, and less controlled by what might happen. May the peace of Christ rule in my heart and show itself in my speech, my decisions, and my presence with others. Through Jesus Christ my Lord. **Amen.**

God of peace, I bring before You the anxiety that so easily rises within me. My thoughts can become restless, my mind can race ahead, and my heart can feel unsettled by things I cannot control.

Yet You are not troubled, and nothing takes You by surprise. So, I ask You to quiet my heart and steady my thoughts.

Help me to bring my concerns to You rather than carrying them alone. Teach me to trust You with what I do not understand and to rest in Your wisdom.

When fear begins to take hold, remind me that You are near and that Your promises remain true.

Let Your peace guard my heart and mind, bringing calm where there has been tension and assurance where there has been uncertainty. **Amen.**

Gracious Father, I confess that I often try to manage my anxieties in my own strength, turning them over repeatedly in my mind without finding peace. Forgive me for this.

Teach me instead to bring every concern to You in prayer. Help me to release what I cannot control and to trust You with the outcomes I cannot see.

Give me a steady confidence that You are working in every situation, even when I do not understand how.

Guard me from anxious thinking that drains my strength and clouds my perspective. Instead, fill my mind with truth and my heart with peace.

Let Your presence become my refuge, and Your promises my anchor in every anxious moment. **Amen.**

Faithful God, You know the burdens that weigh on me and the thoughts that trouble me. I bring them all to You now.

When anxiety rises, help me not to be overwhelmed, but to turn to You quickly and honestly.

Remind me that I am not alone and that You are already present in every situation I face. Give me clarity where my thinking feels tangled and calmness where my heart feels unsettled.

Help me to live one day at a time, trusting You for what lies ahead. Let Your peace replace my striving and Your truth silence my fears.

May I learn to rest in You, even when life feels uncertain and difficult. **Amen.**

Holy Lord, I ask You to establish Your peace deeply within me. Not a temporary calm, but a steady and enduring peace that comes from knowing You.

When my thoughts drift toward worry, draw them back to what is true. When my heart becomes unsettled, anchor it in Your faithfulness.

Help me to resist the urge to imagine worst outcomes or to carry burdens that are not mine to bear. Instead, teach me to trust You with every detail of my life.

Let Your peace shape how I think, how I respond, and how I live.

May I become calmer, more trusting, and more grounded because I have learned to rely on You in every anxious moment. **Amen.**

34. PRAYERS FOR TIMES OF FEAR

Lord God Almighty, I come before You in a time of fear. You know how quickly fear can grip the heart, cloud the mind, and weaken resolve. There are moments when danger feels near, uncertainty feels heavy, and the future seems filled with questions I cannot answer. In such times, I confess that I am often shaken. Yet I thank You that fear does not rule over You. You are never alarmed, never uncertain, and never powerless. So, I come asking that Your presence would be more real to me than the fear that presses upon me.

Your word says, "When I am afraid, I put my trust in You." (Psalm 56:3). Teach me to do exactly that. Not to deny fear, not to pretend courage I do not feel, but to bring my fear honestly into the light of trust. Help me to remember that fear itself is not the end of faith. It is often the place where faith must rise and cling more tightly to You. When fear comes, let it become a summons to prayer and not a doorway to panic.

I place before You the things that frighten me - the unknowns, the threats, the possibilities I cannot control, the losses I dread, and the burdens that make me feel vulnerable. You know them all fully. I ask You not only to change what can be changed, but to steady me while I wait and trust. Let Your word speak more loudly to me than fearful thoughts. Remind me that I am Yours, that Christ is with me, and that nothing can separate me from Your love.

Guard my imagination from running ahead in dark directions. Guard my body from being ruled by tension and my mind from being mastered by dread. Give me calmness to think clearly, wisdom to act rightly, and courage to do the next thing before me. Let fear not drive me inward, but draw me nearer to You.

You are my refuge and my strength. May I find in You a shelter deeper than the storm and a peace stronger than what I fear. Through Jesus Christ my Lord. **Amen.**

Faithful Father, I thank You that in times of fear I do not stand alone. Fear can make the world feel unstable and the heart feel small. It can make dangers seem larger and Your promises seem distant.

Yet You remain the same - holy, wise, strong, and near. You have not ceased to reign because I feel afraid. You have not withdrawn Your care because my heart is trembling. So, I ask You to draw near to me now and to strengthen me with the assurance of Your presence.

Your word says, "So do not fear, for I am with you; do not be dismayed, for I am your God." (Isaiah 41:10). Let that promise settle deeply in me. You do not merely tell me not to fear; You give me the reason. You are with me. You are my God. You will strengthen me and uphold me. Let these words become more than familiar truth - let them become lived reality in the middle of this fearful hour.

I ask You for courage. Not a loud or boastful courage, but the quiet strength that comes from resting in You. Help me not to be ruled by worst-case thinking, by endless what-ifs, or by the feeling that I must secure myself before I can be at peace. Teach me to trust You with what I cannot predict and to obey You in what I can clearly see.

Keep me from isolation in fear. Draw me into prayer, into Your word, and into the support of those who walk with You. Let me not hide in silence when I need help, nor retreat into myself as though I must bear this alone. Give me humility to receive comfort and wisdom from the means You provide.

And let fear not have the final word. Let trust rise. Let peace grow. Let Christ be magnified in the way I endure. If the path remains uncertain, remain unmistakably near.

If my courage falters, uphold me again. And if I must walk through this valley for a time, let me do so with the confidence that the Good Shepherd goes with me. Through Jesus Christ my Saviour. **Amen.**

Lord God, in times of fear I turn to You because I know that You alone are steady and unshaken.

My heart can quickly become troubled, and my thoughts can run ahead into uncertainty and worst-case outcomes. Yet You remain the same - strong, present, and in control of all things.

Help me to bring my fear honestly before You without pretending or hiding it. Teach me to trust You in the very moment when fear rises.

Remind me that You are with me and that nothing I face is beyond Your power or outside Your care. Give me courage to take the next step, even when I feel uncertain.

Let Your presence quiet my heart and replace fear with a growing confidence in Your faithfulness and Your unfailing love toward me. **Amen.**

Gracious Father, You know the fears that trouble me, both spoken and unspoken. Some are clear and immediate, while others sit quietly beneath the surface, shaping my thoughts and reactions. I bring them all to You now.

Help me not to be ruled by fear, but to be guided by truth. Remind me that You are near, that You see what I cannot see, and that You are working even when I do not understand.

Guard me from imagining outcomes that may never come and from allowing fear to control my decisions.

Instead, give me a steady heart and a clear mind.

Let Your promises speak louder than my fears and let Your peace begin to take root where anxiety and uncertainty have held sway for too long. **Amen.**

Faithful God, when fear rises within me, help me to respond by turning toward You rather than retreating into worry or silence. I confess that fear can make me feel small, vulnerable, and unsure of what to do next.

Yet You are my refuge and my strength, always present and always able to help. Remind me that I do not face anything alone.

Give me courage that is not based on my own strength, but on Your presence with me.

Help me to stand firm, to think clearly, and to act wisely even when I feel uncertain. Let fear become a doorway to deeper trust rather than a barrier that keeps me from moving forward in faith and obedience before You. **Amen.**

Holy Lord, I ask You to anchor my heart when fear begins to take hold.

Do not let my thoughts be carried away by uncertainty or by the unknown.

Instead, draw me back to what is true about You - that You are faithful, sovereign, and always near to Your people.

Strengthen me inwardly so that I am not easily shaken by circumstances or overwhelmed by possibilities.

Help me to remember Your past faithfulness and to trust You for what lies ahead. Give me calmness in my spirit, steadiness in my thinking, and courage in my actions.

Let Your peace grow stronger within me than my fear, so that I may live with quiet confidence in You, even in difficult and uncertain times. **Amen.**

35. PRAYERS FOR DISCOURAGEMENT

God of all comfort, I come before You in a time of discouragement. My heart feels heavy, my strength feels low, and my perspective has been clouded by disappointment and weariness. There are moments when progress seems slow, when effort feels fruitless, and when hope begins to fade. I confess that discouragement can quietly take hold, draining joy and weakening faith. Yet I thank You that You are not distant in such times. You are near to the weary, attentive to the burdened, and ready to lift those who feel cast down.

Your word says, "Why, my soul, are you downcast? Why so disturbed within me? Put your hope in God." (Psalm 42:5). Teach me to speak that truth to my own heart. When discouragement settles in, help me not to remain silent under it, but to bring it into the light of Your promises.

I bring before You the things that have led me here - the disappointments I have faced, the efforts that seem unnoticed, the prayers that appear unanswered, and the struggles that feel unending. You know them all fully. I ask You to meet me in this place, not only by changing circumstances, though I ask for Your help, but by renewing my heart within them.

Lift my eyes again to Christ. Let me see His faithfulness, His patience, and His finished work. Remind me that my labour in the Lord is not in vain. Strengthen me to continue, even when I do not see immediate results.

Guard me from giving up. When I am tempted to withdraw, give me courage to press on. When I am tempted to lose heart, renew my hope. Let me take small, faithful steps forward, trusting that You are at work in ways I cannot always see.

And let this season deepen my reliance on You. May discouragement not define me, but refine me. May it lead me into a stronger, steadier hope that rests not on circumstances, but on Your unchanging character. Through Jesus Christ my Lord. **Amen.**

Father God, I thank You that You understand discouragement and that You meet Your people in it. You do not dismiss our weariness or ignore our struggles. Instead, You draw near with patience and compassion. I confess that my heart can become easily discouraged when things do not unfold as I had hoped. So, I ask You to renew me again.

Your word says, "Let us not become weary in doing good, for at the proper time we will reap a harvest if we do not give up." (Galatians 6:9). Help me to hold onto that promise. Even when I do not see the fruit of my efforts, remind me that You are at work. Even when progress seems hidden, remind me that nothing done in faith is wasted. Give me patience to trust Your timing and perseverance to continue in what You have called me to do.

I ask You to strengthen my inner life. Where discouragement has drained energy, restore it. Where it has clouded vision, bring clarity. Where it has weakened resolve, renew it. Help me to return to the simple practices that sustain faith - prayer, Your word, and steady obedience. Let me not neglect these in discouragement but lean into them more deeply.

Guard me from negative thinking that grows unchecked. When my thoughts begin to spiral into defeat, interrupt them with truth. When I am tempted to measure everything by visible results, remind me that You see the heart and value faithfulness. Teach me to walk by faith and not by sight. And let me not walk alone.

Draw me toward others who can encourage and strengthen me. Give me humility to receive help and wisdom to speak honestly about my struggles. Use the fellowship of Your people to lift my spirit and remind me that I am not alone.

May discouragement give way to renewed hope. May weariness give way to quiet strength. And may my life reflect a steady faith that continues to trust You, even when the path is difficult. Through Jesus Christ my Saviour. Amen.

Gracious God, I bring before You the discouragement that has settled on my heart. There are times when I feel weary, when progress seems slow, and when effort appears to bring little result.

In those moments, my strength fades and my hope begins to weaken. Yet You are not discouraged, and Your purposes do not fail.

So, I ask You to lift my heart again. Help me to see beyond what is immediate and to trust in what You are doing, even when it is hidden from me.

Guard me from negative thinking that leads me further down and replace it with truth that strengthens my faith. Remind me that my labour in the Lord is never in vain. Renew my energy, restore my hope, and help me to continue faithfully in what You have called me to do. **Amen.**

Lord, You know how easily I can become discouraged when things do not unfold as I expected. Delays, setbacks, and disappointments can weigh heavily on me, and I can begin to lose heart. I bring all of this to You now.

Help me not to measure everything by visible results, but to trust that You are at work in ways I cannot always see. Give me patience to continue and strength to persevere.

When I feel like stepping back or giving up, draw me forward again with renewed confidence in You. Let Your promises speak more clearly than my circumstances.

Keep my heart steady and my focus fixed on You. May discouragement not take root, but instead lead me to deeper trust and stronger faith in Your unfailing care. **Amen.**

Merciful Lord, I ask You to meet me in my discouragement and bring fresh strength to my soul. You know the quiet burdens I carry and the thoughts that weigh me down.

When I feel overlooked, unproductive, or uncertain, remind me that You see every step of faith and every act of obedience. Help me to continue even when I do not feel motivated or strong.

Guard me from withdrawing or becoming disheartened. Instead, fill my heart with renewed hope and a steady determination to keep going.

Let me not be driven by feelings alone but anchored in Your truth. Strengthen me to take the next step, trusting that You are present, working, and guiding me in every moment of this journey. **Amen.**

Holy Lord, I ask You to lift me from discouragement and give me a renewed perspective.

When my heart feels heavy and my thoughts begin to drift toward defeat, draw me back to what is true. Remind me that You are faithful, that Your plans are good, and that You are not finished with me.

Help me to see discouragement not as a place to remain, but as a place to turn toward You more deeply. Give me courage to continue in obedience, even when it feels difficult.

Let hope rise again within me, not based on changing circumstances, but on Your unchanging character.

Strengthen me to persevere with patience and faith, knowing that You are sustaining me and will bring about Your purposes in Your perfect time. **Amen.**

36. PRAYERS FOR LONELINESS

God who is always present, I come before You in a time of loneliness. You know the ache of it, the quiet sense of distance, the feeling of being unseen or disconnected. Even when surrounded by people, loneliness can linger within. It can make the heart feel heavy and the spirit feel isolated. Yet I thank You that I am never truly alone. You are with me, constant and near, even when others are not.

Your word says, "Never will I leave you; never will I forsake you." (Hebrews 13:5). Let that truth settle deeply into my heart. When loneliness presses in, remind me that Your presence does not come and go. You are not distant, distracted, or unaware. You are attentive, faithful, and near. Help me to believe that more deeply, especially when my feelings tell me otherwise. I bring before You the places where I feel alone - relationships that are missing, connections that have changed, conversations that do not happen, and the quiet moments that feel empty. You know them all. I ask You to meet me in those spaces. Not only by changing my circumstances, though I ask for meaningful connection, but by filling the emptiness with the reality of Your presence.

Teach me to draw near to You in these moments. When I feel alone, let me turn to You rather than withdraw into silence or discouragement. Let prayer become a place of companionship and Your word a voice that speaks into the quiet. Help me to recognise that You are not near in theory, but present in reality.

At the same time, guide me toward others. Keep me from isolation that deepens loneliness. Give me courage to reach out, humility to be honest, and wisdom to build relationships that are genuine and life-giving. Use me also to be a companion to others who may feel alone. Let me reflect Your care in the way I listen, speak, and respond. And let loneliness not define my identity. I belong to You. I am part of Your family. I am known, loved, and remembered. May that truth steady me and give me hope. Through Jesus Christ my Lord. **Amen.**

Faithful Father, I thank You that You see me fully and know me completely. There is no part of my life that is hidden from You, no thought unrecognised, and no feeling ignored. Yet I confess that I can still feel alone. Loneliness can settle quietly, making me feel distant from others and uncertain of where I belong. In those moments, I ask You to draw near to me in a way that I can recognise and rest in.

Your word says, "The Lord is close to the broken-hearted and saves those who are crushed in spirit." (Psalm 34:18). Let me experience that closeness now. When my heart feels heavy, be my comfort. When my thoughts turn inward, remind me of Your presence. Let me not drift into the belief that I am unseen or forgotten. You know me, You care for me, and You remain with me.

Help me also to understand that loneliness is not a sign that You have withdrawn. Even Your people in Scripture knew seasons of isolation, yet You were with them in every moment. Teach me to trust that You are at work, even in this season, shaping my heart and drawing me closer to Yourself.

Give me grace to use this time well. Let loneliness become a place where I seek You more deeply, not less. Let it open space for reflection, prayer, and growth. At the same time, protect me from becoming withdrawn or closed off.
Lead me toward healthy connection, toward friendships that are honest and supportive, and toward fellowship that strengthens my faith.

And where relationships have been lost or strained, bring healing in Your time. Restore what can be restored and comfort what cannot. Give me patience as I wait and hope as I trust.

May Your presence be enough for me in this moment, even as I ask for companionship. Let me know the quiet assurance that I am not alone, not forgotten, and not without hope. Through Jesus Christ my Saviour. **Amen.**

Gracious God, I bring before You the loneliness that weighs on my heart. There are moments when I feel unseen, unheard, or distant from others, even when I am not physically alone.

In those times, my thoughts can turn inward, and the silence can feel heavy. Yet You are not distant from me. You are present, attentive, and near in every moment.

Help me to believe that more deeply. When loneliness presses in, remind me that I am never truly alone because You are with me. Draw me into a deeper awareness of Your presence.

Let me find comfort not only in changing circumstances, but in knowing that I am known and loved by You.

Steady my heart, lift my spirit, and help me to rest in Your faithful and constant care. **Amen.**

Faithful Father, You know the longing within me for connection, for understanding, and for meaningful relationship.

I bring that longing to You without hiding it or trying to ignore it. At times I feel isolated, and it can be difficult to know how to respond. Help me not to withdraw further into myself, but to turn toward You and toward others in healthy ways.

Give me courage to reach out, even when it feels difficult. Guide me into relationships that are genuine, supportive, and life-giving.

At the same time, teach me to be content in Your presence, knowing that You are enough for me in every season.

Let loneliness not define me, but become a place where I grow in trust, dependence, and deeper awareness of Your unfailing love. **Amen.**

Merciful Lord, I ask You to meet me in the quiet places where loneliness is most deeply felt.

You see what others do not see and understand what I cannot always express. When I feel forgotten or overlooked, remind me that I am fully known by You.

When I feel disconnected, draw me into closer fellowship with You. Help me to use these moments not to drift away, but to seek You more intentionally.

Let Your word speak into the silence and Your presence fill what feels empty. Guard me from discouragement and from believing that I am without purpose or place.

Instead, give me renewed confidence that I belong to You and that my life is held securely in Your care. **Amen.**

Holy Lord, I ask You to transform my experience of loneliness into a deeper walk with You.

Do not let it become a place of despair, but a place where I encounter Your presence more clearly. Help me to be honest with You about how I feel and to bring my heart openly before You.

At the same time, guide me toward others and help me to build relationships that reflect Your love and truth.

Give me patience when connection takes time and wisdom in how I relate to others.

Let me not measure my worth by how connected I feel, but by what You have declared about me.

May Your presence steady me, Your love reassure me, and Your grace sustain me through every season. **Amen.**

Merciful God, I come before You in need of healing. You know my body, my mind, and my spirit. You see what is broken, what is weak, and what is burdened. Nothing about my condition is hidden from You. I thank You that You are not distant from suffering, but near to those who are in need. You are compassionate, attentive, and powerful. So, I bring my need to You, asking for Your healing grace.

I know that Your healing may come in different ways and in different times. Sometimes You restore quickly. Sometimes You work gradually. Sometimes You sustain through weakness rather than remove it. But in all things, You remain faithful. So, I ask You to bring healing according to Your will and wisdom.

I ask You to bring physical healing where my body is affected. Strengthen what is weak. Restore what is damaged. Ease what is painful. Bring order where there is disorder. Guide those who care for me, and give them wisdom and skill. Use every means You have provided for my good. Let healing come not only through miracle, but also through the ordinary provisions of care, treatment, and rest.

I ask also for healing within. Where fear has taken hold, bring peace. Where discouragement has settled, bring hope. Where my spirit is weary, renew it. Let this time not draw me away from You, but closer to You. Teach me to trust You in weakness and to depend on You more deeply than before.

Guard me from despair. When progress is slow or uncertain, keep me from losing heart. Let me remember that my life is held in Your hands and that Your purposes are always good. Even in illness, You are at work. Even in weakness, Your grace is sufficient. And whatever the outcome, keep me anchored in Christ. Let me rest in the certainty that my ultimate hope is secure - that one day all sickness will be gone, and I will be made whole in Your presence. Until then, sustain me, strengthen me, and bring healing as You see fit. Through Jesus Christ my Lord. **Amen.**

Faithful Father, I thank You that I may come to You with my need for healing. You invite me to bring my concerns honestly, without fear or hesitation. You are not indifferent to suffering, nor are You unaware of the pain I carry. You see, You understand, and You care. So, I come asking that Your healing hand would be upon me.

Your word says, "He heals the broken-hearted and binds up their wounds." (Psalm 147:3). I ask You to bring that healing into every part of my life. Where there is physical pain, bring relief. Where there is emotional hurt, bring comfort. Where there is spiritual weariness, bring renewal.

Let Your healing touch be both gentle and powerful, restoring what has been damaged and strengthening what has grown weak.

I confess that times of illness can bring many struggles - uncertainty, fear, frustration, and fatigue. Help me not to be overwhelmed by these. Give me patience as I wait, courage as I endure, and peace in the midst of it all. Let me not become defined by my condition, but remain grounded in who I am in Christ.

Guide those who care for me. Give wisdom to doctors, nurses, and all who are involved. Bless their efforts and use them as instruments of Your care. Help me to receive their help with gratitude and trust.

At the same time, guard my heart. When healing does not come as quickly as I hope, keep me from discouragement. When answers are unclear, keep me from anxiety. Teach me to rest in Your sovereignty and to trust in Your timing.

And let this season draw me nearer to You. Let it deepen my prayer life, sharpen my dependence, and strengthen my faith. May I come to know more of Your presence and more of Your grace. And as You bring healing, may I give You the glory, recognising that every good gift comes from Your hand. Through Jesus Christ my Saviour. **Amen.**

Merciful God, I come to You in need of healing, bringing before You the weakness and pain I am experiencing. You know every detail of my condition, and nothing about my situation is hidden from You.

I ask You to bring healing according to Your will, whether through immediate restoration or through a steady process over time. Strengthen what is weak, ease what is painful, and bring order where there is distress.

At the same time, guard my heart from fear and discouragement. Help me to trust You, even when healing does not come as quickly as I hope.

Let me rest in the assurance that You are near, that You care deeply for me, and that Your grace is sufficient for every moment I face. Sustain me and renew me as I look to You. In Jesus precious name I pray. **Amen.**

Faithful Father, I place my need for healing into Your hands, knowing that You are both powerful and compassionate.

You see not only my physical condition, but also the emotional and spiritual strain that comes with it. I ask You to bring relief where there is pain and strength where there is weakness. Guide those who care for me and give them wisdom in every decision they make.

Help me to receive their care with gratitude and trust. When I feel uncertain or weary, remind me that You are at work, even when I cannot see it clearly. Keep me from despair and give me patience as I wait.

Let this time draw me closer to You, deepen my dependence, and strengthen my faith in Your goodness and Your perfect timing. **Amen.**

Gracious Lord, I ask You to bring healing not only to my body, but also to my heart and mind. Times of illness can bring anxiety, frustration, and weariness, and I feel the weight of that now.

So, I ask You to restore me inwardly as well as outwardly. Give me peace where there is fear and hope where there is uncertainty. Help me to trust You day by day, receiving the grace You provide for each moment.

When I feel discouraged, lift my spirit. When I feel tired, renew my strength. Let me not lose sight of Your presence or Your promises.

May this season become one where I experience Your care more deeply and learn to rely on You more fully in every part of my life. **Amen.**

Holy God, I commit my health and my future into Your hands. You are the giver of life and the One who sustains me each day.

I ask You to bring healing in Your way and in Your time, trusting that You know what is best.

Help me to remain steady in faith, even when the path is uncertain or difficult.

Guard me from anxious thoughts and from imagining outcomes that I cannot control.

Instead, teach me to rest in Your sovereignty and to trust in Your goodness. Let Your presence bring comfort, Your word bring assurance, and Your Spirit bring peace.

May I walk through this time with quiet confidence, knowing that I am held securely in Your care and that nothing can separate me from Your love. **Amen.**

38. PRAYERS FOR COMFORT

God of all comfort, I come before You in need of Your gentle and steady care. You know the burdens I carry, the sorrows that weigh on my heart, and the quiet struggles that others may not see. There are times when the soul feels tired, when grief lingers, and when life seems heavier than I expected. Yet I thank You that You are not distant in such moments. You draw near to the broken-hearted and uphold those whose spirits are low. So, I ask You to comfort me with a comfort that is deep, real, and lasting.

Your word says, "Praise be to… the God of all comfort, who comforts us in all our troubles." (2 Corinthians 1:3–4). I hold onto that promise. You are not selective in Your care. You do not comfort only in certain kinds of troubles, but in all of them. I bring now the things that trouble me - the disappointments, the losses, the worries, and the quiet griefs that have settled within me. You know them all fully. Meet me in them, I pray.

Let Your comfort reach beyond surface relief. Bring peace where my thoughts are unsettled. Bring rest where my heart feels weary. Bring assurance where I feel uncertain. Let me not look only for distraction from pain, but for Your presence within it. Remind me that You are near, that You see, and that You care deeply.

Guard me from withdrawing into myself in times of sorrow. Help me to turn to You, to open my heart honestly, and to receive what You give. Let Your word speak into my situation with clarity and hope. Let prayer become a place of quiet strength and not just desperate asking.

And as I receive comfort from You, let it shape me. Make me more compassionate toward others who suffer. Help me to listen, to care, and to offer the same comfort I have received. Let this season not harden me, but soften me. May Your comfort steady me now and remain with me in the days ahead. Through Jesus Christ my Lord. **Amen.**

Faithful Father, I thank You that You are a God who understands suffering and responds with compassion. You do not stand far off, watching from a distance. You draw near, You listen, and You sustain.

I come to You now with a heart that needs comfort. There are things that weigh on me - some clear, some difficult even to express. Yet You know them all, and I trust that You are attentive to every detail.

Your word says, "The Lord is close to the broken-hearted and saves those who are crushed in spirit." (Psalm 34:18). Let me experience that closeness now. When my heart feels heavy, let Your presence be a steadying force. When my spirit feels low, lift me gently. Let me not feel abandoned or alone, but held and supported by Your grace.

I ask for comfort in the midst of pain. Not a quick escape, but a sustaining presence. Help me to carry what I must carry without losing hope. Give me moments of rest within the struggle and glimpses of Your goodness even in difficulty. Remind me that You are working, even when I cannot see how. Guard me from despair. When sorrow feels deep, keep me from believing that it will always remain this way. Let hope quietly grow, even if slowly. Teach me to trust You in the process, not only in the outcome. Let me rest in the knowledge that You are faithful and that Your purposes are good.

Surround me with Your care. Through Your word, speak truth. Through prayer, bring peace. Through others, provide support and kindness. Help me to receive comfort without resistance and to recognise it when it comes.

And in all things, keep my eyes on Christ. He is acquainted with grief and understands suffering fully. In Him I find not only sympathy, but strength.

Let His presence be my comfort and His promises my assurance. May I rest in You and find peace in Your care. Through Jesus Christ my Saviour. **Amen.**

God of all comfort, I come before You with a heart that feels heavy and in need of Your gentle care. You see the burdens I carry, the grief I feel, and the quiet struggles that I may not even be able to put into words.

I ask You to draw near to me in this moment. Let Your presence be real and steady, not distant or uncertain. Bring peace where my thoughts are unsettled and rest where my heart feels weary.

Help me not to look only for distraction from my pain, but to find comfort in knowing that You are with me in it.

Remind me that I am not alone and that You understand what I am facing.

Let Your comfort reach deeply within me and sustain me through this season with quiet strength and enduring hope. Amen.

Faithful Father, I thank You that You are a God who sees and cares for every part of my life. In this time of need, I ask You to surround me with Your comfort.

When my heart feels troubled and my thoughts feel scattered, bring calm and clarity. Help me to rest in the truth that You are near and that nothing I face is outside Your care.

Guard me from becoming overwhelmed by what I feel, and instead anchor me in what is true about You. Let Your promises steady my heart and give me confidence to continue.

Even when circumstances remain difficult, help me to experience Your sustaining presence.

May Your comfort not only ease my burden, but also strengthen my faith and deepen my trust in You each day. **Amen.**

Gracious Lord, I ask You to meet me in the place where I most need comfort. You know the areas of pain, disappointment, and weariness that I carry, and I bring them honestly before You.

Help me not to hide from You or to carry these burdens alone. Instead, draw me into closer fellowship with You.

Let Your word speak into my situation with truth and reassurance.

When my heart feels low, lift it. When my strength feels small, renew it. Give me moments of rest within the struggle and reminders of Your goodness even in difficult times.

Let Your comfort become a steady presence in my life, helping me to endure and to trust You more deeply through every part of this journey. **Amen.**

Holy God, I ask You to fill my life with the comfort that comes from knowing You. Not a temporary relief, but a deep and lasting peace that steadies my heart.

When I feel unsettled or burdened, help me to turn to You quickly and honestly.

Let me find refuge in Your presence and assurance in Your promises. Guard me from despair and from the sense that things will never change.

Instead, remind me that You are at work, even when I cannot see it clearly. Surround me with Your care and provide encouragement through Your word and through others.

May Your comfort carry me through this time and lead me into a deeper confidence in Your faithful and unchanging love. In Jesus' name I pray. **Amen.**

39. PRAYERS FOR THE BROKEN-HEARTED

Merciful Father, I come before You with a broken heart. You know the pain I carry, the disappointment I feel, and the sorrow that has settled deep within me.

There are wounds that are not easily seen and hurts that do not quickly fade. Yet I thank You that You are near to the broken-hearted and that You do not turn away from those who are crushed in spirit.

I bring my heart to You as it is, not trying to hide or minimise what I feel.

Your word says, "The Lord is close to the broken-hearted and saves those who are crushed in spirit." (Psalm 34:18). Let that promise become real to me now.

Draw near and make Your presence known in a way that steadies me. When I feel overwhelmed, be my refuge. When I feel weak, be my strength. Help me not to carry this pain alone, but to entrust it to You.

I ask You to bring healing in Your time. Where my heart has been wounded, restore it. Where trust has been shaken, rebuild it. Where hope has been diminished, renew it.

Let Your grace reach into the deepest parts of my life and begin the work of restoration.

Guard me from bitterness, from despair, and from closing my heart. Instead, keep me soft, open, and trusting in You. Teach me to walk through this season with faith, even when I do not understand.

And in all of this, keep my eyes on Christ, who knows suffering and bears my pain.

Let His presence comfort me and His love sustain me, now and always. **Amen.**

Faithful God, I bring before You the brokenness within my heart.

There are things I have lost, things that have not turned out as I hoped, and wounds that still feel fresh.

At times I struggle to understand why things have unfolded as they have, and I feel the weight of that deeply.

Yet I come to You because I know that You are compassionate, that You see my pain, and that You care for me.

Your word says, "He heals the broken-hearted and binds up their wounds." (Psalm 147:3). I hold onto that truth and ask You to begin that healing work in me.

Bind up what is wounded, bring comfort where there is sorrow, and restore what feels shattered.

Help me to trust that You are at work, even when the healing feels slow.

Give me patience in this process. Keep me from expecting instant relief and help me to walk step by step with You.

Let Your presence be enough for me in each moment, even as I look for Your restoring hand.

Surround me with Your care.

Through Your word, speak truth. Through prayer, bring peace. Through others, provide encouragement and support.

Let me not walk this path alone.

And as You heal me, let my heart become stronger, deeper, and more rooted in You.

May this brokenness lead me into a greater awareness of Your grace and a deeper trust in Your faithful love. **Amen.**

Gracious God, I bring before You my broken heart.

You know the pain I feel and the wounds I carry, even the ones I cannot fully explain. At times the weight of it feels overwhelming, and I struggle to find peace.

Yet I thank You that You are near to me in this place. Help me to turn toward You rather than withdrawing into myself.

Let Your presence bring comfort where there is sorrow and calm where there is unrest. Remind me that I am not alone and that You see me fully.

Begin Your healing work within me, even if it comes slowly. Give me patience to trust You and courage to keep going.

May Your love steady my heart and gently restore what has been broken within me. **Amen.**

Faithful Father, You see the brokenness in my heart and understand the pain I carry. I bring it to You honestly, without hiding or pretending.

Help me to trust that You care for me and that You are working even in this difficult season. Guard me from bitterness, from discouragement, and from losing hope.

Instead, fill my heart with the quiet assurance that You are near.

Teach me to rest in Your presence and to bring my thoughts back to what is true when they begin to drift. Let Your grace meet me in this place and begin to restore my strength.

May I learn to rely on You more deeply and to find comfort in Your unchanging love. **Amen.**

Merciful Lord, I ask You to bring healing to my broken heart.

There are wounds that feel deep and difficult to move past, and I do not have the strength to fix them myself.

So, I bring them to You. Help me to release what I cannot control and to trust You with what I do not understand.

Let Your peace settle over my heart and quiet the pain within me. Remind me that this season will not last forever and that You are leading me through it.

Give me strength to face each day and hope for what lies ahead.

May Your presence comfort me and Your grace sustain me as You gently restore my heart. **Amen.**

Holy Lord, I place my broken heart in Your hands. You are gentle and compassionate, and I trust You to care for me.

When I feel fragile or overwhelmed, hold me steady.

When my thoughts return to what has hurt me, help me to turn again to You.

Guard me from closing my heart or becoming hardened. Instead, keep me open to Your healing and Your truth.

Let this season draw me closer to You and deepen my dependence on Your grace.

Surround me with Your comfort and lead me forward step by step.

May I come to know Your presence more deeply and Your love more fully as You bring healing and renewal to my life. **Amen.**

40. PRAYERS FOR HOPE IN SUFFERING

Faithful God, I come before You in a time of suffering.

You know the pain I carry, the questions I wrestle with, and the weariness that sometimes settles deep within me. Suffering is not easy, and I do not pretend that it is.

Yet I come to You because I know that You are present even here. You have not abandoned me, nor have You lost control. So, I ask You to sustain me and to give me hope that is deeper than what I feel in this moment.

Your word says, "And we know that in all things God works for the good of those who love Him." (Romans 8:28). Help me to hold onto that truth, even when I cannot see how it could be true.

When my understanding is limited, strengthen my trust. When my heart is heavy, remind me that You are at work in ways I cannot yet see.

I ask You to give me endurance in suffering. Help me not to grow bitter or lose heart. Guard my thoughts from despair and my spirit from giving up.

Let suffering not harden me, but deepen my faith. Use this season to shape my character, to refine my trust, and to draw me closer to You.

Let hope rise within me, not based on circumstances, but based on who You are. You are faithful, wise, and good. Remind me that this suffering is not the end of the story. There is a future You have prepared, and there is a day when all things will be made right.

Until then, sustain me by Your grace, comfort me with Your presence, and strengthen me to continue. Through Jesus Christ my Lord. **Amen.**

Merciful Father, I bring before You the reality of suffering in my life. There are things I do not understand and burdens that feel difficult to carry.

At times I feel discouraged, and hope can seem distant. Yet I know that You are not absent in suffering. You see, You know, and You care deeply.

So, I ask You to meet me here and to give me a hope that holds firm.

Your word says, "Not only so, but we also glory in our sufferings, because we know that suffering produces perseverance; perseverance, character; and character, hope." (Romans 5:3–4).

Help me to understand this not only in theory, but in experience. Let suffering produce something lasting in me.

Let it strengthen my faith, deepen my character, and lead me into a stronger hope.

Guard me from despair and from the belief that things will never change.

Remind me that You are working, even when the path is unclear.

Give me patience to wait and trust in Your timing.

Help me to fix my eyes on Christ, who endured suffering and overcame it. In Him I find both understanding and strength.

Let His example guide me and His presence sustain me.
And let hope grow steadily within me. Not a fragile hope, but a firm confidence in Your goodness and Your promises.

May I walk through suffering with faith, knowing that You are with me and that You will bring me through. **Amen.**

Gracious God, in the midst of suffering I ask You to give me a steady and enduring hope. When circumstances feel heavy and the path ahead is unclear, help me not to lose heart.

Remind me that You are present, that You see what I am going through, and that nothing I face is outside Your care. Guard me from thinking that this moment defines everything.

Instead, lift my eyes to see that You are at work, even when I cannot trace Your hand. Strengthen me to endure with patience and trust.

Let hope take root within me, not based on what I feel, but on who You are.

May I walk through this season with confidence in Your faithfulness, knowing that You will sustain me and bring about Your good purposes in time. **Amen.**

Faithful Father, I bring before You the suffering I am experiencing and ask You to sustain me through it.

There are moments when I feel overwhelmed, when the weight of it presses heavily on me, and when hope seems distant.

Yet I know that You are near and that You have not abandoned me. Help me to trust You in this season. Give me strength for each day and grace for each moment.

Guard me from despair and from losing sight of Your promises.

Let me remember that You are working even now, shaping my life in ways I cannot fully see.

May hope rise within me, steadying my heart and giving me courage to continue. **Amen.**

Merciful Lord, I ask You to anchor my heart in hope as I walk through suffering.

Do not let my thoughts be carried away by fear or discouragement. Instead, draw me back to what is true about You - that You are good, that You are faithful, and that You are in control.

Help me to trust You when I do not understand and to remain steady when the way feels difficult. Let suffering not weaken my faith, but deepen it.

Give me a quiet confidence that You are leading me and that this season will not last forever.

May hope grow stronger than my circumstances and guide me forward with patience and trust in You. **Amen.**

Holy Lord, I place my suffering into Your hands and ask You to fill me with hope that endures.

When I feel weary, renew my strength. When I feel uncertain, remind me that You are sovereign and wise.

Help me to take each step in faith, even when I cannot see the outcome.

Guard me from becoming discouraged or withdrawn. Instead, let me draw closer to You and find comfort in Your presence.

Let hope rise within me, not as wishful thinking, but as a firm confidence in Your promises.

May I continue with perseverance, trusting that You are at work and that You will bring me through this season according to Your perfect will. **Amen.**

41. PRAYERS FOR ILLNESS

Merciful Father, I come before You in a time of illness, bringing my weakness and need into Your presence.

You know my body completely, and You understand what I am facing in a way no one else can.

Nothing about this situation is hidden from You. You see the discomfort, the uncertainty, and the weariness that can come with being unwell. Yet I thank You that You are near, attentive, and full of compassion toward me in this moment.

Your word says, "The Lord sustains them on their sickbed and restores them from their bed of illness." (Psalm 41:3). I hold onto that promise and ask You to sustain me now.

Strengthen my body where it is weak and bring healing where it is needed. Ease the discomfort and bring relief in ways that only You can provide.

At the same time, guard my heart from fear and discouragement. When I feel uncertain about what lies ahead, remind me that You are in control and that my life is held securely in Your hands.

Give me patience in this season. Help me not to become frustrated when progress is slow or when answers are unclear. Instead, teach me to trust You day by day, receiving the grace You provide for each moment. Let me not measure everything by how I feel, but by what I know to be true about You.

Surround me with Your care. Guide those who are helping me and give them wisdom in every decision they make. Help me to receive their support with humility and gratitude.

And in all of this, draw me closer to You. Let this time deepen my dependence on Your grace and strengthen my faith in Your goodness. **Amen.**

Faithful God, I bring before You the reality of illness in my life and ask You to meet me in it with Your presence and Your power. There are moments when I feel weak, when my strength is limited, and when I am reminded of how fragile I can be. At times, even simple tasks can feel difficult, and the uncertainty of what lies ahead can weigh heavily on my mind.

Yet I thank You that You are not limited, that You do not grow weary, and that Your care for me never fails. You remain constant, unchanging, and fully able to sustain me, even when I feel unable to sustain myself. Renew my strength where I feel depleted. Restore energy to my body where it has been drained, and bring clarity to my mind where it feels clouded.

Lift my spirit when discouragement begins to settle in. Help me to face each day with courage, even when I do not feel strong. Give me grace for today, without being overwhelmed by tomorrow. I ask also for healing according to Your will. You are able to restore, to renew, and to bring health where there is sickness. I trust You for that, knowing that nothing is beyond Your power. Yet even as I ask for healing, I also ask for grace to endure if this season continues.

Teach me patience when progress feels slow, and steadiness when answers do not come quickly. Let me not lose heart or drift into despair. Instead, keep my eyes fixed on You and my heart anchored in Your promises. Guard my mind from anxious thoughts and from imagining outcomes that I cannot control. When fear begins to rise, remind me of what is true and help me to rest in Your care, in Your sovereignty, and to trust that You are working, even when I cannot see it clearly. Let Your peace steady me and Your presence comfort me in quiet and sustaining ways.

And through this time, draw me nearer to Christ. Let me know Him more deeply and rely on Him more fully. Shape my faith so that it becomes more resilient and more grounded in truth. May my faith be strengthened and my trust in You made more secure through all that I face. **Amen.**

Gracious God, I bring my illness before You and ask for Your help and Your healing.

You know exactly what I am going through, and You understand how it is affecting me physically, emotionally, and spiritually.

At times I feel weak, tired, and uncertain, and I do not always know how to respond. Yet I thank You that You are near and that You care deeply for me. Strengthen my body where it is weak and bring healing according to Your will.

Give me patience as I wait and trust in Your timing. Guard me from discouragement and from anxious thoughts.

Let Your presence bring peace to my heart and steady me through each day. May I rest in Your care and know that I am held securely in Your hands. **Amen.**

Faithful Father, I ask You to sustain me in this time of illness.

There are moments when I feel overwhelmed by weakness and uncertainty, and I need Your strength.

Help me to trust You when I do not understand what is happening or how long it will last.

Give me grace for each day and help me to take things one step at a time.

Guide those who are caring for me and give them wisdom in every decision they make. Let me receive their help with gratitude and trust. Guard my heart from fear and fill me with Your peace.

May I learn to depend on You more deeply and to rest in Your faithful and unchanging care through this season. **Amen.**

Merciful Lord, I ask You to bring healing and renewal into my life.

You are the giver of life and the One who sustains me, and I place my trust in You.

When I feel discouraged or weary, lift my spirit and remind me that You are near. Help me not to lose heart, even when progress feels slow or uncertain.

Let Your grace be sufficient for me in every moment. Strengthen me inwardly as well as outwardly, and help me to rely on You more fully.

Guard me from negative thinking and from imagining the worst. Instead, fill my mind with truth and my heart with hope.

May I walk through this time with steady faith, trusting in Your goodness and Your perfect care. **Amen.**

Holy Lord, I place my health and my future into Your hands. You are sovereign, wise, and good, and I trust You with all that I am facing.

When I feel uncertain, remind me that You are in control. When I feel weak, strengthen me by Your grace.

Help me to rest in Your presence and to find comfort in Your promises.

Let me not become overwhelmed by what I feel, but anchored in what is true about You.

Give me peace in the midst of this situation and hope for what lies ahead. May this time draw me closer to You and deepen my faith. Let Your presence sustain me and Your love surround me each day. **Amen.**

Merciful Father, I come before You in the reality of pain, bringing my discomfort and weakness into Your presence.

You know exactly what I am experiencing, both in my body and in my spirit. Pain can be exhausting, persistent, and at times overwhelming, and I confess that it can affect my thoughts, my emotions, and my outlook on each day.

Yet I thank You that You are not distant from me in this condition. You are near, attentive, and full of compassion toward me in every moment.

Your word says, "My grace is sufficient for you, for My power is made perfect in weakness." (2 Corinthians 12:9). I ask You to make that truth real to me now.

In the midst of pain, let Your grace sustain me. When I feel weary, renew my strength. When the pain feels constant, give me patience to endure and courage to keep going. Help me not to become discouraged or overwhelmed, but to remain steady in faith.

I also ask for healing and recovery according to Your will. Bring relief where there is pain and restoration where there is damage. Guide those who are caring for me and give them wisdom and skill. Help me to follow the path of recovery with diligence and trust.

Guard my heart during this time. Keep me from frustration, from negative thinking, and from losing hope. Instead, let this season draw me closer to You.

Teach me to rely on You more deeply and to find strength in Your presence.

And as recovery comes, whether quickly or slowly, may I give thanks to You. Sustain me through every step and let Your grace carry me from weakness into renewed strength. **Amen.**

Faithful God, I bring before You the ongoing reality of pain and the process of recovery that lies ahead.

You know how difficult it can be to endure discomfort day after day and how discouraging it can feel when progress is slow or uncertain.

Yet I thank You that You are present in every moment and that You care deeply for me. Nothing about this journey is hidden from You.

Your word says, "He gives strength to the weary and increases the power of the weak." (Isaiah 40:29). I ask You to renew my strength as I walk through this season.

When I feel physically weak, strengthen me. When I feel mentally tired, give me clarity.

When I feel emotionally burdened, lift my spirit and remind me of Your presence.

Help me to approach recovery with patience. Let me not rush ahead or become frustrated when improvement takes time.

Instead, teach me to trust the process and to take each step with faith. Give me discipline to follow what is required for healing and perseverance to continue even when it feels difficult.

Guard my mind from discouragement and from focusing only on what is not yet restored.

Help me to notice small signs of progress and to give thanks for them. Let hope grow steadily within me as I see Your hand at work.

And in all of this, draw me closer to Christ. Let me learn dependence, humility, and trust.

May this season not be wasted but used by You to deepen my faith and strengthen my walk with You. **Amen.**

Gracious God, I bring before You the pain I am experiencing and ask for Your help and Your sustaining grace.

You know how difficult it can be when discomfort lingers and affects every part of daily life. At times I feel tired, frustrated, and uncertain, and I need Your strength.

Help me to endure with patience and not lose heart. Remind me that You are near and that You understand what I am facing.

Bring relief where it is needed and guide me through the process of recovery. Guard me from discouragement and from focusing only on what is wrong.

Instead, help me to trust You in each moment and to rest in Your care. Let Your presence bring peace to my heart and steadiness to my mind as I walk through this time. **Amen.**

Faithful Father, I ask You to strengthen me as I walk through pain and recovery. There are moments when I feel overwhelmed and unsure of how long this will last.

Yet I know that You are with me and that You will sustain me. Give me patience to endure and courage to continue.

Help me to take each day as it comes, trusting You for what I need in the moment.

Guide those who are helping me and give them wisdom in their care. Let me not become discouraged when progress feels slow but instead help me to see that You are at work.

May hope grow within me and give me strength to keep moving forward with faith. **Amen.**

Merciful Lord, I place my pain into Your hands and ask You to bring healing and restoration.

You are able to renew what has been weakened and to bring strength where there is limitation. Help me to trust You even when I do not understand the process.

Guard my heart from frustration and from losing hope. Instead, give me a steady spirit and a calm mind.

Let me rely on Your grace each day and not on my own strength.

When I feel weary, lift me. When I feel discouraged, remind me of Your promises.

May this time draw me closer to You and deepen my dependence on Your care and Your faithfulness. **Amen.**

Holy Lord, I ask You to sustain me through this time of pain and recovery.

You know how difficult it can be to wait and to trust when healing takes time.

Help me not to rush ahead or become discouraged. Instead, teach me to walk patiently and faithfully.

Give me strength to follow through with what is needed for recovery and perseverance to continue when it feels hard.

Let me not focus only on what is lacking, but also on the progress that is being made. Fill my heart with hope and my mind with peace.

May Your presence be with me in every step, guiding me and strengthening me as I move toward healing. **Amen.**

43. PRAYERS FOR MEDICAL TREATMENT

Gracious Father, I come before You as I face medical treatment, placing myself into Your care and asking for Your guidance and peace. You know every detail of my condition and every step that lies ahead.

Nothing about this process is hidden from You. While there may be uncertainty in my mind, there is no uncertainty in You. You are wise, powerful, and present with me in every moment. Even when I do not fully understand what is happening, I can trust that You do.

Your word says, "The Lord will guide you always; He will satisfy your needs in a sun-scorched land and will strengthen your frame." (Isaiah 58:11). I ask You to guide me now.

Direct every decision that is made and give wisdom to those who are responsible for my care. Give them clarity, skill, and insight as they treat me. Help them to act carefully and thoughtfully in every step they take.

I also ask You to guard my heart. When I feel anxious or uncertain, bring peace. When I feel overwhelmed, steady my thoughts.

Help me not to imagine outcomes that I cannot control, but to trust that You are working through every part of this process. Let Your peace settle deeply within me.

Give me patience as I walk through treatment and strength to endure what is required. Help me to cooperate fully and to remain steady in faith. Let this time not draw me away from You, but closer to You, deepening my trust and dependence. And in all of this, remind me that my life is in Your hands.

Whether the path is straightforward or difficult, You are with me. Let Your presence comfort me and Your grace sustain me every step of the way. **Amen.**

Faithful God, I place myself into Your hands as I undergo medical treatment, trusting that You are sovereign over every detail. You see the beginning and the end, and You know what is needed far better than I do.

While I may feel uncertain about what lies ahead, I rest in the truth that You are never uncertain. You are not reacting or adjusting, but working with perfect knowledge and purpose in every moment.

Your word says, "Cast all your anxiety on Him because He cares for you." (1 Peter 5:7). I bring my concerns to You now. Take my fears, my questions, and my worries, and replace them with Your peace.

Help me not to carry what You have invited me to release. When anxious thoughts return, remind me again to place them into Your hands, trusting that Your care for me is constant and personal.

I ask You to bless the treatment I receive. Use it for my good and bring healing through it according to Your will. Guide the hands and decisions of every medical professional involved. Let their work be marked by care, precision, and wisdom. Help them to respond wisely to each situation and to act with diligence and understanding throughout the process.

Give me endurance as I move through this process. When I feel tired or discouraged, renew my strength. When progress seems slow, give me patience. Let me take each step with trust rather than fear. Help me not to rush ahead in my thinking, but to remain present and steady in each stage of treatment.

And through this time, draw me closer to Christ. Let me learn to depend on You more deeply and to find comfort in Your presence. When I feel alone, remind me that You are near.

May this season strengthen my faith and remind me that I am always held securely in Your care. **Amen.**

Merciful Lord, I bring before You the medical treatment I am facing and ask for Your peace to settle my heart.

There are many things I do not fully understand, and it is easy for my thoughts to become anxious and unsettled. Yet You understand everything completely, and nothing takes You by surprise.

Help me to trust You with each step of this process. Give me confidence in Your care and assurance that You are present with me.

Guide the doctors and medical staff who are treating me and give them wisdom and skill in every decision they make. When I feel uncertain, steady my heart.

When I feel afraid, remind me that You are near. Let me walk through this time with quiet trust, knowing that my life is safely held in Your hands. **Amen.**

Gracious Father, I ask You to strengthen me as I go through medical treatment. You know the physical demands, the emotional strain, and the uncertainty that can come with it.

At times I feel overwhelmed, and I need Your help. Give me endurance for each stage and patience when things take longer than expected. Help me not to dwell on fears or worst-case thoughts, but to fix my mind on what is true.

Remind me that You are with me in every appointment, every procedure, and every moment of waiting. Let Your presence bring calm to my heart and clarity to my thinking.

Teach me to take one step at a time, trusting that You are guiding the process and working for my good in ways I cannot always see. **Amen.**

Faithful God, I place my treatment into Your hands and ask You to work through it for my healing and restoration.

You are able to use both extraordinary and ordinary means, and I trust You in both. Help me to approach this process with faith and not with fear. Give me a steady spirit and a hopeful outlook, even when the path feels uncertain.

Guard my heart from discouragement and from losing confidence. Instead, strengthen me inwardly and remind me that You are at work.

Help me to cooperate with what is required and to remain patient through each stage.

Let me not feel alone in this journey, but aware that You are with me at every moment, sustaining me and guiding me through. **Amen.**

Holy Lord, I ask You to give me peace as I walk through medical treatment. When my thoughts begin to race or my heart feels unsettled, draw me back to Your truth.

Remind me that You are sovereign, that You are good, and that You are present with me. Help me to trust You not only with the outcome, but with the entire process.

Give me strength when I feel weak, patience when I feel frustrated, and hope when I feel uncertain.

Surround me with people who will encourage and support me and help me to receive their care with gratitude.

Let this time deepen my faith and strengthen my reliance on You. May I walk through it with confidence, knowing that I am never outside Your care. **Amen.**

44. PRAYERS FOR CARING FOR A LOVED ONE

Gracious Father, I come before You as I care for someone I love, bringing both my concern for them and my own need for strength into Your presence. You know their condition, their needs, and the path they are walking.

You also know the weight that caring brings - the responsibilities, the emotional strain, and the moments of uncertainty that can quietly build.

Yet I thank You that neither their need nor my burden is hidden from You.

Your word says, "Cast all your anxiety on Him because He cares for you." (1 Peter 5:7). I bring both their needs and my own to You now. I ask You first to watch over them.

Bring healing where it is needed, comfort where there is pain, and peace where there is fear. Let them know Your presence in a real and sustaining way.

And for me, I ask for strength. Help me to care with patience, with compassion, and with endurance.

When I feel tired, renew me. When I feel overwhelmed, steady me. When I feel unsure of what to do, give me wisdom and clarity.

Guard my heart from frustration and from discouragement. Let me not serve out of pressure alone, but out of love strengthened by Your grace.

Help me to be present, attentive, and faithful in what I can do, while trusting You with what I cannot control.

And through this season, draw both of us closer to You. Let this time deepen our dependence on Your grace and strengthen our faith in Your goodness. **Amen.**

Faithful God, I bring before You the responsibility of caring for someone I love, knowing that this role is both a privilege and a challenge.

There are moments of tenderness and care, but also moments of fatigue, concern, and uncertainty.

You see every part of this journey, and I ask You to meet me in it with Your sustaining grace.

Your word says, "The Lord is my strength and my shield; my heart trusts in Him, and He helps me." (Psalm 28:7).

I ask You to be my strength now.

When I feel physically tired, give me endurance. When I feel emotionally stretched, give me peace. When I feel unsure, give me wisdom.

Help me to care well. Give me patience when it is needed, gentleness in my words, and attentiveness in my actions.

Let me not grow weary in doing good, even when the demands feel constant.

Teach me to take moments of rest when needed and not to carry more than You have asked me to carry.

I also place my loved one into Your hands. You care for them more deeply than I ever could.

Bring comfort, healing, and peace into their life. Let them feel supported, not only by me, but by Your presence.

And in all of this, help me to trust You. Let me not feel that everything depends on me.

Instead, remind me that You are the ultimate caregiver, and I am simply serving under Your care. **Amen.**

Merciful Lord, I bring before You the responsibility of caring for someone I love, and I ask You to strengthen me for this role.

There are moments when I feel tired, stretched, and unsure if I am doing enough. Yet You see both my efforts and my limitations.

Help me to care with patience, kindness, and steadiness. Give me wisdom in the decisions I need to make and clarity in the moments when I feel uncertain.

When I feel overwhelmed, remind me that I am not alone in this. You are present, guiding me and sustaining me.

Guard my heart from frustration and from becoming discouraged. Instead, let Your grace renew me day by day, so that I can continue to serve faithfully, trusting You to supply all that I need. **Amen.**

Gracious Father, I ask You to give me endurance as I care for my loved one. You know the emotional weight, the physical demands, and the ongoing concern that comes with this responsibility.

At times it feels overwhelming, and I do not always know how to respond. Yet I trust that You are with me in every moment.

Help me to take each day as it comes, relying on Your strength rather than my own.

Give me patience when progress is slow and peace when uncertainty remains. Let me not become anxious about what lies ahead, but steady in trusting You.

May my care reflect Your compassion, and may Your presence give me the strength I need to continue faithfully. **Amen.**

Faithful God, I place both my loved one and myself into Your hands as we walk through this season together.

You know their needs more fully than I do, and You care for them even more deeply than I can. Help me to trust You with what I cannot fix or control.

Give me grace to serve with a willing heart and a steady spirit. When I feel discouraged or weary, lift me up and remind me that You are at work.

Let me not carry this burden alone, but share it with You through prayer.

Surround us with Your peace, and provide support through others where it is needed. May this time draw us both closer to You and strengthen our faith in Your care. **Amen.**

Holy Lord, I ask You to guard my heart as I care for someone I love. Help me not to become overwhelmed by responsibility or burdened by what I cannot change.

Instead, teach me to rest in Your sovereignty and to trust in Your wisdom. Give me a calm spirit, a clear mind, and a compassionate heart.

Let me serve with love, not out of pressure, but out of grace. When I feel weak, strengthen me. When I feel uncertain, guide me.

Remind me that You are the one who ultimately sustains both of us.

May I walk through this season with faith, patience, and quiet confidence, knowing that You are present and at work in every moment. **Amen.**

45. PRAYERS FOR THE ELDERLY

Gracious Father, I come before You with thankfulness for the gift of life and for the years You have given. Each stage has been held within Your care, and I recognise that my life has not unfolded by chance, but under Your wise and gracious hand. You have been faithful through every season - in times of strength and in times of weakness, in days of joy and in days of trial. You have never left me, and Your care has never failed. Even in moments when I did not fully understand what You were doing, You were present, guiding and sustaining me. Looking back, I can see that Your faithfulness has been constant and Your provision sure.

As I grow older, I place this stage of life into Your hands, trusting that You are still at work and that my life remains under Your loving care. Help me not to see these years as a time of diminishing purpose, but as a season in which Your work continues in new and meaningful ways.

Strengthen me where I feel weak and steady me where I feel uncertain. When my body slows or my energy fades, remind me that Your strength remains constant and that Your grace is sufficient for each day. Help me to live these years with wisdom, patience, and trust. Guard me from fear about the future and from dwelling on what I can no longer do.

When I am tempted to look back with regret or forward with anxiety, bring my focus back to You. Instead, help me to give thanks for what You have done and to remain faithful in what You still call me to do.

Let my life continue to bear fruit. May my words bring encouragement, my presence bring peace, and my faith point others to You. Use even quiet moments and simple interactions for Your purposes. And through every stage, keep my heart close to Christ, my hope fixed on eternity, and my trust anchored in Your unchanging love. May I continue to walk with You steadily, trusting You fully every day. **Amen.**

Faithful God, I thank You for the journey of life and for Your presence through every season. You have been with me in times of strength and in times of weakness, in seasons of clarity and in seasons of uncertainty. Looking back, I can see that You have never failed me. Even when I was not fully aware of it, Your hand has guided me and Your grace has sustained me.

As I grow older, I become more aware of both my limitations and my need for You. I recognise that my strength is not what it once was and that my dependence on You is greater than ever.

Yet I also see more clearly Your faithfulness and Your sustaining grace. What I may lack in strength, You provide in wisdom, patience, and a deeper understanding of Your ways. I place this season before You and ask You to guide me through it with peace and confidence.

Your word says, "They will still bear fruit in old age, they will stay fresh and green." (Psalm 92:14). I ask You to make that true in my life. Let these years not be marked by decline alone, but by continued growth in faith, wisdom, and usefulness. Help me to remain engaged, prayerful, and attentive to Your voice. Let my life continue to have purpose, even in ways that may look different from earlier years.

When I feel isolated or overlooked, remind me that my life still has value in Your plan. Help me not to withdraw or lose heart, but to remain open and responsive to the opportunities You place before me. When I feel uncertain about the future, help me to rest in the assurance that You are in control. Give me peace in my heart and confidence in Your promises.

And as I look ahead, fix my eyes on the hope of eternal life. Let me face the future not with fear, but with faith. Teach me to hold this world more lightly and to look forward with confidence to what You have prepared.

May my life, in every season, reflect Your goodness and Your grace, as I continue to trust You fully until the end. **Amen.**

Merciful Lord, I bring before You the later years of life and ask for Your sustaining grace in every moment. You know the changes that come with age - the slowing of the body, the shifts in energy, and the adjustments that are required.

At times these changes can feel unsettling, and I can be tempted to focus on what has been lost. Yet I thank You that You remain the same and that Your care does not diminish.

Help me to rest in that truth. Give me peace in my heart and confidence in Your presence. Strengthen me to face each day with faith and not with fear.

Let me continue to live with purpose, gratitude, and trust. May these years be marked not by decline alone, but by a deepening relationship with You and a growing awareness of Your faithfulness in every part of my life. **Amen.**

Gracious Father, I ask You to guide and sustain those who are advancing in years, giving them strength, dignity, and peace.

You know the unique challenges that come with this stage of life, including physical weakness, changing circumstances, and at times a sense of isolation.

I ask You to be especially near in these moments. Bring comfort where there is loneliness, strength where there is weakness, and encouragement where there is discouragement.

Help them to know that they are not forgotten and that their lives still have great value in Your sight. Let them experience Your presence in a real and sustaining way.

Surround them with care, support, and kindness from others. May their hearts be filled with peace and their minds with the assurance that You are with them in every season. **Amen.**

Faithful God, I thank You for the wisdom and experience that come with the passing of years. I ask You to continue to work in the lives of the elderly, strengthening their faith and sustaining their hope.

When they feel weak, be their strength. When they feel uncertain, be their guide. When they feel alone, remind them that You are near.

Help them to look back with gratitude and forward with confidence in Your promises.

Let them not feel that their usefulness has passed, but that they still have a role to play in encouraging and supporting others. Fill their hearts with peace and their minds with truth.

May they rest in Your care and find comfort in knowing that their lives are held securely in Your hands. **Amen.**

Holy Lord, I ask You to bring peace and assurance to those in their later years. Help them to trust You with the future and to rest in Your promises.

Guard them from fear about what lies ahead and from dwelling on uncertainty.

Instead, fill their hearts with calmness and their minds with truth. Let them know that You are with them and that You will never leave them.

Give them strength for each day and grace for every moment. Surround them with loving support and meaningful connection.

May they experience Your presence deeply and find comfort in Your unchanging love. Let their lives continue to reflect Your faithfulness and bring glory to Your name. **Amen.**

Gracious Father, I come before You aware of my frailty and my need for Your sustaining grace. There are times when I feel the limits of my strength more clearly, when my body feels weaker, and when I am reminded that I am not as capable as I once was. These changes can be difficult to accept, and I bring them honestly before You.

Yet in these moments, I thank You that You remain strong, unchanging, and faithful. My weakness does not diminish Your power, and my limitations do not limit Your care. You are not affected by the passing of time, and Your strength does not fade. You remain the same, and Your faithfulness continues without interruption.

Strengthen my spirit even when my body feels weak. Let my faith grow deeper even as my strength fades. Help me to value what You are doing within me, even when outward change feels difficult.

Help me to accept my frailty without fear or frustration. Guard me from discouragement and from comparing myself to what I once was. When I am tempted to dwell on loss or limitation, redirect my thoughts toward Your presence and Your promises. Instead, teach me to live in the present with trust and contentment.

Give me patience in this season. Help me to adjust with grace and to receive help from others with humility, recognising that this too is part of Your provision. Surround me with those who will care for me and encourage me and help me to receive their support with gratitude.

And in all things, fix my hope on Christ and on the promise of eternal life. Let my weakness draw me closer to You and remind me that my true strength is found in You alone. May this season deepen my faith, steady my heart, and strengthen my trust in Your unfailing love. **Amen.**

Faithful God, I bring before You my sense of frailty and ask You to sustain me through it. There are moments when I feel vulnerable, when my strength is limited, and when I am reminded that I am not in control as I once thought. At times, this awareness can feel unsettling, as I realise how much I once relied on my own ability and stability.

Yet in these moments, I turn to You, knowing that what feels uncertain to me is always secure in Your hands. I thank You that You are always in control and that You hold my life firmly and safely within Your care.

Psalm 73:26 says, "My flesh and my heart may fail, but God is the strength of my heart and my portion forever." Let that truth take root within me. When I feel weak, remind me that You are my strength. When I feel uncertain, remind me that You are my security. When I feel unsettled, help me to return to what is true and to rest again in Your unchanging character.

Help me to walk through this season with faith and not fear. Guard my thoughts from anxiety and from imagining what I cannot control.

When my mind begins to wander toward worry, draw it back to Your promises. Instead, fill my mind with Your truth and my heart with Your peace, so that I may remain steady even when circumstances are not.

Give me grace to live well in this season. Help me to be patient, to remain thankful, and to continue trusting You each day. When I feel frustrated by limitations, give me acceptance.

When I feel discouraged, give me renewed strength. Let me not withdraw or lose heart, but remain engaged in what You have given me to do, even if that looks different from before.

And as I face my frailty, draw me closer to Christ. Let me find comfort in His presence and confidence in His promises. May my life reflect quiet trust in You, even in weakness, and may my faith grow deeper as I learn to rely on You more fully each day. **Amen.**

Merciful Lord, I bring before You my frailty and ask for Your sustaining grace. There are times when I feel the limits of my strength and the weight of my weakness, and it can be difficult to adjust.

Yet I thank You that You are not limited and that Your strength never fails. Help me to rest in that truth. Teach me to accept what I cannot change without frustration or fear. Give me peace in my heart and steadiness in my thinking.

When I feel vulnerable, remind me that I am held securely in Your care. Strengthen me inwardly even when I feel weak outwardly. Let me depend on You more deeply each day and find comfort in Your presence.

May my life reflect trust, patience, and quiet confidence in You, even in this season of weakness. **Amen.**

Gracious Father, I ask You to guide me as I live with increasing frailty.

You know the challenges I face and the adjustments I must make, and I bring them all to You. Help me not to become discouraged or overwhelmed. Instead, give me a calm spirit and a trusting heart.

Teach me to take each day as it comes, relying on Your strength for what I need. When I feel frustrated, give me patience. When I feel uncertain, give me peace.

Surround me with people who will support and encourage me, and help me to receive their help with humility. Let me not feel defined by my weakness, but by Your grace.

May I continue to live with purpose, trust, and a deep awareness of Your presence with me. **Amen.**

Faithful God, I place my weakness into Your hands and ask You to sustain me.

You understand my condition fully, and You care for me deeply. When I feel my strength fading, remind me that You are my strength.

Help me to rely on You more fully and to trust in Your provision each day.

Guard my heart from fear and from dwelling on what I cannot control.

Instead, fill my mind with truth and my heart with peace. Give me grace to adjust to this season and to live faithfully within it.

Let me not withdraw or lose hope but continue to trust You. May my life be marked by quiet faith, steady trust, and confidence in Your unfailing care. **Amen.**

Holy Lord, I ask You to bring comfort and assurance as I face the reality of frailty. Help me to trust You with the future and to rest in Your promises.

When I feel uncertain, remind me that You are sovereign and that nothing is outside Your care.

Give me strength for each day and grace for every moment. Help me to focus on what is true and to let go of unnecessary worry.

Surround me with Your peace and with the support of others who care for me. Let me continue to live with dignity, purpose, and faith.

May my life reflect Your faithfulness, even in weakness, and bring glory to Your name in every season. **Amen.**

47. PRAYERS FOR THE FINAL SEASON OF LIFE

Faithful Father, I come before You in the awareness that life moves toward its final season, and I place that reality into Your hands with both humility and trust. You have been with me from the beginning, through every stage and every circumstance, and You have never once failed me.

Now, as I consider the later days of life, I rest in the assurance that You will continue to be with me, guiding, sustaining, and strengthening me to the very end.

Your word says, "Even to your old age and grey hairs I am He, I am He who will sustain you." (Isaiah 46:4). I hold firmly to that promise. When I feel uncertain about what lies ahead, remind me that You are already there.

When I feel the limits of my strength, help me to rely more deeply on Your strength. Let me not face this season with fear, but with a growing confidence in Your faithfulness.

Help me to live these days well. Give me wisdom to order my life rightly, to speak words that encourage others, and to remain faithful in the responsibilities

You still entrust to me. Guard me from regret over the past and from anxiety about the future. Instead, help me to live in the present with gratitude, trust, and peace.

Draw my heart closer to Christ in these days. Let my love for Him deepen and my awareness of His presence grow stronger. Help me to fix my hope not on this life alone, but on the promise of eternal life that is mine in Him.

And when the time comes for me to leave this life, give me peace. Let me face that moment with assurance, knowing that I am held securely in Your hands and that nothing can separate me from Your love. Sustain me, guide me, and carry me through this final season with grace and strength. **Amen.**

Merciful God, I place before You the final season of life, entrusting both my present days and what lies ahead into Your care. As I look toward the future, I am aware that there is much I do not know, and at times that uncertainty can stir concern within me.

Yet I come to You with this, because I know that what is unknown to me is fully known to You. You see the whole path, and nothing lies outside Your wisdom or Your care.

Your word says, "The Lord is my shepherd… even though I walk through the darkest valley, I will fear no evil, for You are with me." (Psalm 23:1,4). Let that truth steady my heart.

When I think about what may come, remind me that I will never walk alone. You will be with me in every step, in every change, and in every moment. When the path feels uncertain, help me to rest in Your guidance.

Help me to approach this season with faith rather than fear. Guard my mind from anxious thoughts and from dwelling on possibilities that I cannot control.

When my thoughts begin to drift toward worry, draw them back to Your promises. Fill my heart with peace and give me a quiet confidence that You will provide what I need for each day.

Let these days be marked by steady trust and thoughtful living. Help me to continue to love, to pray, and to encourage others.

Let my life remain engaged and purposeful, even as circumstances change.

And as I look toward eternity, fix my hope firmly on Christ. Let me find comfort in His presence and assurance in His promises.

May I face the future with peace, knowing that You are my God, my shepherd, and my eternal refuge. **Amen.**

Gracious Lord, I bring before You this final season of life and ask You to fill it with Your peace and Your presence.

There are moments when I feel uncertain about what lies ahead, and I can be tempted to fear what I do not understand.

Yet I thank You that You are already there, holding my future securely in Your hands. Help me to trust You more deeply with each passing day.

Give me calmness in my heart and steadiness in my thoughts. Let me not dwell on fear, but on Your faithfulness.

Teach me to live these days with purpose, gratitude, and quiet confidence in You.

May Your presence comfort me, Your promises guide me, and Your grace sustain me as I walk forward in trust. **Amen.**

Faithful Father, I ask You to sustain me as I move through the later years of life. You know the changes, the challenges, and the uncertainties that come with this season.

At times I feel the weight of these things, and I need Your help. Strengthen me inwardly and give me peace that remains steady.

Help me to take each day as it comes, trusting You for what I need in the moment. Guard my heart from fear about the future and from dwelling on what I cannot control.

Instead, remind me that You are with me and that You will never leave me.

Let me walk forward with confidence, knowing that You are guiding me and holding me securely in Your care. **Amen.**

Merciful God, I place my life into Your hands as I consider what lies ahead.

There is much that I do not know, but I know that You are faithful. Help me to trust You fully with the future. When I feel uncertain, give me peace.

When I feel weak, give me strength.

Let me not be overwhelmed by what may come, but anchored in what is true about You.

Teach me to rest in Your presence and to rely on Your promises.

May I continue to live with faith, with hope, and with a deep awareness that my life is held securely in Your care.

Let this season draw me closer to You and strengthen my confidence in Your unfailing love. **Amen.**

Holy Lord, I ask You to fill this season of life with Your grace and Your peace. Help me to trust You with what lies ahead and to rest in Your promises.

When I feel anxious, remind me that You are in control. When I feel uncertain, remind me that You are near. Give me strength for each day and grace for every moment.

Let me not be consumed by fear, but strengthened by faith. Surround me with Your presence and with the care of others.

May I walk through this season with dignity, with trust, and with quiet confidence in You.

Let my life reflect Your faithfulness and bring glory to Your name in every step I take. **Amen.**

48. PRAYERS FOR DYING WELL

Faithful Father, I come before You with a sober awareness that life on this earth will one day come to an end, and I place that reality into Your hands with trust and hope.

You have been my God from the beginning, guiding me through every season, sustaining me through every trial, and showing Your faithfulness again and again.

As I consider the final moments of life, I do not want to be ruled by fear, but to be grounded in the assurance that You are with me and that You will not leave me.

Your word says, "To me, to live is Christ and to die is gain." (Philippians 1:21). Help me to understand that truth deeply. Let me not view death as loss alone, but as the doorway into the fullness of life with Christ.

When fear arises, remind me that Jesus has conquered death and that through Him I have eternal life.

Prepare my heart for that final moment. Help me to let go of this life with peace, not clinging in fear, but trusting in Your promises.

Give me clarity of mind, steadiness of faith, and a deep sense of Your presence. Surround me with those who will encourage me and remind me of Your truth.

Guard me from anxiety about the unknown. Instead, fill me with quiet confidence in what is certain - that I belong to You, that Christ has secured my salvation, and that I will be with Him forever.

And when that moment comes, grant me peace. Let me entrust my spirit into Your hands with assurance and hope.

May my final moments reflect faith, trust, and a deep confidence in Your unfailing love. **Amen.**

Merciful God, I place before You the reality of death and ask You to help me face it with faith and peace.

It is not something I can fully understand, and at times it can feel overwhelming to consider.

Yet I thank You that You have not left me without hope. Through Christ, death has been defeated, and eternal life has been secured. I hold onto that truth now.

Your word says, "Even though I walk through the darkest valley, I will fear no evil, for You are with me." (Psalm 23:4).

Let that promise steady my heart.

When I think about the final journey, remind me that I will not walk it alone. You will be with me, guiding me, comforting me, and carrying me through.

Help me to prepare well. Give me wisdom to put things in order, to speak words that need to be spoken, and to rest in Your grace.

Let me not be burdened by regret, but assured of Your forgiveness and acceptance in Christ.

As the time draws near, give me peace in my heart and clarity in my mind. Remove fear and replace it with confidence in Your promises.

Let me rest in the certainty that my life is held in Your hands and that nothing can separate me from Your love.

And when I pass from this life, receive me into Your presence. Let my final breath be one of trust, and my final thoughts be fixed on Christ.

May I enter eternity with peace, knowing that I am coming home to You. **Amen.**

Gracious Lord, I bring before You the reality of my final days and ask You to fill my heart with peace and steady confidence.

There are moments when I think about death and feel uncertain or afraid, and I confess that I do not fully understand what lies ahead. Yet I thank You that You do.

You have prepared the way through Christ, and You have promised to be with me always. Help me to trust You more deeply in this. When fear begins to rise, remind me that death is not the end, but the beginning of eternal life with You.

Give me a calm and settled spirit that rests in Your promises. Let me not be overwhelmed by what I cannot see but anchored in what I know to be true about You.

May my heart be filled with peace as I look ahead, trusting that You will carry me safely into Your presence. **Amen.**

Faithful Father, I ask You to prepare my heart for the end of life in a way that is marked by trust and peace. You know my thoughts, my questions, and the concerns that sometimes arise when I think about what is to come.

Help me not to avoid these thoughts, but to bring them honestly before You. Remind me that my life is secure in Christ and that my future is held in Your hands.

Give me confidence in the promises of eternal life and assurance that I will be with You. When uncertainty comes, steady my heart. When fear appears, replace it with faith. Let me walk toward that final moment not with hesitation, but with quiet confidence in Your goodness and Your care.

May I be ready in spirit, trusting fully in Your grace and resting in Your unfailing love. **Amen.**

Merciful God, I place my final days into Your care and ask You to guide me through them with Your presence and Your peace.

There is much that I do not know, and at times that uncertainty can feel overwhelming. Yet I thank You that You know all things and that You hold my life securely.

Help me to trust You completely with what lies ahead. Give me courage to face the future with faith and not fear. Let my heart be anchored in Your promises and my mind filled with Your truth.

Surround me with those who will encourage me and remind me of Your love.

May my final days be marked not by anxiety, but by peace, trust, and a deep awareness that I am held securely in Your hands and being led into Your presence. **Amen.**

Holy Lord, I ask You to give me grace for the final moments of life. Help me to face them with calmness, trust, and assurance in You.

When I feel uncertain or afraid, remind me that You are with me and that You will never leave me. Give me strength for what I will face and peace that remains steady.

Let me not be overwhelmed by the unknown but comforted by what is certain - that I belong to You and that Christ has secured my future.

Help me to entrust my life fully into Your hands.

May my final moments reflect faith, hope, and confidence in Your love, and may I enter into Your presence with peace and assurance. **Amen.**

49. PRAYERS FOR THE HOPE OF ETERNAL LIFE

Gracious Father, I come before You with a heart that longs to understand more deeply the hope of eternal life that You have given through Jesus Christ.

In a world that is often uncertain and fleeting, I thank You that You have given me a hope that is secure, unchanging, and everlasting.

This life is not all there is, and my future is not uncertain, because it rests in Your promises.

Your word says, "And this is the testimony: God has given us eternal life, and this life is in His Son." (1 John 5:11). I hold onto that truth with gratitude.

Thank You that eternal life is not something I must earn, but something You have freely given in Christ. Help me to live in the light of that reality each day.

When I feel weighed down by the struggles of this life, lift my eyes to what is eternal. When I feel uncertain about the future, remind me that my destiny is secure in You.

Let this hope shape how I think, how I live, and how I respond to the challenges I face.

Help me not to cling too tightly to what is temporary, but to live with a perspective that is shaped by eternity. Give me wisdom to invest my time, my energy, and my life in what truly matters.

And as I look ahead, fill my heart with joy and confidence. Eternal life is not distant or uncertain, but a reality already secured in Christ.

Let that truth steady me, comfort me, and fill me with peace as I walk each day in Your presence. **Amen.**

Faithful God, I thank You for the sure and certain hope of eternal life that You have given through Christ.

In the midst of a world that changes and passes away, You have given me something that cannot be taken, something that is secure and everlasting.

While so much around me is temporary and uncertain, this hope remains firm and unshaken. I come before You with gratitude and ask You to deepen my understanding of this hope.

Your word says, "He will wipe every tear from their eyes. There will be no more death or mourning or crying or pain." (Revelation 21:4). Let that promise take root in my heart. Let it become more than words to me, but a steady source of comfort and confidence.

When I experience sorrow or loss, remind me that this is not the final chapter. There is a future You have prepared that is beyond anything I can fully imagine.

Help me to live with eternity in view. Let my priorities be shaped by what will last and not by what will fade. Give me a clearer perspective on what truly matters, so that I invest my time and energy wisely.

Give me a heart that values what You value and a life that reflects the hope I have in You.

Guard me from fear of death and from uncertainty about the future. Instead, fill me with confidence in Christ and assurance in Your promises.

Let the reality of eternal life bring peace to my heart and strength to my faith.

And as I live each day, help me to do so with joy and purpose, knowing that my life is leading toward an eternal future with You. May this hope shape everything I do and bring glory to Your name. **Amen**

Merciful Lord, I thank You for the hope of eternal life that You have given through Jesus Christ.

In a world where so much is uncertain and temporary, I am grateful that my future is secure in You. Help me to understand this hope more deeply and to live in the light of it each day.

When I feel weighed down by the challenges of this life, lift my eyes to what is eternal and unchanging. Remind me that this present life is not the end of the story, but only a part of what You have prepared for me.

Let this hope steady my heart and bring peace to my mind. Help me to trust Your promises fully and to rest in the assurance that I will be with You forever.

May this truth shape my perspective, strengthen my faith, and fill me with quiet confidence in Your unfailing love. **Amen.**

Gracious Father, I ask You to deepen my confidence in the promise of eternal life.

At times I can become so focused on the present that I lose sight of what is to come. Yet You have given me a future that is secure and full of hope.

Help me to live with that perspective clearly in mind. When I face difficulties, remind me that they are temporary. When I feel uncertain, remind me that my future is certain in Christ. Guard my heart from fear and from clinging too tightly to what will pass away.

Instead, fill me with joy as I consider what You have prepared. Let this hope shape how I live, how I respond, and how I trust You. May I walk each day with a growing awareness that I am moving toward an eternal life with You. **Amen.**

Faithful God, I place my hope fully in the eternal life You have promised. You have not left my future uncertain, but have secured it through Christ.

Help me to rest in that truth and to draw strength from it each day.

When I feel discouraged or overwhelmed, remind me that this life is not the end, and that something far greater lies ahead.

Let my heart be anchored in Your promises and my mind focused on what is true.

Help me to live with purpose, knowing that what I do now has eternal significance. Guard me from fear of what lies ahead and replace it with confidence in Your care.

May the hope of eternal life bring peace to my heart and shape my life in a way that honours You. **Amen.**

Holy Lord, I thank You that my future is secure in You and that eternal life is already mine in Christ.

Help me to live in the light of that truth each day. When I am tempted to worry about what lies ahead, remind me that You are in control and that my destiny is safe in Your hands.

Give me a heart that is not troubled by uncertainty but strengthened by hope.

Let me not be consumed by the temporary but focused on what is eternal. Help me to live with confidence, peace, and joy, knowing that I will one day be with You.

May this hope guide my steps, steady my heart, and fill my life with purpose as I walk faithfully before You. **Amen.**

50. PRAYERS FOR HEAVEN'S COMFORT

Gracious Father, I come before You seeking the comfort that comes from the hope of heaven. There are times when this life feels heavy, when sorrow lingers, and when burdens seem difficult to carry.

In those moments, I need more than temporary relief. I need a deeper comfort - one that reaches beyond this life and anchors my heart in what is eternal.

I thank You that You have given that comfort through the promise of heaven.

Your word says, "He will wipe every tear from their eyes. There will be no more death or mourning or crying or pain." (Revelation 21:4). Let that promise take hold of my heart.

When I feel overwhelmed by the brokenness of this world, remind me that this is not the end. There is a future You have prepared that is free from suffering, full of joy, and secure in Your presence.

Help me to draw comfort not only from the thought of heaven, but from the certainty of it. This is not a distant possibility, but a promised reality in Christ.

Let that truth steady me in times of grief and strengthen me in times of trial.

Guard me from losing perspective and from becoming consumed by what is temporary. Instead, lift my eyes to what is eternal.

Help me to live with a heart that is anchored in heaven, even as I walk through this world.

And as I hold onto this hope, let it bring peace to my heart and strength to my soul. May the comfort of heaven sustain me now and shape how I live each day before You. **Amen.**

Faithful God, I thank You for the deep and lasting comfort that comes from knowing that heaven is real and that it is my future in Christ. This is not a vague hope or a distant idea, but a certain promise grounded in Your word and secured through the work of Jesus.

In a world that is often marked by pain, loss, and uncertainty, You have given a promise that does not fade or fail. When circumstances feel unstable or difficult, this hope remains steady and unchanging. I come to You now asking that this hope would not remain distant but would become a present source of strength and comfort in my life, shaping how I think, how I respond, and how I endure.

Your word says in Philippians 3:20, "Our citizenship is in heaven. And we eagerly await a Savior from there, the Lord Jesus Christ." Let that truth shape my perspective. Help me to remember that this world is not my final home, and that my life is part of something far greater. When I feel unsettled by the difficulties of this life, remind me where I truly belong. When I feel discouraged, remind me of the future that is secure in You. Help me to draw comfort from the reality that heaven is not only a place, but the fullness of life in Your presence. There, all things will be made right, every wrong will be addressed, and every sorrow will be replaced with joy. Let that hope strengthen me when I feel weak and steady me when I feel uncertain.

Guard my heart from despair and from thinking that this life is all there is. Protect me from becoming overwhelmed by present difficulties or losing sight of what is eternal. Instead, fill me with confidence in what lies ahead. Let the promise of heaven bring calmness to my spirit and reassurance to my mind, especially in moments when life feels heavy or unclear.
And as I live each day, help me to do so with eternity in view. Let this hope shape my priorities, my decisions, and my responses. May the comfort of heaven deepen my trust, strengthen my faith, and fill my life with peace and quiet confidence in You. **Amen.**

Merciful Lord, I ask You to fill my heart with the comfort that comes from the hope of heaven.

There are times when the burdens of this life feel heavy, and I can become overwhelmed by what I see and experience. In those moments, I need more than temporary relief.

I need a deeper assurance that this is not the end of the story. Help me to remember that You have prepared something far greater than anything I face now. Let the promise of heaven bring peace to my heart and calm to my thoughts.

When I feel discouraged, lift my eyes to what is eternal. When I feel weary, remind me that rest is coming in Your presence.

May this hope sustain me, strengthen me, and give me confidence to continue, knowing that my future is secure with You forever. **Amen.**

Gracious Father, I thank You for the promise of heaven and the comfort it brings to my life.

In a world that is often uncertain and difficult, You have given me a hope that is secure and unchanging. Help me to live in the light of that truth. When I feel troubled or anxious, remind me that my future is not in doubt.

Let this assurance steady my heart and bring peace to my mind. Guard me from focusing only on what is temporary and passing away.

Instead, help me to fix my thoughts on what is eternal. Let the reality of heaven shape how I respond to challenges and how I view my circumstances.

May this hope give me strength to endure, patience to wait, and confidence to trust You fully in every season. **Amen.**

Faithful God, I place my hope in the comfort that comes from knowing that heaven is my future in Christ.

You have not left me without hope, but have given me a promise that is sure and certain. Help me to rest in that promise more deeply.

When I feel overwhelmed by grief or difficulty, remind me that this life is not the final chapter.

There is a future filled with joy, peace, and Your presence. Let that truth steady my heart and strengthen my faith.

Guard me from discouragement and from losing perspective.

Instead, fill me with a quiet confidence in Your plans. May the hope of heaven bring comfort to my soul and help me to walk through this life with trust and peace. **Amen.**

Holy Lord, I ask You to let the comfort of heaven become real to me in the present.

It is easy to think of heaven as distant, but You have given it as a living hope that strengthens me now. Help me to draw from that hope each day.

When I feel weary, remind me of the rest that is to come. When I feel sorrow, remind me of the joy that awaits. When I feel uncertain, remind me that my future is secure in You.

Let this hope shape my thoughts, steady my emotions, and guide my life. May I live with a growing awareness that I belong to You and that my eternal home is with You.

Let that truth bring peace, confidence, and strength to my heart each day. **Amen.**

Gracious Father, I come before You with thankfulness for the gift of marriage, recognising that it is Your design and Your provision. You have brought two lives together, not by accident, but with purpose.

I thank You for the blessing of companionship, for the sharing of life, and for the opportunity to reflect something of Your love through this relationship. Yet I also acknowledge that marriage requires care, patience, and constant dependence on Your grace.

Your word says, "Be completely humble and gentle; be patient, bearing with one another in love." (Ephesians 4:2). I ask You to make that true within my marriage.

Help me to be humble rather than proud, gentle rather than harsh, and patient rather than easily frustrated. Teach me to love consistently, not only when it is easy, but also when it requires sacrifice and understanding.

Guard my heart from selfishness and from expecting more than I am willing to give. Help me to listen carefully, to speak wisely, and to act with kindness in all situations. When misunderstandings arise, give me grace to respond with clarity and peace. When tension comes, help me to pursue unity rather than conflict.

Strengthen the bond between us. Let our relationship grow deeper, not weaker, over time. Build trust, strengthen communication, and deepen affection. Help us to support one another, to encourage one another, and to walk together in faith.

Above all, place Christ at the centre of our marriage. Let our relationship be shaped by His love, His truth, and His example. May our marriage reflect Your grace, bring glory to Your name, and be a source of strength and blessing in our lives. **Amen.**

Faithful God, I place my marriage into Your hands and ask You to guide and sustain it according to Your will. You know every part of our relationship - the strengths we share and the challenges we face. You see the moments of joy and the times of tension, the areas where we connect easily and the areas where we struggle to understand one another. Nothing is hidden from You. I ask You to work within our marriage in a way that brings unity, peace, and growth.

Your word says, "Above all, love each other deeply, because love covers over a multitude of sins." (1 Peter 4:8). Help me to love deeply, not superficially or only when it is easy. Teach me to be quick to forgive, slow to take offence, and ready to extend grace. When I am tempted to hold onto past hurts, help me to release them. Guard me from allowing small issues to grow into larger divisions and help me to address concerns with patience and humility.

Give me wisdom in how I speak and act. Let my words build up rather than tear down. Help me to express appreciation regularly, to show kindness in practical ways, and to remain attentive to the needs of my spouse. When misunderstandings arise, give me the willingness to listen carefully and to seek clarity rather than reacting quickly. Help us to communicate openly and honestly, with respect and care.

Strengthen our commitment to one another. Let our marriage be marked by faithfulness, trust, and mutual respect. Help us to stand together through both easy and difficult times, supporting one another with consistency and sincerity.

Help us to grow together spiritually, encouraging one another in our walk with You. Let prayer, truth, and faith be part of our shared life, shaping our decisions and guiding our relationship. And in all things, let our marriage reflect Christ.

May it be a place of grace, of truth, and of love that honours You. Sustain us, guide us, and continue to build our relationship according to Your good purposes. **Amen.**

Gracious Lord, I bring my marriage before You and ask You to strengthen it with Your grace and truth. You know the daily realities of our relationship, the moments of joy and the moments of tension, and I place them all into Your hands.

Help me to approach my spouse with humility, patience, and genuine love. Guard me from selfishness and from expecting more than I am willing to give. Instead, teach me to serve, to listen, and to respond with kindness.

When misunderstandings arise, help me to seek clarity rather than conflict. When differences appear, help me to pursue unity rather than division.

Let Your Spirit guide my words and shape my actions so that they reflect Christ.

May our marriage grow stronger through every season, rooted in Your grace and sustained by Your faithful love. **Amen.**

Faithful Father, I ask You to deepen the love within my marriage and to strengthen the bond we share. At times it is easy to become distracted, to take one another for granted, or to lose sight of what truly matters.

Bring us back to what is essential. Help us to value one another, to show appreciation, and to remain committed through every circumstance.

Give me wisdom to recognise what my spouse needs and grace to respond in a way that builds up and encourages.

Guard our relationship from bitterness, from neglect, and from unspoken tension. Instead, let honesty, kindness, and patience grow between us. May our marriage reflect Your love and be a place of peace, support, and shared faith as we walk together before You each day. **Amen.**

Merciful God, I place the challenges within my marriage before You and ask for Your help in working through them.

You know where there has been misunderstanding, where communication has been strained, and where patience has been tested. I ask You to bring healing and restoration.

Help me to take responsibility for my part and to respond with humility rather than defensiveness. Give me a willingness to listen carefully and to speak truthfully with grace. Guard me from holding onto hurt or allowing resentment to grow.

Instead, teach me to forgive as I have been forgiven. Strengthen our ability to work through difficulties together, rather than allowing them to divide us.

May Your grace lead us forward into greater unity, understanding, and strength in our relationship. **Amen.**

Holy Lord, I ask You to place Christ firmly at the centre of my marriage. Without Him, we can drift, struggle, and rely too much on our own understanding.

But with Him, there is guidance, grace, and strength for every situation. Help us to seek You together, to pray together, and to build our relationship on Your truth.

Let our marriage not be shaped by the patterns of the world, but by the example of Christ. Give us a shared desire to grow in faith and to encourage one another spiritually.

May our home be a place where Your presence is known and where Your word is honoured. Strengthen our commitment, deepen our love, and guide us in every step so that our marriage reflects Your goodness and brings glory to Your name. **Amen.**

52. PRAYERS FOR HUSBANDS

Gracious Father, I come before You as a husband, recognising both the privilege and the responsibility You have given me. This is not a role I have created for myself, but one that You have entrusted to me, and I desire to honour You in it.

Marriage is Your design, and the role You have entrusted to me is not something to take lightly. I thank You for the gift of my wife and for the life we share together. Thank You for her presence, her support, and the ways she contributes to our life as a couple. Yet I also acknowledge my need for Your help, because I cannot fulfil this role well in my own strength. Your word says I should love my wife as Christ loved the Church and gave Himself up for her." This is a high and humbling calling. Help me to love sacrificially, not selfishly.

Guard my heart from pride, from impatience, and from neglect. When I am tempted to be self-focused or careless, correct me. Help me to be attentive, to listen carefully, and to respond with kindness and understanding. Give me sensitivity to her needs and a willingness to respond with care.

Give me wisdom in how I speak and how I act, so that my words build up rather than tear down. When challenges arise, help me to respond with steadiness rather than frustration, and with understanding rather than defensiveness. Teach me to pursue peace and to work through difficulties with patience.

Strengthen me to lead well. Not with control or harshness, but with gentleness, integrity, and a desire to honour You. Help me to set a spiritual tone in the home, encouraging faith, prayer, and trust in You. Give me consistency in my example and sincerity in my leadership.

And above all, shape my life after Christ. Let His example guide me and His love define me. May my marriage reflect Your grace, and may I honour You in the way I love, lead, and serve each day. **Amen**

Faithful God, I place my role as a husband into Your hands and ask You to shape me according to Your will. This is not a role I can fulfil by instinct or effort alone, but one that requires Your ongoing work in my life. You know my strengths and my weaknesses, and You see where I fall short.

You are aware of my tendencies, my habits, and the ways I sometimes fail to love as I should. Yet You are patient with me and continue to work in my life. I ask You to grow me into the husband You have called me to be, shaping my character over time.

Your word says, "Be devoted to one another in love. Honour one another above yourselves." (Romans 12:10). Help me to live that out in my marriage. Let me be devoted, not distracted; attentive, not indifferent; and honouring, not self-centred. Teach me to show consistent care, not only in words, but in actions that are thoughtful and intentional. Help me to value my wife highly and to demonstrate that in how I treat her each day.

Give me self-control in how I respond, especially in moments of stress or disagreement. When emotions rise or tension increases, help me to pause and respond wisely rather than reacting quickly. Help me to speak with gentleness and to act with patience. Guard me from harshness, defensiveness, or withdrawal, and instead lead me into steady, faithful engagement. Teach me to remain present and to work through challenges with maturity.

Help me to support my wife well. Give me insight into her needs and a willingness to respond with love and care. Help me to notice what matters to her and to act in ways that strengthen our relationship. Strengthen our communication and deepen our trust, so that we grow together rather than apart.

And as I walk in this role, draw me closer to Christ. Let my relationship with Him shape everything else. May my marriage be strengthened by Your grace, and may my life reflect Your faithfulness in all I do. **Amen.**

Merciful Lord, I bring before You my role as a husband and ask You to strengthen me to live it out faithfully. You know the pressures, the responsibilities, and the expectations that come with this calling, and I acknowledge my need for Your help.

Teach me to love my wife with patience, kindness, and consistency. Help me to listen carefully and to respond thoughtfully, rather than reacting quickly or carelessly.

Guard my heart from selfishness and from becoming distant or distracted. Instead, give me a steady commitment to care, to serve, and to support.

Let my words build up and my actions reflect genuine love. Help me to lead with humility and integrity, setting a tone in the home that honours You. May my life reflect Christ in the way I love and serve within my marriage. **Amen.**

Gracious Father, I ask You to shape me into a husband who reflects Your love and Your grace. At times I fall short in patience, in understanding, and in consistency, and I need Your help to grow.

Teach me to be attentive to my wife, to notice her needs, and to respond with care. Help me not to take her for granted, but to value and honour her in both word and action.

Give me wisdom in how I communicate, so that I speak with clarity, kindness, and respect. Guard me from harshness or withdrawal when difficulties arise.

Instead, help me to remain engaged, calm, and willing to work through challenges together.

Let my presence in the home bring stability, encouragement, and peace, as I seek to honour You in all I do. **Amen.**

Faithful God, I place my marriage before You and ask You to strengthen me in my role as a husband.

You see where I struggle and where I need to grow, and I bring those areas to You honestly.

Help me to be dependable, trustworthy, and consistent in my love. Give me self-control in my reactions and patience in my responses.

When I feel stressed or overwhelmed, help me not to withdraw or become irritable, but to turn to You for strength.

Guide me in how I support and encourage my wife, and give me a heart that seeks her good.

Let me not focus on what I receive, but on how I can serve. May my actions reflect Christ's love and bring strength and unity to our marriage. **Amen.**

Holy Lord, I ask You to help me keep Christ at the centre of my life and my marriage. Without Him, I will fall into selfish patterns and weak responses, but with Him, there is grace and strength for every moment.

Help me to seek You daily and to let that shape how I live and relate. Give me a desire to grow spiritually and to lead in a way that encourages faith within our home.

Let my life be marked by integrity, humility, and steady love. When I fail, help me to respond with repentance and humility rather than defensiveness.

Strengthen my commitment and deepen my understanding of what it means to love well. May my life as a husband reflect Your goodness and bring honour to Your name. **Amen.**

53. PRAYERS FOR WIVES

Gracious Father, I come before You as a wife, acknowledging the gift and calling that marriage is. You have brought this relationship together according to Your purpose, and I thank You for the life that I share with my husband. Yet I also recognise my need for Your wisdom, Your grace, and Your strength as I seek to live out this role in a way that honours You.

Your word says, "Clothe yourselves with compassion, kindness, humility, gentleness and patience." (Colossians 3:12). I ask You to shape these qualities within me.

Help me to respond with kindness rather than irritation, with patience rather than frustration, and with humility rather than pride. Teach me to speak in a way that builds up and encourages, not in a way that discourages or wounds.

Guard my heart from comparison, from discontent, and from allowing small frustrations to grow into larger tensions. Instead, help me to cultivate gratitude for what You have given.

Strengthen my ability to support, to encourage, and to walk alongside my husband with faithfulness and grace.

Give me wisdom in how I communicate. Help me to listen well, to express myself clearly, and to seek understanding rather than assumption. When difficulties arise, guide me to respond with calmness and a desire for unity.

Above all, help me to walk closely with Christ. Let my relationship with Him shape every part of my life and my marriage.

May my words, my actions, and my attitudes reflect His love and His truth. Let my life as a wife bring honour to You and contribute to a marriage that is strong, faithful, and rooted in Your grace. **Amen.**

Faithful God, I place my role as a wife into Your hands and ask You to guide me and strengthen me in it. This is a calling that touches every part of daily life, and I recognise my need for Your help in it. You know the daily realities of my marriage, the joys and the challenges, the moments of ease and the moments of strain, and You see where I need to grow. I ask You to work within me so that my life reflects Your grace in every part of this relationship.

Your word says, "Do everything in love." (1 Corinthians 16:14). Help me to live that out consistently, not only when it feels natural, but also when it requires effort and patience. Let love guide my words, my responses, and my attitudes. Help me to choose kindness even in difficult moments and to act with care in the small, everyday interactions that shape our relationship.

Help me not to react quickly or speak carelessly, but to pause and respond with thoughtfulness and grace. Teach me to bring my emotions to You rather than allowing them to control my actions.

Guard my heart from resentment and from holding onto past hurts. When disappointments arise, help me to address them with honesty and humility rather than allowing them to grow. Help me to forgive quickly and to seek reconciliation where it is needed. Let me not withdraw or become distant, but remain engaged with honesty and grace, willing to work through challenges together.

Strengthen our communication and deepen our trust. Help me to contribute to a home that is stable, supportive, and marked by understanding. Let our home be marked by peace, respect, and mutual support. Help me to play my part in creating an environment where both of us can grow and feel secure.

And as I walk in this role, draw me closer to Christ. Let my identity be grounded in Him, not in circumstances. May my life as a wife reflect Your goodness and contribute to a marriage that honours You and stands firm through every season. **Amen.**

Merciful Lord, I bring before You my role as a wife and ask You to strengthen me to live it out with grace and wisdom.

You know the daily rhythms of my life, the responsibilities I carry, and the areas where I find it easy or difficult. I ask You to shape my heart so that I respond with kindness, patience, and humility. Guard me from reacting quickly in frustration or speaking carelessly in moments of tension.

Instead, help me to pause, to think, and to respond in a way that brings peace and understanding. Give me a heart that seeks unity rather than division, and a spirit that is willing to listen as well as speak.

Let my words be encouraging and my actions thoughtful. May I contribute to a marriage that is steady, respectful, and shaped by Your grace. **Amen.**

Gracious Father, I ask You to deepen my love and commitment within my marriage. At times it is easy to become distracted, to lose focus, or to take my husband for granted.

Bring me back to what truly matters. Help me to value him, to express appreciation, and to show care in practical ways. Give me insight into his needs and a willingness to respond with patience and understanding.

Guard my heart from comparison, from discontent, and from allowing small frustrations to grow.

Instead, fill me with gratitude and a desire to build rather than to criticise. Help me to communicate clearly and kindly, especially when things are difficult.

Let my presence in the marriage bring encouragement, stability, and peace, as I seek to honour You in how I love. **Amen.**

Faithful God, I place the challenges within my marriage before You and ask for Your help in working through them.

You know where there have been misunderstandings, where communication has been strained, and where patience has been tested. I ask You to bring healing and restoration.

Help me to take responsibility for my part and to respond with humility rather than defensiveness. Give me a willingness to listen carefully and to speak truthfully with grace.

Guard me from holding onto hurt or allowing resentment to take root. Instead, teach me to forgive as I have been forgiven.

Strengthen our ability to work through difficulties together rather than allowing them to divide us. May Your grace guide our relationship forward into greater unity, understanding, and strength. **Amen.**

Holy Lord, I ask You to keep Christ at the centre of my life and my marriage. Without Him, I can easily drift into self-centred thinking and unhelpful patterns. But with Him, there is grace, strength, and guidance for every moment.

Help me to seek You daily and to let that shape how I live and respond. Give me a desire to grow spiritually and to reflect Your character in my words and actions.

Let my life be marked by gentleness, faithfulness, and steady love. When I fail, help me to respond with humility and a willingness to grow.

Strengthen my commitment to my marriage and deepen my understanding of what it means to love well. May my life reflect Your goodness and bring honour to Your name in every season. **Amen.**

54. PRAYERS FOR PARENTS

Gracious Father, I come before You as a parent, recognising both the gift and the responsibility that You have entrusted to me. Children are a blessing from Your hand, and I thank You for the privilege of caring for them, guiding them, and helping to shape their lives.

Yet I also acknowledge how deeply I need Your wisdom and Your grace, because I cannot fulfil this role faithfully in my own strength.

Your word says, "Start children off on the way they should go, and even when they are old they will not turn from it." (Proverbs 22:6).

I ask You to help me live this out with faithfulness and care. Give me wisdom in how I teach, how I correct, and how I guide. Help me to be consistent, patient, and loving in all that I do.

Guard my heart from frustration and from reacting in ways that are unhelpful or unkind. When I feel tired or overwhelmed, renew my strength. When I am uncertain, give me clarity and direction.

Help me to respond thoughtfully rather than react quickly, especially in challenging moments.

Let my life be an example. Help me to model faith, humility, and integrity so that my children see not only what I say, but how I live. Give me opportunities to speak truth into their lives and the courage to do so with grace.

Above all, I entrust my children to You. You love them more deeply than I ever could. Work in their hearts, draw them to Yourself, and guide their lives according to Your purposes. Help me to trust You with what I cannot control and to remain faithful in what You have given me to do. **Amen.**

Faithful God, I place my role as a parent into Your hands and ask You to guide me in every aspect of it. This responsibility is both a privilege and a challenge, and I recognise how much I need Your wisdom each day. You know my children fully - their personalities, their strengths, their struggles, and their needs.

You also know where I feel confident and where I feel uncertain. There are moments when I feel capable, and others when I feel unsure of what to say or do. I ask You to meet me in both, giving me clarity when I lack direction and steadiness when I feel overwhelmed. Help me not to rely on my own understanding, but to seek Your guidance in both small decisions and significant ones.

Your word says, "Fathers, do not exasperate your children; instead, bring them up in the training and instruction of the Lord." (Ephesians 6:4). Help me to live this out wisely. Guard me from being overly harsh or overly passive. Instead, give me balance - firmness with love, correction with grace, and guidance with patience.

Help me to build strong relationships with my children. Give me time to listen, to understand, and to be fully present in their lives. Let them feel safe, valued, and loved. Give me patience to listen before I speak and wisdom to respond in ways that strengthen trust.

When challenges arise, give me wisdom to respond well. When I feel frustrated or uncertain, help me to pause and seek Your direction. When I make mistakes, give me humility to acknowledge them and to grow.

And as I raise my children, keep my focus on what matters most - their relationship with You. Help me to model faith in a way that is genuine and consistent. Use me as an instrument in Your hands to point them to Christ through both my words and my example. May my parenting reflect Your love and bring glory to Your name. **Amen.**

Merciful Lord, I bring before You my role as a parent and ask for Your wisdom and strength in every part of it.

You know the daily responsibilities, the decisions that must be made, and the challenges that arise unexpectedly.

At times I feel uncertain about what to do or how to respond, and I need Your guidance. Help me to be patient, consistent, and loving in my parenting.

Guard me from reacting out of frustration or speaking in ways that discourage. Instead, give me a calm and thoughtful spirit. Help me to listen carefully to my children and to understand their needs.

Let my words be clear and encouraging, and my actions reflect genuine care. May my parenting be shaped by Your truth and sustained by Your grace each day. **Amen.**

Gracious Father, I ask You to help me raise my children in a way that honours You and guides them toward truth. You know their hearts and their paths better than I do, and I entrust them to Your care.

Give me wisdom in how I teach, how I correct, and how I encourage them. Help me to be consistent and fair, showing both firmness and kindness. Guard my heart from comparison and from unrealistic expectations.

Instead, help me to see each child as uniquely created and to respond accordingly. Give me patience when progress feels slow and perseverance when challenges arise.

Let my home be a place of stability, truth, and love. May my parenting reflect Your character and point my children toward You in every season of life. **Amen.**

Faithful God, I place my children into Your hands and ask You to work in their lives in ways I cannot. There are many things I cannot control, and I feel the weight of that at times.

Yet I trust that You are greater and that Your purposes are good. Help me to remain faithful in what You have given me to do, while trusting You with what I cannot manage.

Give me a steady heart and a calm spirit as I guide them. When I feel overwhelmed, remind me that You are with me. When I feel uncertain, give me clarity.

Help me to pray regularly for my children and to seek Your guidance in every decision. May I parent with faith, trusting that You are at work in their lives even when I cannot see it clearly. **Amen.**

Holy Lord, I ask You to shape my parenting so that it reflects Your love and Your truth. Help me to model faith, integrity, and humility in my daily life.

Let my children see in me a genuine relationship with You, not just words, but actions that are consistent and sincere. Give me wisdom in how I respond to both their successes and their failures.

Help me to encourage them without pride and to correct them without harshness. Guard our home from tension, from misunderstanding, and from neglect. Instead, fill it with peace, communication, and mutual respect.

Strengthen the relationships within our family and help us to grow together in faith. May my parenting honour You and leave a lasting impact for good in the lives of my children. In Jesus' name I pray. **Amen.**

55. PRAYERS FOR CHILDREN

Gracious Father, I bring before You the children You have placed in my life and thank You for them.

They are a gift from Your hand, entrusted to my care for a time, and I recognise both the joy and the responsibility that comes with that trust.

You know each child fully - their personality, their strengths, their struggles, and the path that lies ahead of them. Nothing about their lives is hidden from You, and I place them into Your loving care.

Your word says, "Children are a heritage from the Lord, offspring a reward from Him." (Psalm 127:3). I hold onto that truth with gratitude. Help me to treat them with care, patience, and understanding.

Give me wisdom in how I guide them, how I speak to them, and how I respond to them in both joyful and difficult moments.

Guard their hearts and minds. Protect them from influences that would lead them away from truth. Surround them with good influences, wise guidance, and strong examples. Help them to grow in character, in wisdom, and in understanding. Above all, draw them to Yourself.

Let them come to know Christ personally and to walk in faith from an early age. Give them a desire to know Your word, to seek Your presence, and to live according to Your truth.

And for me, give strength and consistency. Help me to model faith, humility, and integrity so that they see in me a genuine example. Teach me to trust You with their lives, even in the areas I cannot control.

May they grow under Your care and be guided by Your hand all the days of their lives. **Amen.**

Faithful God, I place the children in my life into Your hands and ask You to guide and protect them as they grow. You know each of them fully - their personalities, their strengths, their struggles, and the path that lies ahead of them. You understand the world they are growing up in, the challenges they will face, and the decisions they will one day make. Nothing about their lives is hidden from You. I ask You to watch over them carefully and to lead them according to Your purposes, even in ways I may not always see.

Your word says, "Start children off on the way they should go, and even when they are old they will not turn from it." (Proverbs 22:6). Help me to be faithful in that calling. Give me wisdom to teach them what is right and courage to guide them when correction is needed. Help me to be consistent, patient, and loving in all that I do. Let my example support my words.

Strengthen their character. Help them to be honest, kind, respectful, and thoughtful in their actions. Give them discernment to recognise what is right and the courage to choose it, even when it is not easy. Guard their hearts and minds from influences that would lead them away from what is good. Surround them with friends, mentors, and influences that will encourage them in positive and godly ways.

When they face challenges, be their strength. When they feel uncertain, be their guide. When they are discouraged, be their comfort. In moments when I cannot be there, remind me that You are always present with them.

And as they grow, help me to trust You more fully. There are things I cannot control and outcomes I cannot determine, but I know that You are able. Help me to release my concerns into Your hands and to rest in Your care.

I place them in Your care, asking that You would guide their lives and lead them into all that You have prepared for them. May they come to know You, trust You, and walk with You all their days. **Amen.**

Merciful Lord, I bring before You the children You have entrusted to my care and ask You to guide me as I seek to raise and support them. You know their hearts, their needs, and their personalities far better than I do.

At times I feel uncertain about how best to respond to them, especially in moments of challenge or change. So, I ask You for wisdom. Help me to speak with patience and to act with consistency.

Guard me from reacting in frustration or from overlooking what truly matters. Instead, give me a steady and thoughtful approach to parenting.

Help me to listen carefully, to understand what is beneath their words, and to respond in ways that build trust and security. May my presence in their lives reflect Your care and point them toward truth and stability. **Amen.**

Gracious Father, I ask You to watch over the children in my life and to guide them as they grow. You see the world they are navigating and the influences that surround them, and I entrust them to Your care.

Protect their hearts and minds from what would lead them away from truth. Give them discernment to recognise what is right and courage to choose it.

Surround them with good friendships and wise influences that will strengthen their character. Help them to grow in kindness, respect, and understanding. When they face difficulties, be their strength. When they feel uncertain, give them clarity. Let them know that they are loved and valued.

May their lives be shaped by Your truth and guided by Your hand in every stage of their growth. **Amen.**

Faithful God, I place the future of these children into Your hands and ask You to guide them according to Your purposes.

There are many things I cannot see and many decisions that will one day be theirs to make. Yet I trust that You are able to lead them. Help me to be faithful in what I can do - to teach, to guide, and to encourage them.

Give me patience when progress feels slow and perseverance when challenges arise. Guard my heart from anxiety about what lies ahead. Instead, help me to trust You with their future. Let me pray consistently for them and rely on Your wisdom in every step.

May their lives be shaped by Your grace, and may they grow to know You, trust You, and walk with You throughout their lives. **Amen.**

Holy Lord, I ask You to help me model a life of faith before the children in my care. Let them see in me a genuine relationship with You, not just in words, but in daily actions and attitudes.

Give me integrity in how I live, consistency in how I respond, and humility when I make mistakes.

Help me to teach them not only through instruction, but through example. Let our home or environment be one where Your truth is honoured and Your presence is known.

Strengthen the bond between us and help us to communicate openly and honestly.

May the children in my care grow in confidence, in wisdom, and in faith, and may my influence point them toward a lifelong relationship with You. **Amen.**

56. PRAYERS FOR FAMILY UNITY

Gracious Father, I come before You with my family, recognising that every relationship within it is known to You and held within Your care.

You have brought us together in ways that are unique, and You understand both the strengths we share and the tensions we sometimes experience.

I thank You for the gift of family, yet I also acknowledge how easily unity can be strained by misunderstanding, difference, and the pressures of daily life. I bring all of this before You now.

Your word says, "Make every effort to keep the unity of the Spirit through the bond of peace." (Ephesians 4:3). I ask You to make that a reality within our family. Help us to pursue unity intentionally, not passively.

Give us hearts that are willing to listen, to understand, and to respond with patience and kindness. Guard us from harsh words, from quick reactions, and from allowing small disagreements to grow into lasting division.

Where there has been tension, bring healing. Where communication has broken down, restore it. Where hurt has taken root, give grace to forgive and to move forward. Help each of us to take responsibility for our own attitudes and responses, rather than focusing only on others.

Strengthen the bonds between us. Let our relationships grow in trust, respect, and mutual support. Help us to value one another, even when we differ, and to remain committed to one another through every season.

Above all, place Christ at the centre of our family. Let His love shape our relationships and His truth guide our interactions. May our family reflect Your grace and become a place of peace, strength, and encouragement for each one within it. **Amen.**

Faithful God, I place my family into Your hands and ask You to build and strengthen our unity. You know every dynamic within our relationships - the closeness we enjoy and the areas where distance or tension may exist. You see the spoken words and the unspoken thoughts, the moments of connection and the times of misunderstanding.

Your word says, "Above all these put on love, which binds them all together in perfect unity." (Colossians 3:14). Help us to live this out in practical and consistent ways. Teach us to love not only in words, but in actions that are thoughtful and sincere. Let our love be patient when tensions arise, forgiving when mistakes are made, and enduring when challenges come.

Guard our family from division. Protect us from misunderstanding, from pride, and from the tendency to withdraw when things become difficult. When differences arise, help us not to avoid them, but to face them with honesty and care. Give us courage to address issues openly and grace to do so gently, seeking restoration rather than winning arguments.

Help us to communicate well. Give us the ability to listen carefully, to speak thoughtfully, and to seek understanding rather than assumption. When emotions are strong, help us to slow down and respond wisely. Let our conversations be marked by respect, patience, and a genuine desire for unity. Strengthen our commitment to one another.

Let our family be a place where each person feels valued, supported, and encouraged. Help us to show appreciation regularly and to stand alongside one another through both joyful and difficult seasons. Give us perseverance to remain united even when circumstances test us.

And in all things, let Christ be at the centre. May our family reflect His love, His truth, and His grace in everyday life. Shape our home into a place of peace and stability, bringing honour to Your name and strength to each one within it. **Amen.**

Merciful Lord, I bring before You the relationships within my family and ask You to strengthen our unity. You know the areas where we are close and the areas where tension or misunderstanding can arise.

I ask You to work in each of our hearts so that we may respond to one another with patience, kindness, and understanding. Help me to take responsibility for my own words and actions, rather than focusing on the faults of others.

Guard me from reacting quickly or speaking harshly, especially in moments of stress. Instead, give me a calm and thoughtful spirit that seeks peace. Help me to listen carefully and to value what others are saying.

Let my contribution to the family be one that builds up rather than creates division. May our relationships grow stronger as we learn to walk in grace and truth together. **Amen.**

Gracious Father, I ask You to bring healing where there has been tension or distance within my family. You know the history, the conversations, and the moments that have shaped our relationships, and I place them all into Your hands.

Where there has been hurt, bring restoration. Where communication has broken down, help us to begin again with humility and honesty. Give me a willing heart to forgive and a desire to seek reconciliation.

Guard me from holding onto past grievances or allowing resentment to grow. Instead, fill my heart with grace and a readiness to move forward. Help us to rebuild trust step by step, with patience and care.

May our family become a place where healing is experienced and where unity is strengthened through Your grace. **Amen.**

Faithful God, I place the unity of my family into Your care and ask You to strengthen it according to Your will. You know the pressures we face and how easily they can affect our relationships.

Help us not to drift apart, but to remain connected and committed to one another. Give us time to be together, to communicate openly, and to support one another in meaningful ways.

Help me to be intentional in building relationships within my family, rather than assuming they will grow on their own. Guard us from distraction, from neglect, and from taking one another for granted. Instead, help us to value the gift of family and to invest in it with care and attention.

May our relationships be marked by trust, encouragement, and a shared desire to honour You. **Amen.**

Holy Lord, I ask You to place Christ at the centre of our family so that true unity may grow.

Without Him, we can easily fall into patterns of selfishness, misunderstanding, and division. But with Him, there is grace, truth, and strength to build something lasting.

Help us to seek You together, to pray together, and to allow Your word to shape our lives. Give us a shared desire to grow in faith and to support one another spiritually.

Let our home be a place where Your presence is known and where Your peace is experienced. Strengthen our relationships so that they reflect Your love and bring glory to Your name.

May our unity not be fragile but rooted in You and sustained by Your grace each day. **Amen.**

57. PRAYERS FOR FRIENDSHIP

Gracious Father, I thank You for the gift of friendship and for the relationships You have placed in my life. True friendship is a blessing, a source of encouragement, support, and shared joy. I recognise that these relationships are not accidental, but part of Your provision and care.

You know each friendship I have - the ones that are strong, the ones that are growing, and the ones that may be strained or uncertain. I bring them all before You now.

Your word says, "A friend loves at all times, and a brother is born for a time of adversity." (Proverbs 17:17). Help me to be that kind of friend.

Teach me to love consistently, not only when it is easy, but also when it requires patience, understanding, and sacrifice. Give me a heart that is willing to listen, to support, and to stand alongside others in both joy and difficulty.

Guard my friendships from selfishness, from neglect, and from misunderstanding. Help me to communicate clearly and kindly, and to seek unity rather than division.

When challenges arise, give me grace to respond with humility and a willingness to work through difficulties.
Help me to choose friendships wisely and to nurture those relationships with care. Let my presence in the lives of others bring encouragement, honesty, and strength.

Lord, give me the discernment to know when to speak and when to listen.

Above all, let my friendships be shaped by Christ. May His love, His truth, and His example guide how I relate to others.

Let these relationships reflect Your grace and be a source of blessing and encouragement to all involved. **Amen.**

Faithful God, I place my friendships into Your hands and ask You to guide and strengthen them according to Your will. These relationships are a significant part of my life, and I recognise that they are an important part of Your provision.

You know the importance of these connections and the role they play in shaping my thoughts, my character, and my direction. I thank You for the people You have placed around me, for the encouragement they bring and the support they provide. I ask that You would deepen these relationships in ways that honour You and strengthen my walk with You. Your word says, "As iron sharpens iron, so one person sharpens another." (Proverbs 27:17). Let that be true in my friendships.

Give me a willingness to speak truth with grace and to receive it with humility. Guard me from avoiding necessary conversations and help me to grow through the influence of others who seek to walk faithfully with You.

Guard my heart from superficial relationships that lack depth or honesty. Instead, lead me into friendships that are genuine, supportive, and rooted in truth. Help me to invest time and effort into these relationships, rather than taking them for granted or allowing them to drift. Give me a desire to be present, attentive, and consistent in how I engage with others. When misunderstandings occur, give me patience and clarity.

Help me to address issues directly and kindly, seeking restoration rather than allowing distance to grow. When I am tempted to withdraw or remain silent, give me courage to engage with honesty and grace. Let forgiveness be quick and communication be open, so that relationships may be strengthened rather than weakened.

And in all of this, draw my friendships closer to Christ. May they be marked by faith, by mutual encouragement, and by a shared desire to grow. Let these relationships strengthen my walk with You, and may they reflect Your love in ways that are real, steady, and meaningful. **Amen.**

Merciful Lord, I thank You for the friendships You have placed in my life and ask You to help me be a faithful and consistent friend. You know how easily relationships can be neglected when life becomes busy or when priorities shift.

Guard me from taking friendships for granted or from becoming distant without realising it. Help me to be intentional in staying connected, in showing care, and in making time for meaningful interaction.

Give me a heart that is willing to listen patiently and to respond with understanding. Let my words bring encouragement rather than discouragement, and my actions reflect genuine concern.

When friends are going through difficult times, help me to be present and supportive. May my friendships grow stronger through honesty, kindness, and shared trust, reflecting Your love in a practical and lasting way. **Amen.**

Gracious Father, I ask You to deepen the quality of my friendships so that they are not only enjoyable but also strengthening and encouraging.

Help me to move beyond surface-level interaction and to engage with others in a way that builds trust and understanding. Give me courage to be honest where needed and wisdom to speak with grace. Guard me from avoiding important conversations or allowing misunderstandings to linger. Instead, help me to address issues with patience and clarity. Let my friendships be marked by mutual respect, support, and encouragement.

Teach me to celebrate the successes of others and to stand with them in their struggles. May my presence in their lives bring stability and strength, and may these relationships reflect Your truth and Your grace in every interaction. **Amen.**

Faithful God, I place my friendships into Your care and ask You to guide them according to Your will. You know which relationships are strong and which need attention, and I ask You to give me discernment in how I respond.

me to invest in the right relationships and to nurture them with consistency and care. Guard me from being influenced in unhelpful ways or from drifting into friendships that pull me away from truth. Instead, lead me into relationships that encourage growth, faith, and integrity.

Give me a willingness to give as well as to receive, to support as well as to be supported. Let my friendships be balanced, healthy, and rooted in what is good.

May they strengthen my life and help me to walk faithfully before You. **Amen.**

Holy Lord, I ask You to place Christ at the centre of my friendships so that they may be shaped by His love and His truth.

Without Him, relationships can become shallow or self-focused, but with Him, they can grow in depth and purpose. Help me to seek friendships that encourage spiritual growth and to be a friend who reflects Your character.

Give me a desire to pray for my friends, to support them in their faith, and to speak truth with kindness. Let our conversations be meaningful and our time together purposeful. Guard our relationships from misunderstanding, from pride, and from neglect.

Instead, let them grow in trust, honesty, and mutual encouragement. May my friendships honour You and be a source of strength and blessing in every season. **Amen.**

58. PRAYERS FOR STRAINED RELATIONSHIPS

Merciful Father, I come today with the weight of strained relationships, bringing before You the tension, the misunderstanding, and the distance that has developed.

You know every detail of what has taken place - the words that have been spoken, the moments that have caused hurt, and the silence that has followed. Nothing is hidden from You, and I ask You to meet me in this situation with Your grace and wisdom.

Your word says, "If it is possible, as far as it depends on you, live at peace with everyone." (Romans 12:18). I ask You to help me live this out faithfully. Show me what is within my responsibility and give me the courage to act on it.

Help me to take an honest look at my own attitudes, words, and actions. Where I have been wrong, give me humility to acknowledge it and a willingness to seek forgiveness.

Guard my heart from bitterness, from defensiveness, and from holding onto past hurt. Instead, teach me to forgive as I have been forgiven in Christ.

This is not always easy, but I ask You to give me the grace to release what I am holding onto and to entrust the situation to You.

Where restoration is possible, guide the way forward. Give clarity in communication, patience in listening, and gentleness in responding. Help me not to escalate tension, but to bring calm and understanding into the situation.

And where resolution takes time, give me endurance and peace. Help me to trust You with what I cannot control and to remain faithful in what I can do.

May this situation be transformed by Your grace, and may my response reflect Your truth and Your love. **Amen.**

Faithful God, I place before You the relationships in my life that are strained or broken, asking You to bring healing and restoration according to Your will.

You know how difficult these situations can be and how deeply they can affect my thoughts, my emotions, and my sense of peace.

I bring all of this to You, trusting that You are able to work in ways I cannot.

Your word says, "Be kind and compassionate to one another, forgiving each other, just as in Christ God forgave you." (Ephesians 4:32).

I ask You to make this real in my heart. Help me to respond with kindness rather than harshness, with compassion rather than judgement, and with forgiveness rather than resentment.

Give me wisdom in how to approach this situation. Help me to know when to speak, what to say, and how to say it. Guard me from reacting out of emotion or from allowing frustration to guide my actions. Instead, give me a calm and steady spirit.

Where trust has been damaged, I ask You to begin the process of rebuilding it. Where communication has broken down, open the way for honest and respectful conversation.

Where there is distance, create opportunities for reconnection.

At the same time, help me to accept that I cannot control every outcome. Teach me to do what is right and to leave the results with You.

Let my actions be shaped by obedience to You rather than by the response of others.

And in all things, let Christ be my example. May my response reflect His grace, His truth, and His patience, bringing honour to Your name. **Amen.**

Gracious Lord, I bring before You a relationship that has become strained, and I ask for Your help in responding with wisdom and grace.

You know what has happened, what has been said, and how it has affected me. At times I feel hurt, frustrated, or uncertain about how to move forward. Yet I do not want my response to be driven by emotion alone.

Help me to pause, to reflect, and to respond in a way that honours You. Show me where I may need to take responsibility and give me humility to do so honestly. Guard my heart from becoming hardened or defensive.

Instead, help me to remain open, willing to listen, and ready to seek peace where it is possible. Let my words be thoughtful and my actions measured. May I contribute to healing rather than further division. **Amen.**

Merciful Father, I ask You to bring healing into a relationship that has been affected by misunderstanding or hurt. You know the details far better than I do, and I place them into Your hands.

me not to replay past moments or dwell on what has gone wrong. Instead, give me a forward-looking perspective shaped by Your grace. Teach me to forgive sincerely, not superficially, and to release what I cannot change.

Where communication is needed, give me courage to speak with honesty and gentleness. Where patience is required, help me to wait without becoming frustrated. Guard me from bitterness and from allowing this situation to shape my attitude negatively. Let Your peace guide me and Your truth direct me. May this relationship, if it is Your will, be restored and strengthened through Your grace. **Amen.**

Faithful God, I place this strained relationship into Your care and ask You to guide the path forward.

I recognise that I cannot control the response of the other person, and that can be difficult to accept.

Yet I trust that You are at work beyond what I can see. Help me to focus on what You are calling me to do. Give me clarity in my thinking and steadiness in my actions.

I feel uncertain, remind me to seek Your wisdom. When I feel discouraged, remind me that You are present. Let me not withdraw or avoid the situation but approach it with care and maturity.

May my response reflect Your character, and may I act in a way that honours You, regardless of the outcome. **Amen.**

Holy Lord, I ask You to guard my heart as I walk through this situation. It is easy for hurt to turn into resentment and for frustration to become distance.

Protect me from that. Help me to remain soft in heart and open in spirit. Give me the strength to forgive, the wisdom to speak, and the patience to wait.

Let me not be defined by this difficulty but shaped by how I respond to it. Surround me with Your peace and remind me that You are in control.

Whether this relationship is restored quickly or slowly, help me to trust You fully.

May my life reflect Your grace in this situation, and may Your work be evident in how I think, speak, and act each day. **Amen.**

Gracious Father, I come before You in this season of singleness, acknowledging that You know my life fully and have ordered my days according to Your wisdom.

This is not a forgotten or lesser season, but one that is known to You and held within Your purposes. I thank You that my identity is not defined by my relationship status, but by my relationship with Christ, and that in Him I am fully known, fully loved, and fully accepted.

Your word says, "I have learned to be content whatever the circumstances." (Philippians 4:11). I ask You to teach me this contentment.

There are times when I feel the weight of longing, the questions about the future, and the uncertainty that can come with this season. Yet I do not want those feelings to lead me into discontent or restlessness.

Instead, help me to rest in Your timing and to trust Your plan for my life.

Guard my heart from comparison and from measuring my life against others. Help me to value what You are doing in me now. Give me a sense of purpose in this season, and help me to use my time, energy, and gifts in ways that honour You. Strengthen me to walk faithfully.

Let my life be marked by integrity, by devotion to You, and by a willingness to serve. Help me to build meaningful relationships, to invest in friendships, and to remain connected within the Church.

And as I look ahead, I place my future into Your hands. Whether You lead me into marriage or call me to continued singleness, help me to trust You fully. Let my life be shaped not by uncertainty, but by confidence in Your goodness and Your perfect will. **Amen.**

Faithful God, I bring before You the reality of living as a single Christian and ask You to meet me in this season with Your grace and Your presence.

You know both the joys and the challenges that come with it. There are freedoms and opportunities, but also moments of loneliness, longing, and uncertainty.

At times, I feel content and focused, and at other times I feel the weight of what is not yet fulfilled. I bring all of this to You honestly, without hiding or pretending.

Your word says, "Seek first His kingdom and His righteousness, and all these things will be given to you as well." (Matthew 6:33). Help me to live this out daily.

Let my focus be on You, not on what I feel is missing. Give me a heart that is fully devoted to You and a life that is centred on Your purposes. Help me to see this season as one that has meaning and value in Your plan.

Guard me from becoming discouraged or distracted. Help me to use this season well, investing in my relationship with You, growing in faith, and serving others with willingness and joy.

Give me clarity about how to live purposefully and faithfully, making wise choices with my time and energy.

When I feel lonely, remind me that I am not alone. Your presence is constant, and Your love is sufficient. Surround me with meaningful relationships and opportunities for connection that bring encouragement and support.

And as I think about the future, give me peace. Help me to trust Your timing and to wait without anxiety. Whether my path includes marriage or continued singleness, I place it into Your hands.

May my life reflect Your grace and bring honour to Your name in every season. **Amen**

Merciful Lord, I bring before You this season of singleness and ask You to help me live it with purpose and peace. You know my thoughts, my desires, and the questions that sometimes arise about the future.

At times I can feel uncertain or even restless, and I need Your help to remain steady. Teach me to trust You more deeply with my life. Help me not to measure my worth by my circumstances, but to rest in the truth that I am fully known and loved in Christ.

Guard my heart from comparison and from looking at the lives of others in a way that leads to discontent. Instead, give me a sense of purpose in this season.

Help me to invest in my relationship with You, to build strong friendships, and to serve faithfully. May this time be one of growth, stability, and deepening trust in Your care. **Amen.**

Gracious Father, I ask You to give me contentment and confidence as I walk through this season of life. There are moments when I feel the weight of being alone and I wonder what lies ahead. I bring those thoughts to You honestly now.

Help me not to be controlled by them. Instead, give me a calm and settled heart that rests in Your sovereignty. Teach me to use this season wisely, not waiting for something else to begin, but living fully in what You have given me now.

Give me meaningful relationships, opportunities to serve, and a clear sense of purpose. Guard me from isolation and from withdrawing unnecessarily.

Let my life be active, engaged, and fruitful. May I walk with confidence, knowing that You are guiding me and that my future is secure in Your hands. **Amen.**

Faithful God, I place my future into Your hands and ask You to help me trust You with what lies ahead.

I do not always know what You have planned, and at times that uncertainty can feel difficult.

Yet I know that You are good and that Your plans are wise. Help me to rest in that truth.

Give me patience as I wait and strength to remain faithful in the present. Let me not become anxious or distracted but focused on what You have called me to do now.

Help me to grow spiritually, to deepen my understanding of Your word, and to walk closely with You each day.

May this season not be wasted but used to strengthen my faith and prepare me for whatever lies ahead. **Amen.**

Holy Lord, I ask You to keep Christ at the centre of my life in this season of singleness. Without Him, I can easily drift into distraction, discouragement, or misplaced priorities.

But with Him, there is clarity, purpose, and peace. Help me to seek You daily and to let that shape how I live.

Give me a desire to grow in faith, to serve with willingness, and to invest in relationships that are healthy and encouraging.

Guard my heart from loneliness that leads to unhealthy choices or from seeking fulfilment in the wrong places. Instead, let me find my deepest satisfaction in You.

May my life reflect Your grace, Your truth, and Your goodness, and may I walk forward with confidence, knowing that You are leading me in every step. **Amen.**

60. PRAYERS FOR THE HOME

Gracious Father, I come before You with thankfulness for the home You have provided. Whether large or small, busy or quiet, it is a place of shelter, of daily life, and of shared relationships.

I recognise that a home is more than a physical space. It is shaped by attitudes, words, and actions, and I ask You to make this home a place that reflects Your presence and Your peace. Your word says, "Unless the Lord builds the house, the builders labour in vain." (Psalm 127:1).

I ask You to be the foundation of this home. Guide how we live, how we speak, and how we relate to one another. Let everything within this home be shaped by Your truth and sustained by Your grace.

Guard this home from tension, from harsh words, and from neglect. Help us to communicate with kindness, to listen with patience, and to respond with understanding.

Where there has been strain, bring healing. Where there has been distance, bring restoration.

Let this home be a place of peace. When pressures from outside increase, let this be a place where rest is found. When difficulties arise, let this be a place where support is given.

Strengthen the relationships within it so that they are marked by trust, respect, and care.

Above all, let Christ be at the centre. May Your word be honoured here, Your presence sought, and Your name lifted up.

Let this home not only serve those who live in it, but also be a place of welcome, encouragement, and blessing to others. Build this home according to Your will and let it reflect Your goodness in every part. **Amen.**

Faithful God, I place my home into Your hands and ask You to guide and shape it according to Your purposes. You know the rhythms of daily life, the interactions that take place, and the challenges that arise.

You see the tone of our conversations, the attitudes we carry, and the patterns that develop over time. Nothing is hidden from You. I ask You to be actively at work within this home, bringing unity, peace, and strength. Let Your presence be evident in both the ordinary and significant moments of our life together.

Your word says, "As for me and my household, we will serve the Lord." (Joshua 24:15). Help us to live this out in a real and consistent way. Let this home be marked by a desire to honour You in both small and significant things. Give us a shared commitment to truth, to faith, and to living in a way that reflects Your character. Help us to encourage one another daily, reminding each other of what matters most.

Guard this home from distraction, from busyness that crowds out what matters, and from patterns that weaken relationships. Instead, help us to be intentional in how we live together.

Give us time to connect, to listen, and to support one another. Help us to prioritise what strengthens our relationships rather than what pulls us apart, and to create space for meaningful interaction.

Strengthen the atmosphere of this home. Let it be a place of encouragement rather than criticism, of patience rather than frustration, and of grace rather than judgement. Help each person to contribute positively and to take responsibility for their words and actions.

And in all of this, let Your presence be known. May this home reflect Your love, provide stability for those within it, and be a place where faith grows and is lived out daily. **Amen**

Merciful Lord, I bring before You the home in which I live and ask You to shape it according to Your will. You know the daily interactions, the conversations, and the atmosphere that exists within it.

I ask You to guide all of these things so that this home becomes a place of peace and stability. Help me to contribute positively through my words and actions. Guard me from speaking carelessly or reacting in ways that create tension.

Instead, give me patience, kindness, and a willingness to listen. Help me to respond thoughtfully, especially in moments of pressure or disagreement. Let my presence in the home bring encouragement rather than frustration.

May this home grow stronger as we learn to relate to one another with grace and understanding, reflecting Your love in practical and consistent ways. **Amen.**

Gracious Father, I ask You to strengthen the relationships within this home so that they are marked by trust, respect, and care. You know the different personalities, needs, and pressures that exist, and I ask You to bring unity among us.

Help us not to drift apart through busyness or misunderstanding. Instead, give us a desire to connect, to communicate, and to support one another.

Teach me to be intentional in building relationships within this home, rather than assuming they will develop on their own.

Give me wisdom in how I speak and how I listen. Let my actions reflect genuine concern and commitment. May this home become a place where each person feels valued, supported, and understood, and where relationships continue to grow stronger over time. **Amen.**

Faithful God, I place the atmosphere of this home into Your hands and ask You to fill it with Your peace. There are times when stress, pressure, or outside influences can affect how we relate to one another, and I need Your help to keep things steady.

Guard this home from tension that builds and remains unresolved. Help us to address issues calmly and honestly, seeking resolution rather than allowing division to grow. Give me a steady spirit that does not react quickly but responds thoughtfully.

Let my presence contribute to peace rather than conflict. Help us to create an environment where honesty is welcomed, forgiveness is practised, and understanding is sought.

May this home reflect Your presence and provide a place of rest and strength for all who live here. **Amen.**

Holy Lord, I ask You to place Christ firmly at the centre of this home so that everything flows from Him. Without Him, we can easily fall into patterns that weaken relationships and create distance. But with Him, there is guidance, grace, and strength.

Help us to seek You together, to value Your word, and to allow Your truth to shape how we live. Give me a desire to lead by example, showing faith, humility, and consistency in my daily life.

Let this home be a place where Your presence is known and where Your peace is experienced. May it not only serve those who live here but also be a place of welcome and encouragement to others.

Strengthen this home according to Your will and let it reflect Your goodness in every way. **Amen.**

61. PRAYERS FOR WORK

Gracious Father, I come before You and place my work into Your hands. Thank You that work is not merely a necessity of life, but part of Your good design for human living. From the beginning, You gave people meaningful tasks, responsibility, and the dignity of labour. I thank You, therefore, for the opportunity to work, to serve, to contribute, and to use the abilities You have given me.

Your word says, "Whatever you do, work at it with all your heart, as working for the Lord, not for human masters." (Colossians 3:23). Let that truth shape my whole attitude to work. Keep me from laziness, resentment, and half-hearted effort. Guard me from treating work as a burden to endure only, and teach me instead to approach it as a sphere in which I may honour Christ. Help me to be diligent, reliable, and faithful in the tasks that are entrusted to me.

When work feels repetitive, give me perseverance. When it feels demanding, give me strength. When it feels unnoticed, remind me that You see all things clearly. Keep me from grumbling in my spirit or becoming careless in my habits. Let me work with integrity, with patience, and with a desire to serve well. Help me to speak graciously, to act honestly, and to carry out my responsibilities with a clear conscience before You.

I also ask for wisdom in my work. Help me to make good decisions, to manage my time well, and to respond calmly under pressure. Guard me from pride when things go well and from discouragement when they do not. Let my work be marked by steadiness, humility, and trust in You.

Above all, keep Christ at the centre of my life so that work does not become an idol or a source of identity apart from Him. May I labour faithfully, rest wisely, and live each day knowing that my true worth is found in being Yours. Let my work become an offering of gratitude to You and a testimony of Your grace in my daily life. **Amen.**

Faithful God, I thank You that You are present not only in times of worship and prayer, but also in the ordinary responsibilities of daily work. Too easily I can divide life into what seems spiritual and what seems ordinary, forgetting that every part of life belongs under Your lordship. So, I ask You to help me see my work in the light of Your truth and to carry it out in a way that pleases You.

Your word says, "Commit to the Lord whatever you do, and He will establish your plans." (Proverbs 16:3). I bring my work before You now and ask that You would govern it, direct it, and bless it according to Your will. Give me clarity of mind for the tasks before me and wisdom in the decisions I must make. Help me to work carefully and responsibly, not cutting corners, not acting dishonestly, and not allowing frustration to rule my spirit.

Guard me in my relationships at work. Help me to deal fairly with others, to be respectful in speech, and to show patience when difficulties arise. Keep me from gossip, complaint, and unnecessary conflict. Instead, let my conduct reflect the character of Christ. May others see in me honesty, steadiness, kindness, and self-control.

When work becomes tiring or stressful, renew my strength. When it becomes monotonous, give me faithfulness in small things. When I face pressure, teach me to pray rather than panic. And when I feel dissatisfied, help me to remember that my first calling is not to seek personal advancement above all else, but to honour You where You have placed me.

I ask also that my work would be useful to others. Let it contribute to what is good, serve real needs, and be done with a sincere desire to bless rather than merely to achieve. Keep me from making work my master, and help me instead to serve Christ through it.

May I labour with gratitude, humility, and diligence, trusting that nothing done faithfully before You is wasted. **Amen.**

Gracious Lord, I bring before You the work that lies ahead of me and ask for Your help in approaching it with the right attitude and spirit.

You know the tasks, the pressures, and the expectations that I will face, and I ask You to give me strength and clarity as I begin.

Help me not to approach my work reluctantly or carelessly, but with a willing and steady heart.

Guard me from distraction and from allowing my mind to wander when I should be focused. Instead, help me to give proper attention to what is before me.

Let my work be marked by diligence, consistency, and care. May I carry out my responsibilities faithfully, knowing that I ultimately serve You in all that I do. **Amen.**

Faithful Father, I ask You to guide me throughout the working day and to help me remain steady in both my actions and my attitude.

There are moments when work becomes demanding, when pressure increases, or when things do not go as planned.

In those moments, help me not to become frustrated or overwhelmed. Instead, give me a calm and thoughtful spirit.

Help me to pause, to think clearly, and to respond wisely. Guard my speech so that my words are measured, respectful, and helpful. Let my actions reflect integrity and reliability.

May those I work with see consistency in me, and may my conduct reflect Your grace in practical ways throughout the day. **Amen.**

Merciful God, I place my work relationships into Your hands and ask You to guide how I relate to others.

You know the personalities I interact with, the challenges that may arise, and the dynamics that exist. Help me to deal fairly and kindly with everyone. Guard me from impatience, from harshness, and from speaking carelessly.

Instead, give me a spirit of patience and understanding. Help me to listen well and to respond with wisdom.

When difficulties arise, give me the ability to remain calm and to seek resolution rather than conflict.

Let my presence in the workplace contribute to stability and cooperation. May my relationships be marked by honesty, respect, and a genuine desire to do what is right. **Amen.**

Holy Lord, I ask You to keep my work in its proper place in my life. It is easy for work to become consuming, to take over my thoughts, or to shape my identity more than it should.

Guard my heart from making work my source of worth or security. Instead, remind me that my identity is found in Christ and not in what I achieve.

Help me to work diligently, but also to rest when it is time to rest. Give me balance and wisdom in how I manage my time and energy.

Let me not neglect other responsibilities or relationships because of work.

May I honour You in both my labour and my rest, living each day with a right perspective and a steady trust in Your provision. **Amen.**

62. PRAYERS FOR FAITHFULNESS AT WORK

Gracious Father, I come before You and ask for Your help to be faithful in the work You have given me to do. You know the responsibilities I carry, the expectations placed upon me, and the daily tasks that can sometimes feel routine or demanding.

I thank You that none of this is outside Your care. Help me to see my work not simply as a duty, but as a calling in which I may honour You and serve others.

Your word says, "Now it is required that those who have been given a trust must prove faithful." (1 Corinthians 4:2). I ask You to make me faithful in all that has been entrusted to me.

Help me to carry out my work with diligence, reliability, and integrity. Guard me from cutting corners, from being careless, or from doing only what is necessary to get by. Instead, give me a steady commitment to do my work well, even when no one is watching.

When work becomes repetitive, help me to remain consistent. When it becomes difficult, give me endurance. When it feels unnoticed, remind me that You see everything clearly.

Keep my heart from discouragement and from losing motivation. Let me not measure my faithfulness by recognition from others, but by obedience to You.

Give me wisdom in my decisions and discipline in my habits. Help me to manage my time well and to remain focused on what is important. Guard me from distraction and from becoming scattered in my efforts.

Above all, help me to remember that faithfulness in small things matters before You. Let my work reflect a quiet consistency that honours Christ. May my attitude, my actions, and my perseverance point to a life shaped by Your grace and sustained by Your strength. **Amen.**

Faithful God, I bring my work before You and ask that You would strengthen me to be consistent and trustworthy in all that I do.

You know how easy it is to begin well and then lose focus, to be diligent at times and careless at others.

I ask You to form within me a steady faithfulness that does not depend on circumstances or mood, but is rooted in a desire to honour You.

Your word says, "Whoever can be trusted with very little can also be trusted with much." (Luke 16:10). Help me to take seriously the small responsibilities that fill my day.

Let me not overlook them or treat them lightly. Instead, teach me to approach each task with care and attention, knowing that faithfulness is built in these moments.

Guard my heart from inconsistency. When I feel tired or unmotivated, give me perseverance.

When I am tempted to delay or avoid responsibility, give me discipline. Help me to follow through on what I begin and to complete my work with care.

Give me integrity in all situations. Let my words be honest and my actions dependable. Help me to be someone others can rely on, not because I am seeking approval, but because I desire to live rightly before You.

And when I fail or fall short, give me humility to acknowledge it and grace to begin again. Let me not become discouraged, but continue to grow in faithfulness over time.

May my work be marked by consistency, trustworthiness, and quiet diligence. Let my life reflect the character of Christ in both small and significant things, so that everything I do is shaped by a desire to honour You. **Amen.**

Gracious Lord, I ask You to help me remain faithful in the daily work that You have given me.

You know how easy it is to begin tasks with good intentions and then lose focus or motivation along the way. I ask You to give me a steady and consistent spirit.

Help me to approach each responsibility with care, even when it feels small or repetitive. Guard me from cutting corners or becoming careless in my work. Instead, give me a desire to do things properly and to follow through with diligence.

Let me not depend on recognition or approval from others to remain committed. Rather, help me to remember that You see everything and that my faithfulness matters before You.

May my work reflect a quiet consistency that honours You in every detail. **Amen.**

Faithful Father, I ask You to strengthen me in moments when faithfulness feels difficult.

There are times when work becomes tiring, when progress seems slow, or when I feel unmotivated to continue. In those moments, help me not to give in to discouragement. Instead, give me perseverance and renewed focus. Remind me that faithfulness is not measured by how I feel, but by how I continue.

Help me to take one step at a time and to remain committed to what is before me. Guard me from becoming distracted or overwhelmed. Give me clarity in my thinking and steadiness in my actions.

Let me continue to work with patience and care, trusting that consistent effort matters and that You are at work even in what seems ordinary. **Amen.**

Merciful God, I place my habits and patterns of work before You and ask You to shape them according to Your will.

You know where I tend to be inconsistent or easily distracted, and I ask for Your help in these areas. Give me discipline in how I use my time and energy.

Help me to develop routines that support faithfulness rather than hinder it. Guard me from procrastination and from avoiding what needs to be done.

Instead, give me a willingness to engage with my responsibilities promptly and with focus. Let my work not be rushed or careless, but thoughtful and steady.

May my daily habits reflect a growing sense of responsibility and integrity, as I seek to honour You in the way I approach my work. **Amen.**

Holy Lord, I ask You to keep my heart grounded in the right motivation for faithfulness. It is easy to work for recognition, approval, or personal gain, but I ask You to re-centre my thinking. Help me to work first and foremost as an act of obedience to You.

Let my faithfulness flow from a desire to honour Christ rather than to impress others. Guard me from pride when things go well and from discouragement when they do not.

Help me to remain steady, regardless of the circumstances around me. Let my work be marked by integrity, humility, and perseverance.

May I be known as someone who is reliable and trustworthy, not for my own reputation, but as a reflection of Your work in my life. **Amen.**

Gracious Father, I come before You with my financial needs and place them openly in Your hands. You know the pressures I feel, the responsibilities I carry, and the uncertainty that can arise when resources are limited. Nothing about my situation is hidden from You. I thank You that I do not face these concerns alone, but under Your care as a loving and faithful Father.

Your word says, "And my God will meet all your needs according to the riches of His glory in Christ Jesus." (Philippians 4:19). I hold onto that promise and ask You to help me trust it deeply. When I feel anxious about provision, remind me that You are my provider. When I am tempted to worry about the future, steady my heart in the knowledge that You already know what I need.

Give me wisdom in how I manage what You have entrusted to me. Help me to make careful decisions, to avoid unnecessary spending, and to act responsibly in every financial matter. Guard me from impulsive choices and from trying to solve everything in my own strength.

At the same time, I ask for Your provision. Open the right doors, provide the right opportunities, and supply what is needed in ways that are consistent with Your will. Help me to recognise Your hand at work, even in small and unexpected ways.

Guard my heart from fear and from allowing financial pressure to control my thinking. Instead, give me peace that rests in Your faithfulness. Help me to live with gratitude for what I have and trust for what I need.

Above all, keep my heart anchored in Christ. Let me not measure my security by finances, but by Your unchanging love. May I walk forward with wisdom, responsibility, and quiet confidence that You will provide according to Your perfect plan. **Amen.**

Faithful God, I bring before You my financial concerns and ask You to guide me through them with wisdom and peace.

You know the details of my situation, the commitments I must meet, and the uncertainty that can arise when resources feel limited.

I place all of this before You, trusting that You are able to provide and to lead me wisely.

Your word says, "Keep your lives free from the love of money and be content with what you have, because God has said, 'Never will I leave you; never will I forsake you.'"

Help me to live in that truth. Guard my heart from fear and from placing my security in money. Instead, teach me to rest in Your presence and Your promises.

Give me wisdom in every decision I make. Help me to manage my finances carefully, to plan responsibly, and to act with integrity in all things.

Protect me from poor choices that could make matters worse, and give me clarity when I feel uncertain about what to do next.

I ask also for Your provision. Where there is need, supply what is required. Where there are obstacles, provide a way forward.

Help me to see opportunities clearly and to act wisely when they arise.

At the same time, teach me contentment. Help me to live with gratitude for what You have already given and to resist the pressure to constantly want more. Let my heart be satisfied in You, not in material things.

May this season deepen my trust in You. Let it teach me dependence, patience, and gratitude. And through it all, help me to walk forward with faith, knowing that You are faithful in every circumstance. **Amen.**

Merciful Lord, I bring before You my financial concerns and ask You to steady my heart with Your peace.

You know the pressures I feel and the responsibilities I carry, and I ask You to help me not to become overwhelmed by them.

Guard my mind from constant worry and from imagining worst-case outcomes. Instead, remind me that You are present and that You care for every detail of my life. Give me clarity in my thinking and calmness in my decisions.

Help me to approach each financial matter carefully and responsibly, rather than reacting out of fear. Let me take one step at a time, trusting You for what lies ahead.

May Your peace guard my heart and mind as I place these concerns into Your hands. **Amen.**

Gracious Father, I ask You to guide me in how I manage the resources You have given me. Help me to be wise, careful, and responsible in every decision.

Guard me from impulsive spending and from making choices that I may later regret. Instead, give me a thoughtful and disciplined approach.

Help me to prioritise what is important and to make decisions that reflect good stewardship.

When I feel uncertain, give me clarity. When I feel pressured, give me patience to pause and think carefully. Let my actions reflect integrity and responsibility.

May I handle what I have with care, trusting that faithful stewardship matters before You and contributes to greater stability in my life. **Amen.**

Faithful God, I place my need for provision into Your hands and ask You to supply what is required in Your timing.

You know the specific needs I have, even those I may not yet fully see. I ask You to open the right opportunities and to provide in ways that are consistent with Your will.

Help me to recognise Your provision, even when it comes in unexpected ways. Guard me from becoming discouraged if answers are not immediate.

Instead, give me patience to wait and faith to trust. Let me not lose heart, but continue to look to You with confidence.

May this season strengthen my dependence on You and deepen my trust in Your faithful care. **Amen.**

Holy Lord, I ask You to guard my heart from placing too much importance on money and material security.

It is easy to become anxious, to compare myself with others, or to feel unsettled when finances are uncertain. Protect me from these patterns.

Help me to find my security in You and not in what I have or do not have. Give me a spirit of contentment and gratitude, even in challenging circumstances.

Let me recognise the many blessings that You have already poured out upon my life.

Help me to live with a balanced perspective, working responsibly while trusting fully in Your provision.

May my heart remain steady, my faith remain strong, and my trust remain firmly anchored in You. **Amen.**

64. PRAYERS FOR CONTENTMENT

Gracious Father, I come before You asking that You would teach me the grace of contentment. You know how easily my heart can become restless, how quickly I can begin to compare my circumstances with those of others, and how often I can feel that something is missing.

Yet I know that true contentment is not found in changing circumstances, but in knowing You and trusting in Your care.

Your word says, "I have learned to be content whatever the circumstances." (Philippians 4:11). I ask You to teach me this same lesson. Help me to be content not because everything is easy or ideal, but because I trust that You are present and at work in every part of my life. Guard my heart from dissatisfaction and from constantly looking for something more to bring fulfilment.

When I am tempted to compare myself with others, remind me that You have given me a unique path. Help me to value what You have entrusted to me and not to overlook the blessings already present in my life. Open my eyes to see Your provision, even in small and ordinary things.

Give me a spirit of gratitude. Help me to notice what I have rather than focusing on what I lack. Teach me to give thanks in all circumstances, recognising that Your goodness is constant even when situations change.

At the same time, keep me from complacency. Let contentment not become an excuse for passivity, but a foundation for faithful living. Help me to work diligently, to pursue what is right, and to trust You with the outcome.

Above all, anchor my heart in Christ. Let my deepest satisfaction be found in Him, not in possessions, achievements, or circumstances. May my life reflect a quiet confidence in Your goodness and a steady trust in Your provision. **Amen.**

Faithful God, I bring before You the restlessness that can so easily take hold of my heart.

There are times when I feel unsettled, when I look at my circumstances and wish they were different, or when I compare myself with others and feel that I am lacking.

I confess these things to You and ask that You would reshape my thinking and my desires according to Your truth.

Your word says, "But godliness with contentment is great gain." (1 Timothy 6:6). Help me to understand this deeply.

Teach me that true gain is not found in having more, but in living with a heart that rests in You.

Guard me from the constant pressure to want more, to achieve more, or to measure my life by what I possess.

Give me peace in the present. Help me to live fully in the circumstances You have placed me in, rather than always looking ahead or wishing things were different.

Let me find stability in Your unchanging character, even when everything else feels uncertain.

Help me to be thankful. Open my eyes to see the ways You have provided and the blessings You have already given.

Let gratitude shape my thinking and my outlook.

And when I feel discontent rising, remind me of what is true.

Remind me that You are sufficient, that Your grace is enough, and that my life is held securely in Your hands.

May my heart grow steady, my thoughts become settled, and my life reflect a deep and lasting contentment that comes from trusting You in every season. **Amen.**

Merciful Lord, I ask You to quiet the restlessness in my heart and to teach me contentment.

You know how easily I can become dissatisfied with my circumstances or begin to compare my life with others. In those moments, my focus shifts away from You, and I lose sight of what is true.

Help me to recognise when this is happening and to bring my thoughts back under Your truth. Give me a calm and settled spirit that is not easily shaken by what I see around me.

Remind me that my life is not lacking anything that You have chosen to withhold for my good.

Help me to trust Your wisdom in what You have given and what You have not. May I learn to rest in Your care and to live with a growing sense of peace and trust. **Amen.**

Gracious Father, I ask You to help me develop a heart of gratitude that supports true contentment. It is easy to overlook what I have and to focus on what I feel is missing.

Guard me from this pattern. Open my eyes to see Your provision in my daily life, both in obvious and in subtle ways.

Help me to recognise the many small blessings that I often take for granted. Give me a habit of giving thanks, even in ordinary moments.

Let gratitude reshape my perspective so that I begin to see my life differently. When I am tempted to complain or feel dissatisfied, remind me of Your faithfulness.

May a thankful heart grow within me, strengthening my contentment and helping me to live with greater joy and peace. In Jesus' name. **Amen.**

Faithful God, I place my desires before You and ask You to bring them into alignment with Your will.

There are things I want, goals I pursue, and changes I hope for, and at times these desires can lead to discontent when they are not fulfilled.

Help me to hold these things with open hands.

Teach me to pursue what is right while remaining content in the present. Guard me from becoming driven by constant striving or from measuring my worth by what I achieve.

Instead, help me to live with balance, working faithfully while trusting You with the outcome. Let my desires be shaped by Your truth and guided by Your wisdom. May I learn to rest in You, even as I move forward in life. **Amen.**

Holy Lord, I ask You to anchor my heart firmly in Christ so that true contentment may grow within me.

Without Him, I will continue to look for satisfaction in things that cannot truly satisfy. But with Him, there is fullness and peace. Help me to return again and again to this truth.

When I feel unsettled, remind me that I belong to You. When I feel dissatisfied, remind me that You are enough.

Let my identity be rooted in Christ and not in my circumstances.

Give me a steady confidence that comes from knowing that my life is held in Your hands.

May my heart grow more settled, my thoughts more peaceful, and my life more reflective of the contentment that comes from trusting You fully. **Amen.**

65. Prayers for Rest

Gracious Father, I come before You aware of my need for rest. You have created me with limits, yet I often live as though I have none. I carry responsibilities, pressures, and expectations, and at times I become weary in body, mind, and spirit.

I thank You that You understand my weakness and that You invite me not to strive endlessly, but to come to You and find rest.

Your word says, "Come to Me, all you who are weary and burdened, and I will give you rest." (Matthew 11:28). I come to You now with that invitation in mind. Help me to lay down what I have been carrying - the anxieties, the unfinished tasks, the concerns about tomorrow, and the pressure I place upon myself. Teach me to release these things into Your hands and to trust that You are able to hold them far better than I can.

Give me wisdom to rest rightly. Help me not to see rest as laziness or avoidance, but as a necessary part of faithful living. Guard me from the constant pressure to do more and to achieve more, even when I am already tired. Instead, help me to recognise when I need to pause and to receive rest as a gift from You, not something I must earn.

Restore my strength. Renew my mind where it feels tired and scattered. Bring calm to my thoughts and peace to my heart.

Help me to step away from what drains me and to return with clarity and steadiness. Teach me to rest not only physically, but mentally and emotionally, releasing the need to control everything.

Above all, let me find deeper rest in Christ. Not only physical rest, but rest for my soul. Let me rest in Your sovereignty, Your care, and Your faithfulness. May I learn to live with a healthy rhythm of work and rest that honours You and sustains me for the life You have called me to live. **Amen**

Faithful God, I bring before You the weariness that I sometimes carry and ask You to refresh and restore me.

There are times when I feel physically tired, mentally drained, or emotionally stretched, and I recognise that I cannot continue well without rest.

Yet I also confess that I do not always rest wisely. I can push too hard, delay rest unnecessarily, or fill my time with activity that does not truly restore me.

Your word says, "In repentance and rest is your salvation, in quietness and trust is your strength." (Isaiah 30:15). Teach me to understand this truth. Help me to embrace rest not as weakness, but as strength found in trusting You.

Give me the humility to slow down and the wisdom to step back when needed.

Guard me from restlessness that keeps me from resting. When my mind continues to race or my thoughts remain unsettled, bring calm and clarity.

Help me to quiet my thoughts and to trust that You are in control, even when I am not active.

Give me discernment in how I use my time. Help me to set aside space for rest that is genuine and restoring. Keep me from filling that time with distractions that leave me just as tired as before.

And as I rest, draw me closer to You. Let times of rest become moments of renewed awareness of Your presence.

Strengthen me not only physically, but spiritually, so that I may return to my responsibilities with greater clarity, patience, and faithfulness.

May I learn to rest well, trusting that You are at work even when I am still. **Amen.**

Merciful Lord, I come before You feeling the weight of weariness and ask You to bring rest to my body and my mind.

You know the demands that have been placed upon me and how easily I can become tired without realising it fully. Help me to recognise my need for rest and not to ignore it.

Guard me from pushing beyond what is wise or necessary. Instead, give me permission in my own heart to pause and to slow down. Help me to step away from constant activity and to create space where I can be still.

Let my mind settle and my body relax. May I not feel guilty for resting, but receive it as a gift from You. Restore my strength and prepare me to continue faithfully in the responsibilities You have given me. **Amen.**

Gracious Father, I ask You to bring calm to my thoughts and peace to my heart so that I may truly rest.

Even when I stop working, my mind can continue to move, replaying situations, planning ahead, or worrying about what is still to be done.

I ask You to quiet these thoughts. Help me to release them into Your care and to trust that You are in control.

Give me a settled spirit that does not feel the need to hold everything together. Teach me to let go and to rest in Your presence.

Let this time of rest be genuine and refreshing, not filled with distraction or unrest.

May my thoughts become clearer, my heart more peaceful, and my spirit more steady as I learn to rest in You. **Amen.**

Faithful God, I place my daily rhythm before You and ask You to help me find a healthy balance between work and rest.

You know how easily one can take over the other, and I need Your wisdom to manage both well.

Help me to work diligently when it is time to work and to rest fully when it is time to rest.

Guard me from overworking out of pressure or fear, and from avoiding responsibilities under the guise of rest. Give me discernment to know what is needed in each moment.

Let my life be marked by steadiness rather than extremes. May I learn to live with a rhythm that honours You and sustains me over time, so that I may remain faithful in all that You have called me to do. **Amen.**

Holy Lord, I ask You to lead me into deeper rest in Christ. Beyond physical rest, I need rest for my soul - rest from striving, from proving myself, and from carrying burdens that are not mine to carry.

Help me to remember that my identity is secure in Him and not in what I accomplish.

When I feel the need to keep going in order to feel worthwhile, remind me that I am already accepted in Christ.

Let my heart find peace in that truth.

Help me to trust that You are at work even when I am still.

May this deeper rest shape my life, bringing calm to my spirit and steadiness to my faith as I learn to rely on You more fully. In Jesus matchless name I pray. **Amen.**

66. PRAYERS FOR SERVING OTHERS

Gracious Father, I come before You and ask for a heart that is willing to serve others faithfully and with the right spirit.

You have not called me to live only for myself, but to love and serve those around me in practical and meaningful ways. Yet I recognise that my natural tendency is often toward comfort, convenience, and self-interest.

I ask You to reshape my heart so that I may reflect the servant-hearted example of Christ.

Your word says, "Serve one another humbly in love." (Galatians 5:13). I ask You to make this true in my life. Help me to serve not reluctantly or out of obligation, but willingly and with sincerity.

Guard me from seeking recognition or praise for what I do. Instead, give me a quiet and genuine desire to be useful to others and to meet real needs.

Open my eyes to opportunities to serve. Help me to notice what others may overlook and to respond with kindness and care.

Give me discernment to know when to act, what to do, and how best to help. Let my service be thoughtful and appropriate, not driven by impulse but guided by wisdom.

When serving becomes difficult or inconvenient, give me perseverance. When I feel unappreciated, remind me that You see all things. Keep my heart from discouragement and from withdrawing when effort is required.

Above all, help me to serve in a way that reflects Christ. He did not come to be served, but to serve, and to give His life for others. Let His example shape my attitude and my actions. May my life be marked by humility, generosity, and a steady willingness to serve wherever You place me. **Amen.**

Faithful God, I bring before You my desire to serve others and ask that You would guide and strengthen me in this calling.

You know the situations I encounter, the people around me, and the needs that exist. I ask You to help me engage with these opportunities in a way that honours You and brings real benefit to others.

Your word says, "Each of you should use whatever gift you have received to serve others, as faithful stewards of God's grace." (1 Peter 4:10). Help me to understand and use what You have given me.

Whether my abilities are visible or behind the scenes, help me to use them faithfully. Guard me from comparing my role with others or feeling that what I do is too small to matter.

Give me a balanced and wise approach to serving. Help me not to overextend myself to the point of exhaustion, but also not to withdraw when I am needed.

Teach me to serve with both willingness and wisdom, recognising my limits while remaining faithful.

Guard my heart from pride when things go well and from discouragement when they do not. Help me to serve steadily, without becoming dependent on recognition or approval.

Let my motivation be rooted in obedience to You and love for others.

And as I serve, shape my character. Let patience, kindness, and humility grow within me. Help me to see service not only as something I do, but as part of who I am becoming in Christ.

May my life reflect a genuine concern for others and a consistent willingness to act. Let my service be useful, thoughtful, and grounded in Your grace, bringing honour to You in all that I do. **Amen.**

Merciful Lord, I ask You to give me a heart that is ready to serve others without hesitation.

You know how easily I can become focused on my own needs, my own schedule, and my own comfort. I ask You to shift my attention outward.

Help me to notice when others need encouragement, support, or practical help. Give me sensitivity so that I do not overlook opportunities to serve. When I see a need, give me the willingness to act rather than to delay or ignore it.

Guard me from excuses that keep me from helping. Instead, give me a spirit that is responsive, thoughtful, and willing. Let my actions reflect genuine care and not just good intentions. May I grow in readiness to serve, responding to others with kindness and consistency in everyday situations. **Amen.**

Gracious Father, I ask You to shape my attitude as I serve so that it reflects humility and grace. It is easy to serve outwardly while inwardly seeking recognition or feeling frustrated when my efforts are unnoticed.

Guard my heart from these patterns. Help me to serve quietly and faithfully, without needing affirmation from others.

Remind me that You see all things and that my service is ultimately before You. When I feel unappreciated, give me steadiness rather than discouragement.

When I feel pride rising, bring humility. Let my motivation be rooted in love and obedience, not in how others respond.

May my service be marked by sincerity, patience, and a genuine desire to bless others, reflecting the servant-hearted example of Christ in both small and significant ways. **Amen.**

Faithful God, I place before You the opportunities I have to serve and ask for wisdom in how I respond.

Not every opportunity is mine to take, and I need Your guidance to know what is right. Help me to recognise where I can be most useful and where my efforts will have the greatest impact.

Give me discernment so that I do not become overwhelmed by trying to do everything, but remain faithful in what You have given me to do.

Help me to serve with focus and intention rather than scattered effort.

Let my service be thoughtful, appropriate, and effective. May I act with clarity and purpose, trusting that faithful service in the right areas matters more than trying to do too much. **Amen.**

Holy Lord, I ask You to shape my life so that serving others becomes a natural expression of my faith. Help me not to separate what I believe from how I live.

Let my faith be active and visible in the way I care for others. Give me a willingness to give my time, my energy, and my attention where it is needed.

Guard me from becoming self-centred or withdrawn. Instead, help me to remain engaged with the people around me. Let my life reflect generosity, kindness, and a readiness to act.

May I grow in consistency so that serving others is not occasional, but a steady part of how I live.

Through it all, let Christ be seen in my actions, and may my service bring honour to Your name. **Amen.**

67. PRAYERS FOR EVANGELISM

Gracious Father, I come before You with a renewed awareness of the call to share the gospel with others. You have brought me to faith through Your grace, and You have entrusted me with the message of Christ.

Yet I confess that I do not always speak as I should. At times I hesitate, I remain silent, or I lack the courage to take opportunities that are before me. I ask You to strengthen me in this area and to help me become more faithful in bearing witness to the truth.

Your word says in 2 Corinthians 5:20, "We are therefore Christ's ambassadors, as though God were making His appeal through us." Help me to take this calling seriously. Give me a sense of responsibility, not driven by pressure, but shaped by love and gratitude. Remind me that the message I carry is not my own, but Yours, and that it is powerful to save.

Give me boldness when opportunities arise. Help me not to be held back by fear of rejection or uncertainty about what to say. Instead, give me clarity, simplicity, and confidence as I speak about Christ. Help me to speak truthfully, graciously, and wisely.

At the same time, give me sensitivity. Help me to listen carefully, to understand the people around me, and to speak in ways that are appropriate and thoughtful. Let my words be marked by respect and care.

Guard my heart from seeing evangelism as a task alone. Instead, help me to see people as individuals who need Christ. Give me compassion and genuine concern for their lives.

Above all, remind me that You are the One who saves. My role is to be faithful; the results belong to You. Help me to trust You with the outcome and to remain consistent in my witness. May my life and my words point clearly to Christ. **Amen.**

Faithful God, I bring before You my desire to share the gospel more faithfully and ask You to guide me in this calling.

You know the people in my life - those I see regularly, those I care about, and those who do not yet know Christ. I ask You to work in their hearts and to prepare them to hear and respond to the truth.

Your word says, "Always be prepared to give an answer to everyone who asks you to give the reason for the hope that you have." (1 Peter 3:15). Help me to be prepared.

Give me a clear understanding of the gospel and the ability to express it simply and accurately. Help me not to overcomplicate what should be clear.

Guard me from fear. At times I hold back because I am unsure or concerned about how I will be received.

In those moments, remind me that I am not speaking for myself, but for Christ. Give me courage to speak when the opportunity is right.

Help me also to live in a way that supports my words. Let my life reflect integrity, kindness, and consistency, so that my witness is not weakened by contradiction.

May others see something genuine in how I live.

Give me patience in this work. Not every conversation will lead to immediate results, and I ask You to help me remain faithful over time.

Let me continue to pray, to speak, and to live as a witness, trusting that You are at work.

May my life be a consistent testimony to Christ, and may You use both my words and my actions to point others to the truth. **Amen.**

Merciful Lord, I ask You to give me boldness to speak about Christ when opportunities arise.

You know how easily I can hesitate or remain silent, even when I sense that I should speak. In those moments, I need Your help. Give me courage that is steady and not forced.

Help me to recognise the right opportunities and to act on them without delay. Guard me from overthinking or becoming paralysed by uncertainty.

Instead, give me a simple and clear way of speaking.

Help me to trust that You are at work and that I do not need to have perfect words. Let me step forward in faith, speaking honestly and respectfully.

May I grow in confidence as I learn to rely on You rather than on my own ability. **Amen.**

Gracious Father, I ask You to give me a genuine concern for those who do not know Christ.

It is easy to become focused on my own life and responsibilities, and to lose sight of the spiritual needs of others. I ask You to awaken my heart again.

Help me to see people as You see them, not simply as acquaintances or colleagues, but as individuals in need of grace. Give me compassion that leads to action, not just awareness.

Let my concern be sincere and not superficial.

Help me to care enough to pray, to listen, and to speak when the opportunity comes. May my interactions be marked by kindness and genuine interest, reflecting a heart that desires the good of others. **Amen.**

Faithful God, I place before You the people in my life who do not yet know You. You know their thoughts, their experiences, and the barriers that may exist.

I ask You to work in their hearts in ways that I cannot. Prepare them to hear the truth and to respond to it.

Open doors for meaningful conversations and give me wisdom to recognise them.

Help me to be patient and not to force situations, but to act when the time is right.

Guard me from discouragement if I do not see immediate results. Instead, remind me that You are always at work.

Let me remain consistent in prayer and faithful in witness, trusting that You will bring fruit in Your time. **Amen.**

Holy Lord, I ask You to shape my life so that it supports the message I speak.

Help me to live with integrity, consistency, and kindness, so that my actions do not contradict my words.

Give me self-control in my speech and wisdom in how I relate to others. Let my life reflect something of the character of Christ in everyday situations.

When others observe how I live, may they see a difference that points beyond me.

Help me to be aware that my witness is not only in what I say, but in how I act.

Let my life and my words work together, creating a clear and consistent testimony to the truth of the gospel. **Amen.**

Gracious Father, I thank You for the gift of the local Church, the community of believers You have called together in Christ. Thank You that I am not called to walk alone, but to belong to a body where faith is shared, strengthened, and expressed in fellowship.

I thank You for those who lead, those who serve, and those who gather week by week. This is Your Church, and I ask You to shape it according to Your will.

Your word says, "And let us consider how we may spur one another on toward love and good deeds." (Hebrews 10:24). I ask You to make this true among us. Help us to encourage one another, to support one another, and to walk together in faith. Guard us from becoming distant, disconnected, or passive in our involvement. Instead, give us a shared commitment to build one another up.

Strengthen the unity of the Church. Where differences exist, help us to respond with grace and understanding. Where misunderstandings arise, bring clarity and patience. Guard us from division, from pride, and from self-centred attitudes that weaken fellowship. Let humility and love shape our relationships.

Give wisdom to those who lead. Guide them in their decisions, strengthen them in their responsibilities, and guard their hearts as they serve. Help them to lead with integrity, faithfulness, and dependence on You.

Help each of us to play our part. Let us not stand back, but engage with willingness and care. Give us a sense of responsibility for the health and growth of the Church.
Above all, let Christ be at the centre. May the Church reflect His truth, His love, and His grace. Let it be a place where people grow in faith, are strengthened in hope, and are equipped to live for You. **Amen.**

Faithful God, I bring before You the local Church and ask that You would continue to build it according to Your purposes.

You know its strengths and its weaknesses, its joys and its challenges.

I ask You to work within it so that it becomes a place of spiritual growth, unity, and faithful witness.

Your word says in Ephesians 4:16, "From Him the whole body… grows and builds itself up in love, as each part does its work." Help this to be true among us.

Let each person understand their place and contribute in a way that strengthens the whole.

Guard us from comparison, from feeling unnecessary, or from withdrawing from involvement.

Instead, give us a shared desire to serve and to build up the body of Christ.

Strengthen the teaching of Your word within the Church. Let it be clear, faithful, and centred on Christ. May those who hear grow in understanding and apply Your truth in their lives.

Guard the Church from distraction. Help it not to lose focus on what truly matters. Keep it centred on the gospel, grounded in Scripture, and committed to living out Your truth.

Give us a heart for those beyond the Church. Let us not become inward-focused, but outward-looking, ready to welcome others and share the message of Christ.

And in all things, let the Church reflect Your character. May it be marked by love, truth, humility, and grace.

Strengthen it for the work You have called it to do, and may it bring honour to Your name. **Amen.**

Merciful Lord, I thank You for the local Church and for the people You have placed around me. I ask You to help me value this community more deeply.

It is easy to become passive or disconnected, attending without truly engaging. Guard me from this pattern. Instead, give me a desire to be involved, to build relationships, and to contribute in meaningful ways.

Help me to take responsibility for my part in the life of the Church. Let me not wait for others to act, but be willing to take initiative where needed. Give me a spirit of cooperation and a willingness to support others.

May my presence strengthen the Church rather than weaken it, and may I grow in commitment to the body of Christ. **Amen.**

Gracious Father, I ask You to strengthen the unity of the Church and to guard it from division.

You know how easily misunderstandings, differences, or personal preferences can create tension. I ask You to bring a spirit of humility among us.

Help me to respond to others with patience and grace, even when I do not fully agree. Guard me from pride, from harsh judgement, and from speaking carelessly.

Instead, give me a desire to preserve unity and to seek peace. Help me to listen well, to communicate clearly, and to act with wisdom.

Let my attitude contribute to harmony rather than conflict. May the Church be marked by love and mutual respect, reflecting the unity that is found in Christ. **Amen.**

Faithful God, I place the leaders of the Church into Your hands and ask You to strengthen them in their work.

You know the responsibilities they carry and the pressures they face. I ask You to give them wisdom in decision-making, clarity in teaching, and strength in leadership.

Guard their hearts from discouragement and from becoming overwhelmed.

Surround them with support and encouragement from those they serve.

Help me to pray for them consistently and to support them in practical ways. Let me not be critical or distant, but engaged and encouraging.

May the leaders of the Church be upheld by Your grace and strengthened for the work You have called them to do. **Amen.**

Holy Lord, I ask You to keep the Church centred on Christ in all things. It is easy for focus to drift, for priorities to shift, and for distractions to take hold.

Guard us from this. Help us to remain grounded in Your word and committed to the gospel. Let every activity, every decision, and every effort be shaped by a desire to honour Christ.

Give us clarity about our purpose and unity in pursuing it.

Help me personally to remain focused on what truly matters and to contribute in a way that supports that focus.

May the Church reflect Your truth and Your grace, standing firm and growing strong as it lives for You. **Amen.**

69. PRAYERS FOR REVIVAL

Gracious Father, I come before You with a longing for revival, both in my own life and among Your people. You know how easily faith can become routine, how quickly hearts can grow cold, and how often we can continue outwardly while lacking inward life and passion.

I ask You to renew us, to awaken us, and to restore a deep and living devotion to Christ.

Your word says, "Will You not revive us again, that Your people may rejoice in You?" (Psalm 85:6). I ask You to do this work again in our time. Begin in my own heart. Search me and reveal anything that has dulled my spiritual sensitivity.

Where I have grown careless, awaken me. Where I have become distracted, refocus me. Where I have lost joy, restore it again.

Cleanse my heart from anything that grieves Your Spirit. Give me a fresh desire for Your word, a renewed commitment to prayer, and a deeper awareness of Your presence. Let my faith not be shallow or inconsistent, but living and active.

And as You work in me, I ask that You would work among Your people. Stir a renewed hunger for truth, a deeper love for Christ, and a greater unity within the Church. Let there be repentance where it is needed, humility where pride has taken hold, and a fresh seriousness about following You.

Guard us from seeking emotional experience without true transformation. Instead, let revival be marked by genuine change, by obedience, and by a lasting impact on how we live. Above all, exalt Christ among us. Let His name be honoured, His truth proclaimed, and His presence known.

May revival begin within and spread outward, bringing renewed life, joy, and faithfulness to Your people. **Amen.**

Faithful God, I bring before You a desire for true spiritual renewal and ask that You would move in power among Your people.

You know the condition of the Church, the challenges we face, and the ways in which we can become distracted or weakened in our faith. I ask You to work deeply and genuinely, bringing renewal that is rooted in truth and sustained over time.

Your word says, "Return to Me, and I will return to you." (Malachi 3:7). Help us to respond to that call. Begin by drawing us back to Yourself.

Turn our hearts away from what has distracted us and bring us again to a place of humility and dependence. Let revival not be something we speak about lightly, but something we pursue with sincerity and seriousness.

Give us a renewed desire for holiness. Help us to take sin seriously and to turn from it fully. Let repentance be real and lasting, not superficial or temporary.

At the same time, restore joy in salvation and confidence in Your grace.

Stir a deeper commitment to Your word. Let it be read, understood, and applied with clarity and conviction. Strengthen the preaching and teaching of Scripture so that it carries weight and authority.

Unite Your people. Remove division, soften hardened attitudes, and create a shared desire to seek You together. Let prayer become central, not peripheral, and give us a renewed sense of urgency in calling upon You.

And in all things, let Christ be lifted high. May revival not centre on people or events, but on the exaltation of Jesus.

Let His name be honoured, His gospel proclaimed, and His work evident among us. **Amen.**

Merciful Lord, I ask You to begin a work of revival in my own heart. It is easy to look outward and desire change in others, yet I know that renewal must begin within me.

Search my heart and show me where I have grown spiritually dull or complacent. Reveal attitudes, habits, or patterns that are not pleasing to You.

Give me the grace to respond honestly and without resistance. Help me not to excuse or ignore what You reveal, but to turn from it with sincerity.

Create in me a fresh desire to seek You, to spend time in Your word, and to pray with greater focus.

Let my faith be renewed from within, not by outward effort alone, but by a genuine work of Your Spirit in my life. **Amen.**

Gracious Father, I ask You to awaken a deeper hunger for You among Your people.

There are times when faith becomes routine, when worship becomes familiar, and when the sense of Your presence feels distant. I ask You to change this.

Stir hearts to seek You with greater desire and seriousness. Let there be a renewed commitment to prayer, not as an obligation, but as a genuine pursuit of Your presence.

Help me to be part of that change, not waiting for others, but responding personally. Give me a willingness to prioritise what matters most.

May there be a fresh movement toward You, marked by sincerity, humility, and a deep longing for spiritual life. **Amen.**

Faithful God, I place the Church before You and ask that You would bring true renewal among Your people.

You know where weakness exists, where distractions have taken hold, and where focus has been lost. I ask You to restore clarity and purpose. Strengthen the teaching of Your word and give it authority among us.

Help us to respond not only with understanding, but with obedience. Remove anything that hinders growth and replace it with a desire for truth and faithfulness.

Let the Church not drift or remain passive, but become active in seeking You.

May there be a renewed seriousness about following Christ and a deeper commitment to living according to Your will. **Amen.**

Holy Lord, I ask You to guard my understanding of revival so that I seek what is true and lasting.

It is easy to desire visible or emotional expressions, but I ask You to focus my heart on what matters most.

Let revival be marked by genuine repentance, renewed obedience, and a deeper love for Christ. Help me not to seek experience alone, but transformation.

Give me discernment so that I recognise what is real and what is superficial. Let my life be shaped by truth and grounded in Your word.

May any renewal I experience lead to lasting change, steady faithfulness, and a deeper commitment to living for You each day. In Jesus' name I pray. **Amen.**

70. PRAYERS FOR FINISHING WELL

Gracious Father, I come before You with a desire to live faithfully and to finish well the life You have given me. You know the path I have walked, the seasons I have passed through, and the challenges that still lie ahead.

I thank You for Your sustaining grace up to this point, and I ask You to continue that work in me so that I may remain steady and faithful to the end.

Your word says, "I have fought the good fight, I have finished the race, I have kept the faith." (2 Timothy 4:7). I long for that to be true of my life. Help me not only to begin well, but to continue well and to finish with faith intact.

Guard me from drifting, from becoming careless, or from losing focus over time. Give me perseverance that does not fade and commitment that does not weaken.

When I face difficulties, give me endurance. When I feel tired, renew my strength. When I am tempted to settle or become complacent, stir me again to remain faithful. Help me to keep my eyes fixed on what truly matters and not to be distracted by what is temporary.

Shape my character over time. Let humility deepen, faith grow stronger, and obedience become more consistent. Help me to learn from each season and to continue growing in Christlikeness.

Above all, keep my heart anchored in Christ. Let Him remain central in my thinking, my decisions, and my desires. May my life reflect a steady trust in Him, not only in moments of strength, but also in times of weakness.

And when my race is complete, may it be said that I remained faithful. Let my life bring honour to You, and may I finish with confidence in Your grace and hope in Your promises. **Amen.**

Faithful God, I place my future into Your hands and ask You to guide me so that I may finish well. You know what lies ahead, though I do not.

There will be changes, challenges, and uncertainties, and I ask You to prepare me for them. Help me to walk forward with steadiness, trusting You in every stage of life.

Your word says, "Let us run with perseverance the race marked out for us, fixing our eyes on Jesus." (Hebrews 12:1–2). Help me to live with that focus.

Let me not become distracted by what is around me or discouraged by what is difficult. Instead, give me a clear sense of direction and a steady commitment to follow Christ.

Guard my heart from weariness that leads to giving up. When progress feels slow or unseen, help me to continue. When I feel alone or uncertain, remind me that You are with me. Strengthen me to take each step faithfully, even when the path is not fully clear.

Give me wisdom in how I use my time and energy. Help me to invest in what matters most and to avoid being consumed by what is temporary. Let my priorities remain aligned with Your purposes.

As I grow older and move through different seasons, help me not to lose zeal or conviction. Instead, let my faith deepen and my trust in You become more settled.

May I continue to serve, to grow, and to remain faithful in whatever You call me to do.

And at the end of my life, may I look back with gratitude, knowing that Your grace sustained me.

Let me finish with faith, with hope, and with confidence in Christ. **Amen.**

Merciful Lord, I ask You to give me perseverance to continue faithfully in the life You have given me.

There are times when I feel tired, when progress seems slow, or when I am tempted to lose focus.

In those moments, I need Your strength. Help me not to give in to discouragement or to settle into complacency.

Instead, give me a renewed sense of purpose and direction. Remind me that each day matters and that faithfulness is built over time. Help me to take one step at a time, trusting You for what lies ahead.

Let me not be overwhelmed by the length of the journey, but strengthened by Your presence in each moment. May I continue steadily, relying on Your grace to carry me forward. **Amen.**

Gracious Father, I ask You to guard my heart from drifting over time.

It is easy to begin with enthusiasm and then slowly lose focus, becoming distracted or complacent.

I ask You to keep my faith active and alive. Help me to remain attentive to Your word and consistent in prayer.

Guard me from habits that weaken my walk and from attitudes that dull my sensitivity to Your truth. Instead, give me a steady desire to grow and to remain close to You.

Let my commitment not depend on circumstances, but on a deepening relationship with Christ.

May I continue to seek You with sincerity, growing in faith and obedience as the years go by. **Amen.**

Faithful God, I place my future before You and ask for wisdom as I move through the different seasons of life.

You know the changes that will come and the challenges I will face. Help me to adapt without losing direction.

Give me clarity about what matters most and the courage to let go of what does not.

Guard me from becoming rigid or resistant to change, but also from losing conviction.

Help me to remain grounded in truth while growing in maturity.

Let each season shape me in a way that prepares me for what lies ahead.

May I move forward with confidence, trusting that You are guiding me every step of the way. **Amen.**

Holy Lord, I ask You to keep Christ at the centre of my life so that I may finish well. Without Him, I will lose direction, strength, and purpose.

But with Him, there is everything I need to continue faithfully.

Help me to fix my eyes on Him daily, to draw strength from His example, and to rely on His grace.

Let my identity remain rooted in Him, not in my achievements or circumstances. Give me a heart that remains humble, teachable, and dependent on You.

May my life reflect a consistent and growing faith, and may I reach the end with confidence, knowing that I have trusted You and followed Christ. **Amen.**

"It matters little what form of prayer we adopt or how many words we use, what matters is the faith which lays hold on God and touches the heart of the Father who knew us long before we came to Him."

(Dietrich Bonhoeffer)